Create Your Future

Jack Healey: Lessons from a life in civil and human rights

Create Your Future

Jack Healey: Lessons from a life in human and civil rights

Published by Human Rights Action Center
www.humanrightsactioncenter.com

Printed in the United States of America
Illustration by Shepard Fairey / obeygiant.com
Photographic reference by Simon Cole

ISBN (pbk)   979-8-9901290-0-9
ISBN (ebk)   979-8-9901290-1-6
ISBN (hc)   979-8-9901290-2-3

Proceeds from the sale of this publication support

Human Rights Action Center.

Thank you for your continued support

Dedications

*In loving memory of my mother, Mary Olivia Gaughan Healey,
who taught me to hear the cries of those without a voice.*

&

*In loving memory of Feryal Gharahi, trusted colleague, life partner,
and friend. Feryal pushed me to think bigger, push harder, and fight
uncompromisingly for the cause of human rights.*

&

*To those whose voices have been
silenced by oppression and tyranny.*

May our voices thunder for you.

Foreword

My teen years included the Civil and Women's Rights Movements, and the Vietnam War, along with the assassinations of JFK, Malcolm X, Dr. King, and Robert Kennedy. At some point during these years, I remember being challenged to keep a running list of five people who were central to my moral and spiritual beliefs. The names on my list have included Dr. King, Gandhi, JFK, and Bro. Tom O'Brien, with one person finding himself on the list since the early '70's—Jack Healey.

My respect for Jack was initially grounded in his fundamental belief in young people, alongside his willingness to stand up against international and national tyranny embedded in violations of basic human rights across the globe. His genius in analyzing national and regional tensions has kept me leaning forward, over many tables, as we shared a meal or watched a Washington Nationals game.

When I returned to DC in 2009 to join President Obama's Administration, I couldn't wait to see Jack again, face-to-face. I was immediately drawn into the issues Jack was tackling in the States and across the world. His resolute determination to free Leonard Peltier and bring attention to the house arrest of numerous international leaders has revealed his deep inner faith. Jack's humility spurred me always to ask, "What can I do?" I highly encourage you to engage the core principles behind Jack's remarkable life.

Greg Darnieder

Former senior advisor to:
First Lady Michelle Obama, Obama Administration
Secretary of Education Arne Duncan, Obama Administration
Steans Family Foundation

Contents

Lesson One

You Can Get Things Done Without Power or Money

Chapter 1

Foundations

1938-1951

I was lucky, and I knew it at an early age, though outsiders wouldn't know it by looking at me. I was the youngest of eleven children, scrawny and nearly blind in one eye.

My father died in a horrific streetcar accident when I was two, and our sole income for years was the small monthly check that arrived in our mailbox courtesy of President Franklin Delano Roosevelt's recently created Social Security program. But I was lucky—I was raised by a mother who gave me a voice.

Mary Olivia Gaughan was a quiet woman with a magnificent face. She was gentle and easy. Peace and calm were her nature. Nothing rocked her in the essentials: her God, her faith, her belief in our people, and her belief in our need to survive and thrive. She was always good, always simple, and her faith was an ever-present focus of her life and loves. That simplicity rattles a less-than-perfect me even now. I secretly envied her those virtues. None of us could misbehave around her. We didn't know how she managed it, but we all behaved, at least until we were out on our own.

I was born March 24, 1938, midway through my mother's 46th year. She and I shared a natural bond. I charmed her, and she provided quiet strength for me to lean on and trust. Her love was always on call. Many people enjoyed spending time with her, from trash collectors to the insurance agent. Workers would often stop by for a cup of coffee or two. She gave solace, which no one discussed, yet everyone felt.

My father, Martin Healey, began working in the Pennsylvania coal mines at age twelve. He managed to get out of the mines and into the steel mill in 1922 and became a self-made metallurgist by the mid-1930s. He started out as a security guard, put himself through night school, and became well-respected in his field. He worked on alloys and heat treatments of iron, steel, and glass at Superior Steel in Carnegie, Pennsylvania—not a bad job with World War II looming. Family history says that Martin Healey was part of the team at Superior Steel that patented a bullet before World War II called SuVeneer, which was used at the Battle of Stalingrad. I do not have the memories of my father that my ten siblings have because he died when I was two. His loss devastated my mother and our family. The streetcar driver who took his life took much more than that. He took away my sisters' handsome hero and my brothers' big daddy, who could do anything. His death crippled most of my family for years.

My father's passing did not make much difference to me as a small child. One powerful person was enough, and she was a force, that mother of mine. At that time, my self-assigned task was to keep my mother happy and feeling good. I decided early on that my job was to take care of her and lift her spirits.

• • • • • • • • • •

We all vied for my mother's attention, but I was the curious one. I asked her questions that nobody else thought to ask. She told me about her time as a teacher, and what it was like for her to teach in the school for the miners' children. I learned about life for Irish Catholics in the mining towns throughout Pennsylvania.

She told me tales of the Molly Maguires, founded by a group of Irish coal miners who banded together to fight the unsafe conditions of the mines. She grieved over the twenty Mollies who were hanged after the deaths of some of the mine supervisors. She taught me that the death penalty was a weapon of the rich and powerful against the poor, and never the other way around. I learned that her grandfather had known John L. Lewis, head of the United Mine Workers Union. My mother made absolutely sure I remembered who he was and what he meant to the Irish.

She told me what happened when a miner died on the job, and I began to understand oppression. My Uncle Tony McHugh, a short guy who used to take me on walks, died in a mine cave-in. When the death cart came from the mine and stopped in front of your home, it was over and there was no more to say. The miner's family descended from impoverished to shambles. Life was different from then on, and it was hard, very hard, for a very long time.

I learned about the 10,000 Ku Klux Klan members who, in 1923, marched through Carnegie's Irishtown protesting against Irish Catholics. The Irish, including my dad, staged a counterdemonstration to the KKK march and things turned violent, resulting in the death of a Klan member named Abbott. An Irishman named Patrick McDermott was accused of Abbott's death; he was tried and found innocent. When World War II came, my mother's two oldest boys went off to fight in Asia. The country under President Franklin Delano Roosevelt needed her boys, and while sending them to war was difficult, that was part of the bargain for being in this country. She said she would gladly give back.

We had an understanding between us that required few words. She told me one day that she did not need to go to my baseball games like she did for the others. She said I didn't need it. She was right. I liked baseball with contact. She would not have approved of that behavior. However, one time she did chase large Gordon Willard around the field with a frying pan to defend me.

The only time I saw my mother cry was when President Roosevelt died. She used to make us thank President Roosevelt out loud when the Social Security checks for the four youngest children arrived in the mail at the end of the month.

During my interview with Amnesty International, they asked me who I was. Squaring my shoulders, I proclaimed, "I am the son of John L. Lewis, Franklin Delano Roosevelt, and Jesus Christ." I was not kidding. Those were the men I considered my fathers, and I was proud of them.

Over the years, our family had won and we had lost. With my dad gone, winning again did not come easy. To me, that was my job, and I knew I could deliver. I was determined not to let the coal mines of Eastern Pennsylvania and steel mills of Western Pennsylvania produce another round of something terrible. I knew I would make things better for my mother.

• • • • • • • • • •

My mother liked children. She used to say that just because kids were small, it did not mean that they didn't know or didn't matter. They were full people, complete people, just small. Words, actions, and behavior were just as important around them as around anyone else. It was this respect for children that led me to practice the only real talent God gave me: speaking. When I was five, I started giving speeches to my mother. Eleven children cannot fit in one car, and on errand day when it was my turn to stay home, I would march to the curb and give a five-minute speech on why she should not go on her errands without me. She would roll down the window and listen to my entire speech. My siblings, my forced audience, would scream, "Tell him to shut up! Get him outta here! Pump the clutch, let's leave without him! Here he comes again to give one of those speeches!" But Mother patiently listened each time.

Strength often comes to women when their husbands die. God does that. My brother Mike and I slept in the attic, which was hot in the summer and cold in the winter. In winter, when my mother came to wake us up, I would poke my feet out so she could put my socks on. I knew she felt bad that her babies lived in a cold attic, but this kindness made it okay. We went down to breakfast smiling every morning.

Mike and I walked a mile to or from school four times each day. He always looked out for me. He was big and tough, and nothing sent him into action faster than a big kid trying to do me in. He was much taller than I was and was a natural athlete. If I learned a new skill in baseball, I would be his teacher for about an hour and then he would surpass me. I was small. I could not use brawn, so I learned to rely on brains, ideas, vision, and speed to solve problems.

Being Irish, we did not speak of our bond, but it was solid. Hints in Irish families are important. If you miss the hint, you miss the love, the affection, the direction, and the flow of the family. I was quick with these essential hints and I would watch my mother for even small ones: how she would look at me, at other people and things. I understood body language. I learned to trust actions and body language more than words. Most people pay attention to words, and they should not. There is more reality in what people do than in what people say. Trust comes from action; distrust comes from inaction. The sermon is always better than the preacher.

Below her calm and ease, my mother possessed a rare steely toughness. "If someone pushes you—push back," she said. "You're not my boy if you don't push back." So, if someone pushed me, he got pushed back pretty damn fast. It was good training that prepared me for life. She often told me that she did not bring me into this world just to survive, but to do something.

• • • • • • • • • •

When I was fourteen, I won a $500 raffle at school, and my sister Naomi brought the money home. "We won $500!" Naomi proclaimed. "Oh, good," my mother replied. She grabbed her hat, put it on her head, and announced, "We're going to Florida." That was the day I discovered my mother loved to travel. She just had never had a chance to go anywhere before. The four of us still at home—Mother, Naomi, Mike, and I—jumped in Naomi's car and drove to Florida, just like that. She did not think about luggage or maps or anything at all. Of course, motels and restaurants were too expensive for us. Instead, we ate apples and oranges and stopped at the Mennonite watering holes.

After what felt like seven years in the car, we finally got to Florida. Mike and I were excited about going to the beach, when my mother asked, "Where is the church?"

"Oh, no," we moaned under our breaths. "We just got to the beach and now we're looking for a church." Catholic Florida was not to be found. We hunted for hours. We finally spotted a church, and of course, she wanted to stay within walking distance of it, which was about seventy-five miles from the ocean.

Her rule was: God first, fun later. God is, and then we are too. That was the order of things and that was that. Her God was an Irish God, giving special protection to widows, orphans, workers, and the poor. No one was to make fun of anyone, especially kids with real problems. For them, we said special prayers to special saints. There are a lot of "specials" in Catholicism, and she called on them for our souls.

Her Catholicism was magical. It was soft and included everyone. I learned more about religion—real religion—at my mother's knee than in all my years in the seminary and monastery. Her faith spoke to universal principles, not to bigotry, divisions, or anger. She prepared me for differences and gave me a curiosity that has never stopped. People were people and that was that, with a reminder that some of the Irish were the worst.

We were always on time for Sunday Mass. We never missed it, ever. One Sunday an ice storm came to Pittsburgh, and the city came to a halt. Ice had formed on everything. We thought for sure God would let us out of Church—and God may have, but not my mother. We pulled her to church on a sled with all of us slipping and sliding and falling behind her. God first, fun later.

She wrecked our ball games with rosaries, novenas, Masses, and extra Masses. When the clock struck 6:55 p.m., we all fought for the bathroom to avoid the daily recitation of the rosary at seven o'clock. We were always glad she said the rosary facing in on her favorite chair, because we would sneak away or get off our knees, or not pray too much. Looking back, I think this was a halftime break for her to think, to pray, to be by herself, and to ask God to take care of us all because it was clearly a bigger job than she felt she could do. We always prayed for the conversion of Russia. Later, when the Soviet Union collapsed without a bullet being fired, I thought about all her praying.

In traditional Irish families, when a grandmother lived alone, it was customary for the oldest granddaughter to go live with her. My mother happened to be the oldest granddaughter, so when her grandfather died, she was sent to live with her grandmother. That shaped Mom's views of her grandparents' era. She learned to say the rosary in Gaelic from her grandmother. I realized later that the Ireland she talked about was the Ireland of the 1860s. It was as if her grandmother was speaking through my mom's words.

My mother was half Druid. Her Ireland of leprechauns and Druids also came from her grandmother. Along with her Catholicism, my mother read tea leaves, cards, and numbers. Itchy hands meant you were getting some money. A bird in a chimney meant someone was dying. She knew all the Druid beliefs and practices. The Catholic priests would tell her to stop doing those things, and I did too. I realized later that I should not have. I learned that St. Patrick and the early Christians in Ireland melded the pre-Christian Irish Druid and Celtic religions with Roman Catholicism, creating a distinctly Irish faith. The Reformation shifted all of Ireland into a new kind of Catholicism. I now have a lot more respect for our true religion than I did at the time.

Her faith gave her the best, but to my mind, it also took too much. Her faith held her back and brought a deep fear. It also gave her clarity about how to treat people. My mother kept driving me to values, concepts, and clear statements. All of that came through her faith, her Church, and her Irishness. Humility and being good were moral imperatives—and that was that.

My mother's Catholicism led me to the seminary and to becoming a priest. Those years lifted her; she wrote me a letter every single day for thirteen years. I was ordained in 1966. I did my job for her, and in that effort, I gave myself the education, training, and focus I would need later.

I once asked her if she was ever scared.

"I was scared the night I looked up and saw twenty-two eyes staring at me after the funeral of your father," she said, "and then I realized I had a job to do, and I just moved on."

In the struggle of my early teens, she challenged me regularly about being a man. She wasn't talking about machismo, but about truth, helping the poor, and fighting for what one believes.

I finally asked, "When will I be a man?"

"When you learn to walk the highways and byways of life," she said, "and learn to listen to the weeping and the wailing of the poor, then and only then will you be a man."

Lord, I thought, I will never ask her another question.

• • • • • • • • • •

The day my father was killed, July 21, 1940, changed our family's finances and my mother's accounting. The big paychecks stopped coming, and there was no money in sight with eleven children to feed, house, and clothe. She spent most of her time at the wash basin in the cellar, or in the kitchen over the stove. We learned never to ask her for money when she was busy at either of these places. Plotting her schedule away from these two places became an art. After prayers was the best time to ask for a dollar or two, though none of us was ever successful at getting the big money. She just did not have it. Or so we thought.

One time I asked her, "What am I getting for Christmas, Mom?"

"The roof over your head," she replied.

For three days, I stared up at our roof. Then I realized I was not getting anything for Christmas. She knows the roof is a gift. There was no apology either. There was a lesson somewhere there.

Okay, I am tough, I thought. I do not need a present. But as soon as I got a dime, she got a present. That is just the way it was. Flowers were never passed on the way home without being snatched. She liked those "gifts."

The same was true for other holidays and our birthdays. She did not apologize. We just wanted her time, her presence. We often slipped into her room to kiss her goodnight; we savored the moment, feeling safe and secure. Most of us learn to like our mothers any way they come to us. Their presence in our lives is enough, with or without goodies. We learn to appreciate what life offers besides material possessions.

My mother avoided unwanted expenses. If we were pulled over for speeding, my mother, from the back seat, would lean out the window and start telling the police officer about how her husband died and how many children she had to feed. She would tell him every sad story that ever occurred to her, and the poor cop would be weeping by the time she was done. In the end, he'd apologize for stopping the car. She wanted no part of that ticket.

Fashion was never a high priority in our house. When my sisters were little, they would ask her, "Mom, how do I look?" Without looking up from her reading, Mom would feel the fabric and declare, "It's perfect; it's wool." When I got dressed, things did not always match. "Mom, I have two different socks on," I would tell her. "Who'll be lookin' at your feet?" she asked. "No one's lookin' at your feet." After that, I never wore a matching pair of socks. I figured if no one is looking at my feet, I'd just put on any damn socks.

In eighth grade, I went for my first overnight stay at my friend Dick Krause's house. When it came time to get ready for bed, his mother asked me, "Where are your PJ's?" "What are PJ's?" I asked. "Pajamas!" She said. I told her I had forgotten them, but I did not know what they were. We never had such things.

When my mother went shopping, Mike and I would meet her at the streetcar to carry her groceries across the bridge and up the hill to our house in zone five of Pittsburgh, Oakwood. By the time we reached the bridge, her hands already had deep creases from the four heavy grocery bags she carried in both hands. There were many times we did not meet her, and I wondered how she got up that hill carrying all that food.

Mom never complained about having to carry those bags; she just worried about how she was going to pay for them. She worried her way through life. We never knew which problems my mother would decide were hers. She sometimes decided that certain things did not apply to her. She would tell us kids, "Don't get sick on my watch, because there is nobody here to take care of you." Somehow, we just did not get sick. We all had perfect attendance records at school. If one of us woke up feeling bad, she would give us a nudge and say, "The fresh air will do you some good. You will feel better by the time you get to school."

When I was thirteen, I smoked my first cigar. I got sick as a dog. I came into the house and landed flat out in the front room. I heard my mother come into the room. She took one look at me and said, "He must be on drugs." She turned around and left the room. Luckily for both of us, I was not on drugs, and I did not like smoking cigars. It was not going to be her problem. My mother did not like to pay medical bills, either. When Mike and I were in eighth grade, Mike broke his leg playing football. Father Lonergan, a big half Irish, half Native American priest who coached the football team, drove us home and carried Mike into the house.

"Father Lonergan," my mother began, "Why would you be bringing him into my house? I do not fix bones. He broke that leg on your property! Take him to the hospital!"

Father Lonergan carried Mike back out to his car and took him to the hospital. He even paid the bill. This widow had decided she was having no part in that problem, even though it was her son.

I thought to myself, "This lady is tough."

• • • • • • • • • •

She used her own remedies when we got hurt so she could avoid the expense of taking us to the doctor. When we came home with a gash or a cut, she'd put a great big wad of bread and milk on the wound and wrap it up. I did not know what it was supposed to do, and I never asked. As I sat there with milk running down my leg, I always wondered if it was doing any good.

One winter day when Mike and I were sledding, he bashed his head on the bumper of the car and got a big cut on his head. My mother looked at him and then turned to my brother-in-law and asked, "Would you mind sewing that up?" Mike and I looked at each other with fear and horror. She was having no part of that medical bill, so my brother-in-law stitched up Mike's head right in front of us. No medical bills that day, just a light scar for Mike.

In my second year of high school, I broke my jaw playing football. I was an eighty-eight-pound guard. The only thing the coach said was, "Take some aspirin." I walked home with a broken jaw. Later that night I had to be taken to the hospital, the pain and swelling were so bad. I was out of school for several weeks, and then the hospital bill came in the mail.

"Jackie, you have to take that bill to the school," she said to me.

"Take it to school? Who do I give it to? There is no one at the school to give this bill to," I explained.

"I'll take it to the school," she told me, so she dragged me along to see the principal. When we got to the principal's office, my mother explained the situation to him.

"My boy was playing football for you when he broke his jaw," she said. "We're not having this bill." The principal did not know what to say, so he took the bill and paid it.

Banks had collapsed in the Depression, and she never trusted them after that. When she died, we discovered that she had $18,000 in cash in her room. We smiled at this because we knew what she would say: "I made it to the end for you and for me. I made it because we all made it." To her, the goal in life was to have dignity at the end, and all you needed to do was make it to the end with enough to end well.

My mother taught us about giving by enforcing a strict rule. She was like the IRS: everyone got taxed. Each person living in the house had to kick in money from whatever jobs they had, no matter how much they earned. The amount was not as important as the act of contributing. My sisters earned most of the money that came in, though each of us gave what we could. Mike worked at a beer distributor down the street, and I moved boxes at a local store for $5 a week. Our mother made each one of us grasp the value of the home by adding to it. Prosperity for all of us came from contributions by each of us. In most cases, my mother was clever about avoiding the bill collectors, but there were times when there was no getting around them. It was then that we all had to share the burden of paying them.

One fateful day, it was my turn to find some money to pay an unexpected bill. This adventure would teach me one of the most important and enduring lessons of my life. Some guys from the neighboring town of Beechview jumped my brother Mike one night along Banksville Road in South Pittsburgh. One of them tripped him and the second held him down so the third could get on top of him and punch him in the face. They had knocked out three teeth by the time a police officer strolled by. The officer helped Mike to his feet but did not bother chasing after the three boys. Maybe he recognized them as sons of members of the powerful Pittsburgh mob who were chummy with many in the police force. Maybe he just did not care.

By the time I got home, my mother had cleaned Mike up and assessed the damage. As the mother of eleven children, she was accustomed to bloody noses, scraped knees, tears, and fights. That afternoon was different. Mike was missing three front teeth, and my mother could not fix him with an ice pack and some Band-Aids. When my mother and Mike came home from the dentist, she asked me to sit with her in the dining room. Quiet as usual, she pulled out a chair and said, "Jackie, I don't have the $300 for your brother's teeth. You will have to get that money for me."

I looked at her and thought, "You've got other kids... why me?" But I didn't say a word. She knew I could talk, and talk, and talk, and this was a time for action. This job was mine, and that was fine. I jumped on a streetcar headed to Mount Washington where the police officer who handled the case was stationed. Mount Washington overlooked Pittsburgh, which, when I was young, was impossible to see because of all the soot from the steel mills. On that day, I could see Pittsburgh clearly, and the city was beautiful.

I found the Irish cop who broke up the fight and asked his advice on how to find $300 for Mike's teeth.

He shook his head. "You would need the best lawyer in Pittsburgh to get a cent out of those families, so just get out of here, kid. You have no idea what you are getting yourself into."

The thing is, I did know what I was getting myself into. I just had no choice. My mother had asked me to fix this. If I needed the best lawyer in Pittsburgh to handle Mike's case, I would find the best lawyer in Pittsburgh. The fact that I did not have any money, or that he might need to be paid in the first place, did not occur to me.

On the streetcar to downtown Pittsburgh, I noticed the menacing jail up ahead. Lawyers go with jails, I figured, so I got off at that stop. I asked the same question to everyone I passed on the street: "Who is the best lawyer in the city of Pittsburgh?" They all pointed to the brownstone a couple blocks away and said one name: Charlie Maloney.

The building directory pointed me to the third floor, so I slid into the building with a uniformed delivery person. I was dressed in my older brother's oversized pants and a faded yellow button-down shirt, which had belonged to at least one other sibling. It must have been immediately clear to the secretary that I was not their typical client. From behind a large wooden desk, she asked, "Can I help you?"

"I am here to see Charlie Maloney."

She must have been on to me, because her next question was, "What time is your appointment?" I did not let that deter me.

"I need Mr. Maloney to represent my brother's case. You see, my brother was beaten up by some ferociously ill-tempered but well-connected local kids. They whacked his teeth out and our family needs the money from their families to repair his choppers," I said, trying to appear as cute, well-humored, and as innocent as possible.

As I spoke, I could see the secretary biting her lip to hold back laughter. Then she stopped smiling, lifted a pencil from her desk, and pointed at the door. "Get out of here kid." Folding my arms, I declared, "Not without an appointment." A staring contest ensued. Little did I know that Charlie Maloney was lurking in the doorway listening to our whole conversation. He must have realized that he would have to intervene to defuse the standoff.

"So, you want me, Charlie Maloney, to take on the case of some fighting schoolboys?" he asked, turning to the secretary and laughing along. Charlie was a handsome and imposing man who spoke with a tone of confidence that made him impossible to ignore. Embarrassed, I turned around to leave the office.

"Hang on, kid" he called after me. "I'll do it." A few months later when my mother, Mike, and I walked into the courtroom with Charlie, even the judge stood up.

"What are you doing on this case?" asked the judge, shocked to see Pittsburgh's best attorney on a case about a few kids who got into a fight. The accused kids' fathers were standing behind them in the courtroom to remind the judge that the boys had the power of the Pittsburgh mob behind them, literally and figuratively. Lucky for us, they were small potatoes compared to Charlie.

"What are you doing on this case?" demanded one of the men.

Charlie stood up tall and put his arm around Mike. "I only come to court for one reason: to win."

The fathers began whispering furiously. Before proceedings began, one of them walked over to my mother and handed her an envelope with $300 inside.

"Case closed!" said Charlie cheerfully. "Jack? Mike? You all want to get a hamburger?" Charlie Maloney had coffee at our home every Monday for the rest of his life.

I learned a valuable lesson from the incident. Those who rule by using wealth and power to intimidate others are only as powerful as everyone else lets them be. Those without guns and capital have morality as a weapon to strike fear into the hearts of the powerful. The coercive power of the Pittsburgh mob melted away when faced by Charlie, who gained power from his reputation as an upstanding person who was genuinely good at his craft. This was the type of person with whom I wanted to surround myself. For the rest of my life, if I wanted something done, I would look for the best, and I would try to be my best.

I also gained confidence. My mother trusted me with a need. Sometimes mothers just want an all-out effort by their kids; mine wanted a victory. Her boy had been hurt, and she was not walking away. I was small and insignificant until I listened to her plea for justice and restitution. She wanted to face the family who hurt her boy. Quietly, she was training me in justice and the pursuit of good over evil.

Her message was clear. "No matter the odds, you get going."

I learned that even without power or money, I could solve a problem. This truth was one of my mother's immense contributions to the rest of my life. It still works for me today.

· · · · · · · · · ·

If I spent most of my time at home sitting quietly in the kitchen or laundry room helping my mother, I spent most of my time in school making life as difficult as possible for my teachers.

I had always been skinny and smaller than my classmates. My sister Naomi started me in school a year early so my mother could have some quiet. This meant Mike and I were in the same grade, which was above my age group peers. It was a great surprise to me later to learn that I may not have been as small as I always felt. I was actually just in school and sports with kids older and thus larger than I was.

I had a lazy eye so severe it required surgery when I was eleven and then again at eighteen. I wore enormous glasses, which did not help my social life much. It earned me the nickname Bug, not exactly a kid's dream come true. This was not too big a problem in elementary school, because I was fast on the baseball field and the track, and I was not afraid to fight. But by my first year of high school, being fast and quick with a sucker punch was no longer enough. I was pretty much invisible in the halls of my high school, the youngest of the Healey kids and not a standout on the sports field or in the classroom.

My reputation changed the day I met Jack Bear. Six foot four and 190 pounds at age 14, Bear towered over the rest of us. The first time I encountered him, he was standing in the middle of the hallway blocking a smaller kid and dangling a cigarette menacingly. Jack's usual trick was to drop his lit cigarette into the cuff of another kid's Levi's. The victims would walk away not realizing they were smoking from their ankles. Most of us had burn holes in our jeans by the end of that year.

That day Ray was the victim. He began hopping around like crazy, shrieking. I laughed. It didn't occur to me that perhaps I could have done something kinder than laugh at Ray, who was taking off his pants to find the offending cigarette. Bear heard me. He stood up and looked down at me, and I shut up fast—we just stared at each other in silence except for the high-pitched shrieks coming from Ray, who was still jumping around behind Jack.

"Hey... so, do you come here often?" I finally stammered.

He just looked blank, and I panicked. What had I been thinking? I should run now because he was going to come for me next.

Bear mimicked me: "Come here often? Come here often? To school? Bug, you are crazy. What is your real name, man?" From then on, I was no longer "Bug." I was known as "the Bug who hangs out with the Bear"—an upgrade for a freshman.

It was the Bear's idea to steal hubcaps. We would steal the hubcaps from a car, and then go a few streets over, find some poor schmuck whose hubcaps had stolen by some other boys looking for beer money, and sell the hubcaps back to him. When we were not defrauding unfortunate car owners into buying back hubcaps every time they went to the grocery store, we found other fun activities to keep us busy.

Bear figured out that it was possible to climb onto the dumpster in the back of the movie theater, disable the fire alarm, and crack the back door so the rest of us could go in. Soon, just breaking in for the double feature did not provide enough excitement. We gathered in groups of six to ten kids and scattered throughout the dark theater. We would wait for the moment the hero was about to be attacked, or the moment the audience feared for the girl about to go into the dark basement alone because the bad guy was down there. At those moments, we would all yell in unison. The entire theater would jump and scream. And then call for the ushers.

When we got bored with this version of the game, we would step it up to the next level. In those days, movie screens were just large pieces of cloth. We would get four or five boys and squeeze in behind the screen before the film began and wait until that perfect moment in the movie. Then, in unison, we would jump out from behind the screen and run toward the audience, yelling at the top of our lungs. This game infuriated the ushers. It was almost impossible to execute without a few of us getting bloody noses or slapped around as we were dragged out of the theater. "We told you last week not to come back here," would be ringing in our ears.

The girls in my grade did not find my friends or me particularly amusing. For a while, this was not much of a problem for me, but then it began to matter for one reason: Marcie Stinner. Marcie was, hands down, the prettiest girl in the freshman class and maybe the entire high school. She was one of those girls who managed to be beautiful without seeming to hold it over others. Because of her looks and her kindness, she was asked out on more dates in the fall of freshman year than I have been on in my life. She turned them all down—the football players and the smart boys, the basketball players, the greasers, the oddballs, and the sons of Pittsburgh's elite. She was very polite and used a very firm, "No, thank you. No."

One day, when her parents were out of town, she threw a party. It seemed the whole school was there. Those who identified as greasers, with slicked-back hair and tight jeans, as well as Socs, with loose jeans and big sweaters, perched in different corners with their own cliques. I arrived with my usual crew of riffraff: Jack Bear, Sal Gaetano, Ed Schroth, Ray Santomo, and T. Malley. Our slicked-back hair, tight jeans, and attitude put us solidly in the greaser subculture. We spent most of our time sitting around a card table, playing blackjack, and making fun of people.

As a prank, Jack Bear decided that he was going to try to jump over our classmates like a gymnast leaps over a pommel horse. Although he was very tall, Jack was not nearly tall enough to clear even the shortest of those present. Instead, he made a running start, then leaped, sending them hurtling to the ground. As usual, our classmates were amused, but in a slightly condescending manner. After a few good laughs, I decided I had had enough, and it was time to leave by myself.

I walked around, giving the usual goodbye high-fives. Then I noticed Marcie, standing by the front door with a bow in her hair and a smile across her round face and my heart palpitations turned into quick thuds. Suddenly, I felt a bit of courage come over me. I approached the door and glanced around to make sure no one else was looking.

"Marcie," I mustered. "May I give you a kiss goodnight?" She leaned her head forward and puckered her lips. I pressed my mouth up against hers, and the four seconds that our lips touched seemed to be the most marvelous of my life. I walked out of the party, coolly, like it was the type of ending that I expected most evenings. The second I was sure everyone was out of sight, I skipped the whole way home.

That kiss changed me. It shattered an invisible barrier not only between Marcie and me but between me and all girls. I had gained acceptance by the other gender. I crossed a social bridge with a sure and steady friend, and it opened the other half of the world to me.

Marcie and I became fast friends. She would pick me up on the way to school. We sat next to each other at lunch, passed notes in class, and walked home together. This drove the jocks crazy because they felt they were more worthy of Marcie's attention. While they were bending over backward to get her to notice them, I had her undivided attention. Suddenly, all those guys who had always ignored and looked down on me wanted to be my friend. Now, I was cool even for them. In one night, I climbed the social ladder at Dormont High School so quickly that I could barely remember what it was like to be at the bottom. My shyness began to melt away.

To this day, I am still not sure why Marcie bothered to speak to me. I suspect it was because of the way that the other students treated her. Beauty is a mixed blessing. People fear and envy beautiful people. Beautiful girls are often ridiculed behind their backs by envious classmates, subjected to awkward conversations with nervous boys, and held to impossible standards by teachers and parents. I think Marcie appreciated my sincerity and that I did not treat her with the fake reverence or hidden disdain that many of the other students did. Later in life at Amnesty, I often found myself surrounded by celebrities whom others treated with similar reverence and disdain. But I always remembered my experiences with Marcie, Dormont High School's local celebrity, and how treating her the same way I treated everyone else was the best way to get to know her.

• • • • • • • • • •

For a while, I was doing okay in high school. I had wrangled my way onto the football team during my freshman and sophomore years. I was an 88-pound guard and without a doubt the scrawniest guy on the field. I was hanging out with Marcie Stinner and getting into a manageable amount of trouble with Bear and the boys. One afternoon on the football field it all came apart. I slammed into the fullback's knee hard, much harder than I had meant to hit him.

It was not until we filed into the locker room that anyone noticed I was injured. I stumbled into the locker room and crawled to the bench. I could tell that my nose was bleeding, but I could not find the proper way to address the problem. I could barely sit up. Then I saw Buzzy Goldberry standing in front of me. He kept saying something repeatedly, but I could not hear him over the ringing in my ears. Finally, he hauled me to my feet and dragged me out the door and towards home.

My mother, ordinarily calm in the face of bumps and bruises, nearly passed out when I walked into the room. My sister Naomi grabbed the car keys, and the three of us raced up the street to the emergency room. The doctors at Mercy Hospital saw my jaw was badly broken. They decided to reset the bone right then, without an anesthetic. I was strapped to a hospital table, kicking and shouting as the doctor jerked the broken bone back into place. We heard a loud snap that signaled that the bone had been set. The pain was intense, and I went into shock. When I woke up, I had a helmet-like contraption over my face. It was to stay on for six to eight weeks. I asked the doctor how many hours a day I would have to wear the giant helmet. "Well," the doctor said, "You will wear it all day and all night." I never missed not having a television before, but as I spent my days lying on my back staring at the ceiling, I wanted a television so badly. I was bored and humiliated.

When I finally returned to school, I discovered that my class had moved on. Moby Dick was covered while I recuperated. When my teacher asked me what literary tool Melville had employed by not killing the whale, I drew a blank. "What whale?" I asked, as my classmates tittered.

In algebra, I turned my parabolas into doodles, only to have them torn up by my irate math teacher. In biology, I failed two quizzes in the first week on the anatomy of the frog that had been dissected in my absence. By the end of my first week, I knew trying to catch up was useless.

As usual, Jack Bear had some ideas. On Friday that first week back, Bear and I passed a note around the class with two words scrawled on it: "Books @ 12:07". At exactly 12:07 that afternoon, twenty minutes before the start of our lunch break, forty large geography textbooks hit the linoleum floor, causing Mrs. Callahan to shriek and drop her chalk.

"Both Jacks—out in the hallway, right now," she hissed. The next day, when 12:07 came and went without incident, Mrs. Callahan looked relieved. At 12:09, the entire class stood up, pointed out the window at nothing and screamed. Without a word, she looked at us and pointed to the door. Bear and I spent the rest of the period behind the gym. We decided to shoot for 12:04 the next day, just to mix things up a bit.

In the past, any trouble I had gotten into had taken place pretty much under the radar. Cops had chased us many times, but we had never been arrested. I was often sent to the principal's office, but I had not been suspended or expelled. The principal called me a barbarian. I took that as a compliment because I thought the barbarians had won.

After my second day back at school, I started lying to mom. Over dinner, she asked me with concern how I was adjusting. "It won't be long until I am caught up with the rest of the class," I said, slopping some potatoes into my mouth. When my mother smiled at the news, the guilt from lying gave me knots in my stomach. Still, I saw no other way. Report cards were an unanticipated problem; they bore the unmistakable record of my new apathy. They came four times a year. The first one had been delivered before my jaw was broken and the second was issued while I was laid up so I was in the clear for those, but there were two more that my mother would be anticipating.

Mike tipped me off as to when the first one was due to be sent home. Every day I tried to intercept the mail. Finally, I saw the 5x6 manila envelope that exposed my lies. I tore it open and hid the evidence under my mattress. To my surprise, Mom never asked for it. A few months later, I hid the final report card under my bed as well, but that one was not forgotten. Mom knew it was due and began to get suspicious. One morning as I was finishing my eggs, she asked me if I had seen it. I knew my charade was up. I fished the report card out from under my bed and reluctantly handed it over.

I stood there, watching her read it. Her expression did not change, and she did not say a word, but I knew that things were going to be different. A few days later, Mom called me into the kitchen. "You have three choices: reform school, military school, or seminary." Though terrified, I was also relieved that there were ways for me to start over. Frank Cipriani, a rotund, quiet kid from my football team, let me know about a retreat for high schoolers interested in seminary life. Understanding this would probably be my best option, I asked if I could join.

The retreat was sort of a soda pop and dine event for Pittsburgh schoolboys and we spent most of our time playing baseball. In the mess hall, the fresh food straight from local farms was the best I had ever tasted. A twenty-seven-year-old priest, Father James, and I bonded instantly. We chatted about sports and getting into mischief in Pittsburgh. Father James had an amazing talent for seeing potential in others. He was such a put-together man that his confidence in me gave me confidence in myself. Toward the end of the trip, he took me aside and told me that I was too smart to keep up my nonsense. When we got back, he joined my family one night for dinner. My mother was elated to have a priest in the house. He spoke a lot about kids needing discipline and how much he loved being a priest. I could tell my mother was smiling because she was imagining me in that position ten years down the line.

Everything was changing around me. Our high school must have had a coordinated effort to expel mischievous kids because that year we were all sent away. Jack Bear left for military school. Several Catholics went off to Catholic school or Kiski, a Pennsylvania boarding school.

The city I grew up in was also changing. Jobs were getting harder and harder to find as the steel mills closed. The loss of employment meant more frustrated parents, and a rise in alcoholism and domestic violence. Though I rarely witnessed such vices firsthand, there was a tangible feeling of decay in the city. I was ready to go.

Father James suggested that I attend a three-week Latin language camp later that summer. At Latin camp, the priests taught us using strict memorization. Nothing made sense to me. All the new vocabulary seemed to float in my head for only a few moments before disappearing again. At the end of the day, it was as if I had learned nothing. Frustrated, I left after only one week and returned home. When I walked back in the door, the look of disappointment on my mother's face was unbearable. I knew I had to go back.

Mary Healey, wrapped by her children (l-r) Agnes, Mike, Jack, Elaine (BB), and Carole.

Mike, Mom, and me at the beach. First, my family went to church, and then we went to the beach.

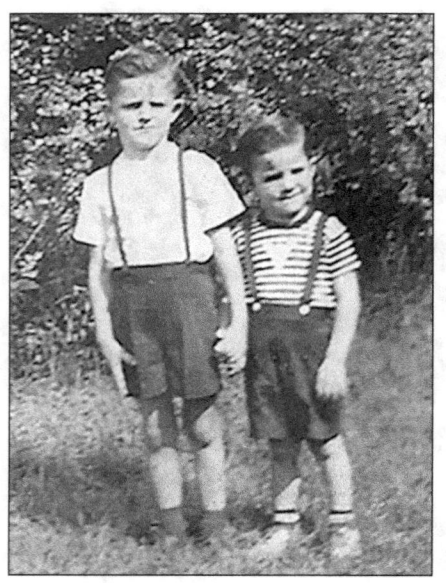

Jack and his brother Mike

Ninth grade school photo. I was in ninth grade when I faced down a gang.

Martin Healey studied metal alloys at Carnegie University.

AT THE BATTLE OF STALINGRAD
SuVeneer fought, too!

Martin Healey was part of the team at Superior Steel that was granted a patent on a type of bullet called the SuVeneer shown in this Superior Steel ad from 1942.

The Healey clan in 2010 at the wedding of Dr. Dennis Manning and Lisa Fulton Manning. Photo by John Madia.

Jack with Elaine and Molly Mc Clelland; Patrick and Elisabeth Healey with daughter Morgan; Debra and Michael Healey.

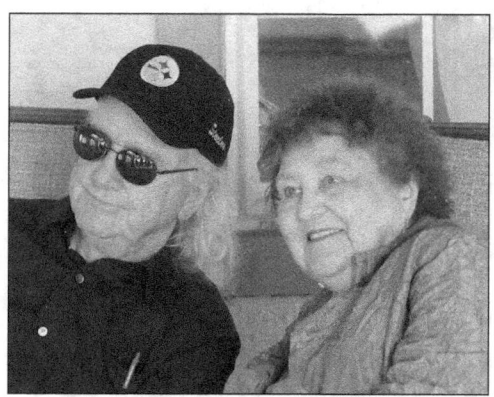

Jack with his sister Elaine.

Chapter 2

The Seminary Years

1953-1962

K eith's knuckles slammed into the back of my head before I'd gotten a chance to shake his hand or introduce myself. For a split second, I considered letting it go and not engaging in a fistfight on my first day at the seminary. I could give my mother a chance to drive out of the parking lot before she was called back to hear about me fighting, but Keith taunted me with threats of future punches. So, I turned around and punched my new neighbor directly in the nose.

Blood spurted out across his pressed shirt, the white sheets of his neatly made bed, and the floor. As Keith and I watched the blood flow, Father Patrick walked into the dorm to see if I had gotten settled in my little alcove. Father Patrick looked at us. No one said anything. The priest calmly put one hand on each of our shoulders and escorted Keith to the infirmary and me to his office.

The Capuchin Franciscan order was extremely strict. The priests took vows of chastity, poverty, and obedience. They were expected to spend their lives dedicated to the Church and to train the next generation of young men.

Certain things, such as smoking, speaking out against the Church, or knocking someone out with a swift uppercut to the nose, were simply not tolerated. The prohibitions were so strong that anyone who did not get the message—me, for example—faced expulsion.

I sat in Father Patrick's office, with its crucifix and photo of Pope Pius XII, in oppressive silence. The prospect of a call to my mother, and of returning to Pittsburgh after failing at this, was not appealing. I wanted to make my mother proud, not embarrassed.

Father Patrick, a short, bald, very Irish 60-year-old, sank into his seat, put his fingertips together, and asked me in his calm, quiet voice why Keith was bleeding in the infirmary. He patiently explained to me that it was the policy of the seminary to expel anyone involved in a physical altercation. He understood that I had failed out of high school and said that he wanted to give me a chance, but I was making it a little difficult.

"He hit me first!" I burst out, stung by the injustice of it all. The fact was that Keith, that coward, had waited until my back was turned to hit me. Father Patrick put a hand up. "Christ," he said. "Christ did not hit back. Not when he was spit on, stoned, attacked, or crucified. Christ did not hit back. Do you understand that?"

I opened my mouth to suggest that perhaps Christ had not met Keith, but Father Patrick was not done. He looked at the ceiling as if seeking advice from above. Finally, he spoke. God was calling on him, he explained, to give me another chance. One more fight and I would find myself in the back of my mother's car headed home, or maybe prison, if I continued down my present path.

• • • • • • • • • •

The seminary and monastery were all about silence. Grand Silence began at 8 p.m. every night and lasted until class began the next day. No outside communication was permitted. No music, no radio, no newspapers, no television, and no magazines. Routine was sacrosanct. I sat next to John Petruha for meals three times a day, every day for twelve years.

We rose at 5:45 a.m. every morning to the bell, which unfortunately doubled as the fire alarm. At 6 a.m. we appeared in chapel for Mass and meditation, kneeling with our heads bowed until it was finally breakfast time. We walked to breakfast single file by age. Many mornings we ate our peanut butter toast in total silence. Since my initial conversation with Father Patrick, I lived in fear of being expelled, so I lined up behind John Petruha every morning, ate my toast in silence, knelt in chapel, and remained still during meditation. I behaved.

As strange as it might seem now, seminary was basically a normal way to grow up. We were a bunch of young guys who played ball together, lived together, studied and worked together. It was very much like a boarding school with a Catholic touch. Overall, it was a good way to spend my teen years. Our school covered the usual high school curriculum: biology, English, and math. The first year was fine because I had already completed almost two years at Dormont High, but my sophomore year did not begin well. The first biology test was an unmitigated disaster. I was only a third of the way through when Father Roch, my teacher, collected our papers.

I had studied for a week, and I knew where that endocrine system was, I could probably even pinpoint it on one of those frogs the Bear and I used to put in people's lockers. But I failed the test. Father Roch called me to his office, where I waited nervously, hoping that he would not call my mother. Father Roch, though, did not say anything about my mother. "Would you mind telling me how Gregor Mendel conducted his first pea experiment?" he asked, putting his feet up on the desk and leaning back in his chair. I started talking about peas and Punnett squares, chlorophyll, and the vascular system of a green, leafy plant, and how it was different from that of a tree until I ran out of breath. Father Roch wanted to know why I had failed the biology test when I knew all the material.

"Dyslexia is a learning disorder characterized by difficulty reading due to problems identifying sounds and learning how they relate to letters and words. Dyslexia is a common learning disability in children." — Mayo Clinic

Father Roch didn't have a name for the reason I failed the test. But he understood that I knew the test material. He did not have the prescribed "variety of educational tools" that can be used now to help treat dyslexia. So, he created his own. He gave me extra credit assignments that allowed me to answer questions verbally. He spent time after each class asking me what we had learned. He called on me to answer questions in class, and I began to get the answers right. Soon, I was raising my hand to talk about Plato, telling my classmates about the connection between God and science, and explaining what St. Thomas Aquinas was referring to in a paragraph. I was participating in debates about the way justice should be enforced in society, the relationship between equality and liberty, and challenging Father Roch on what, specifically, defines a democracy.

All this extra work could not have been easy for Father Roch. He had to develop tools to help me learn and then had to convince the other priests to do the same. He patiently quizzed me verbally every day. He was especially kind to do all this extra work for a kid who was basically there to avoid being sent to jail. He was one of those amazing people who not only practiced what he preached, but he also believed in it. He believed that I deserved forgiveness, patience, and a chance to succeed. Father Roch and the other priests recognized that my struggle to read and write did not reflect my ability. They taught me and treated me with the respect that children with learning difficulties often did not receive.

For two of the summers that I was home from the seminary, I worked at Safeway Steel scaffolding company. The regular staff consisted of nine men and my boss, George Grazorchalk. I scraped off cement, repainted steel equipment, cleaned up the place, and helped move scaffolding on and off trucks. Occasionally, I would even go to an outside job putting scaffolding up the side of a building. I loved the job and the people.

The warehouse was on the south side of Pittsburgh, across the river from the main part of the city. The Southside was the Slavic part of town. Slavs from Eastern Europe populated the area. In Pittsburgh, at that time, if you knew where someone lived, you knew what nationality and/or what church he or she belonged to. I would go bounding over to the business area each day for a sandwich and soda. Each time, I was asked to bring back sandwiches for everyone. Finally, I asked George, "Can't someone else go? I do it all the time."

George said, "These guys cannot get served over there because they're Black." I was surprised and upset. I went home and told my mom. She said, "I know. It is common, prejudiced, and wrong." Those trips for sandwiches strengthened my empathy and I never complained again.

● ● ● ● ● ● ● ● ● ●

The steady decline of steel in the 1960s and 1970s turned into an almost total shut down by 1983. In January of that year, unemployment ranged from 17%-27% in the region. Closed factories left huge tracts of empty, polluted land along the river. Unlike many other Rust Belt towns, Pittsburgh did not have to move people to develop its waterfront. Pittsburgh could rebuild itself. Crucial to the rebuilding of Pittsburgh was the pride the town shared in its sports teams, the Steelers and the Pirates. Each was rebuilt along with the city, all to the immense pride of its citizens. To me, Pittsburgh's transformation has been an affirmation of the possibility of change.

The Pittsburgh Steelers football team owed their revival to the dedication of their legendary owner, Art Rooney. He and I spent time together in the halls and waiting rooms of Mercy Hospital when both of us were visiting relatives there. Art was very Catholic and liked his clergy. His brother was a priest, and Art always gave the church half of any sum he won at the track. He used the other half of his winnings to buy the Steelers.

I asked Art what he did for his parish at Christmas and Easter. Art said he handed them a blank check. "Write in any amount you want, Father," he would say. I asked why he did this. He answered, "I know my priest. He writes in a lot less than I would." After I became a priest, there were many times when I wished that Art were one of my parishioners. The star of the Pittsburgh Pirates in those days was Roberto Clemente. He came to life for me in the middle of a game against the Dodgers I attended in my late teens.

It was my awakening to what a real ballplayer looked, acted, and performed like. I witnessed Clemente scoop up a hard hit into right field as the hitter streaked to third base. His throw from right field was so hard and so straight and so strong that the crowd in Forbes Field just stood in awe and cheered as the runner was tagged out. No one believed me for years, and I thought I made it up until I read the book Clemente, by David Maraniss. It confirmed that day in the stands.

Clemente brought a new language—he spoke in Spanish when he won the Most Valuable Player Award—and a new era to Pittsburgh. His hitting and fielding skills won him a place on fifteen all-star teams and earned him twelve Golden Glove Awards with a lifetime batting average of .317. Clemente embodied Pittsburgh's resurgence. He had talent graced by poise and kindness. Once a year, on his days off from the ballpark, Clemente would drive thirty-five miles north of Pittsburgh to our seminary, jump out of the car, and throw the ball around with us for a while. He was educated by our Order in Puerto Rico, and he came to give back. Once on my way from New Bedford, Massachusetts to the ferry to Martha's Vineyard, I told the Puerto Rican taxi driver this story. He pulled the taxi over to the curb, turned around and said, "Tell me everything again." Clemente was a source of pride in both his native home, Puerto Rico, and his adopted home, Pittsburgh.

Art Rooney and Roberto Clemente rebuilt Pittsburgh's spirit. Both men had integrity, a spark, a fire and a sense of victory, which they passed on to the city. In many ways, they personified Pittsburgh. Like Rooney and Clemente, Pittsburgh did not fail its people. Old Pittsburgh was centered on the steel industry. It held a position of pride and was arguably the most important city during WW II. When steel failed, Pittsburgh transformed itself into a medical, education, and research hub. Unlike most rust belt cities, Pittsburgh climbed out of its depression and made it in the new economy.

I set the direction of my life the moment I chose the seminary over a military academy. For thirteen years, I followed a path of faith and study. It was a choice of solemn meditation over teenage pranks. It was the right decision for me. It was most especially the right move for my mother, who was determined that I grow up to be a man who cares for other people. She visited me faithfully every month. I stopped the acting out which could have led to more serious problems. I moved through high school and into college for two years. My first Latin teacher in high school seminary had been Father Dan. He was a big guy, and freshmen knew to watch out for him because he could be tough. He was a great teacher, and it was not his fault that despite studying Latin for 13 years I still knew basically nothing. I could not read, write, or understand it, although some classes were taught exclusively in Latin, and of course, the prayers and Mass for all those years were in Latin.

In college, I had Father Dan as a teacher again, this time for English literature. I knew in seminary and college that Father Dan was an alcoholic. I liked Father Dan a lot, and I wanted to do something that might help him. So, when assigned to draft a short story, I wrote about a priest, now a hobo on skid row, who continually washed his hands but did nothing else. At the end of the three-page story, he dies and his brother, a fellow priest, offers Mass at his funeral, telling the funeral crowd that the hobo was a good guy gone wrong with booze. The only dignity he had retained was his respect for his long-ago ordination, so he continually washed the hands that had been consecrated. My short story received an A-plus, the only one I ever got. I tried to warn Father Dan, but he died of alcoholism a few years later.

In 1959, after my sophomore year of college, I joined the Capuchin Order in Annapolis, Maryland. I began wearing the brown robes of a Franciscan in 1960 and took the new name of Barnabas to mark the beginning of a new life. I returned to St. Fidelis Seminary for two more years of silence, meditation, and study as required to earn a B.A. in philosophy. During those two years, I lived a hidden monastic life. These were my only years of serious scholarship. While we were not supposed to talk to other people, the difficult concepts of philosophy struggled against the isolation of my own thoughts. The questions of life being raised in my coursework needed a voice, and I needed to act. My view out the window was of a cemetery, and I felt dead. The only comfort was finding the

Papal encyclicals that covered labor rights, living wages, strikes, the labor movement, and the priest worker movement. A copy of the Daily Worker newspaper, written by Dorothy Day, sparked my passion. Those two years were the longest of my seminary years.

The standard procedure for leaving the seminary was simple. Guys simply disappeared. One hot afternoon, in the middle of a soccer match, Brother Davis passed out in the center of the field. He had lost so much weight because of the stress, the silence, the regimented diet, and the lack of human contact that his heart was not functioning properly. He was taken to the infirmary, and simply vanished. We knew he was no longer in the infirmary, but he did not return to the monastery. We were given no information, and we knew not to ask questions. A few weeks later Brother Gabriel collapsed on the way to meditation, and he, too, did not return from the infirmary and simply disappeared. A person was just there, and then not. I wondered if this would happen to me.

I was ready to disappear. I was ready to be done with sitting at desks and repeatedly discussing the same texts until we sucked them dry of new material. We were talking about ancient philosophy and history and ignoring the present. I felt the days were wasting. For thirteen years, I studied the charity part of the gospels. But I felt Jesus was saying "Remember my chains." It was calling me to action. "Get moving already."

I was going through my own awakening just as the nation stirred. It was the 1960s, and a societal revolution was taking place. I learned about the Woolworth sit-ins by reading the newspapers in which my mother wrapped my care packages. We were not allowed to have newspapers, so my mother demonstrated her own defiance of authority by sneaking them in to me.

The sit-ins were straight out of the pages of the Gospels: people standing together to protest injustice. While we studied the Book of John, and ate our morning peanut butter toast, we slept and woke in silence. Much of the country was coming closer to living our faith, fighting for equality and freedom, just as the Gospels described a world of long ago fighting in the name of the Lord.

I did not put this thought together until the third-floor toilet clogged one morning in March during my novice year in Annapolis. If the toilet had not clogged, if the plumber had not been called, maybe those final two years in seminary would not have felt so long. Father Peter was a calm and formal man, about seventy-years-old, who could silence a room with one sharp look. On the day the toilet clogged, he was almost bouncing with excitement as the plumber hauled equipment up and down the narrow staircase.

"You know," he said to the plumber, "the last time I was in the world, Eisenhower was considering making peace with the Soviets. Can you imagine that? Peace with the Soviets. Has it worked?" The plumber just looked at him, shook his head and kept working.

"How about the Yankees? The last time I was in the world, they were winning the World Series. Are they still winning?" Now Father Peter was nearly shouting to be heard over the noise of the electric plunger, squeezing into the bathroom behind the plumber. "What is going on with Hungary? Are they still protesting over there? The last time I was in the world…"

The plumber stood up abruptly and turned around, shutting off the electric plunger, which sputtered into silence. "What in the hell do you mean by 'when I was in the world?' Where in the bloody hell do you think we are now, Father?" As I listened to the plumber and Father Peter, I knew that I did not want to become Father Peter. I was a nice, celibate twenty-one-year-old in the wrong place. I had been sheltered in the seminary. The urge to leave came and went. When I took my simple vows, I made an additional vow to myself: I was not going to leave the world.

I graduated from St. Fidelis College in 1962 with my mother proudly looking on. Next I would begin graduate studies at Catholic University in Washington, D.C. As a child, I had gone to Washington with my mother, my sister Elaine, and my brother-in-law, Skip Manning, on the only trip I ever took with my mother without all our usual numbers. I instantly loved the beauty of Washington, D.C. I was enthralled by the architecture. Skip Manning and I flew paper airplanes out of the top windows of the Harrington Hotel.

Honoring my mother after my ordination. Family Photo.

Chapter 3

I Begin to March

1962-1966

Nineteen-sixty-two was an auspicious year to arrive in Washington. Everything seemed possible. Pope John XXIII had called for the Second Ecumenical Council of the Vatican, seeking to "open the Church windows and let in fresh air" to align the Church with the progressive changes of the time. The seminary was brimming with pride because America had elected its first Catholic president, a prime subject of cafeteria chatter. If you wanted to make new friends, it was always a sure bet to bring up the Catholic president.

No one I knew was more excited by President John F. Kennedy's election than my mother. Though she was enthusiastic about his platform (he had run as "an FDR Democrat"), she was much more excited that he was Irish. A few days after Kennedy defeated Richard Nixon, I received a letter from my mother stating, "The Irish will never be second-class citizens in America again." I laughed out loud when I finished reading her letter. My mother was an Irish American, and I was a dream of Irish descent.

The new president carried with him the hopes of many traditionally marginalized groups. He had campaigned on issues of civil rights and was embraced by anti-segregation activists, including singer Harry Belafonte, who referred to President

Kennedy as the civil rights candidate. There were high hopes for positive changes to come. A certain progressive nationalism was in the air, and why not? The prior two decades had appeared promising for America. The country had helped defeat fascism, war spending had pulled millions of Americans out of poverty, and for the first time, the country had an expansive middle class who lived in houses with one-car garages, and who began to realize their dream of sending their kids to college. History was moving forward, and there were two choices: to be on the side of progress or the losing side. I wanted to be part of this tide of change.

At Catholic University, there was a large group of progressive priests and seminarians involved in the civil rights movement. During the first week of school, they held a meeting for all incoming students interested in getting more involved. My entire seminary class showed up, and we were immediately put to work advertising an upcoming talk by Reverend Walter Fauntroy, a civil rights minister who worked with Dr. Martin Luther King Jr. in the Southern Christian Leadership Conference (SCLC).

I spent hours that weekend hanging fliers on every available post on campus. After that I was hooked. The group spent a lot of its time on popular education, hosting speakers such as the anti-war priests, the Berrigan brothers; Dorothy Day of the Catholic Worker Movement; and Rabbi Abraham Heschel, who had marched alongside Dr. King in Selma, Alabama.

We brought a culture of activism to campus, hosting hootenannies after hours in the campus dining hall. Hootenannies were an important, but not often written about, part of civil rights culture. Groups of folk musicians traveled around the country with acoustic guitars, violins, snare drums, and a few bales of hay (to be used as stage props). Hundreds would gather in the campus dining hall to watch the bands play songs in the folk style of Woody Guthrie, such as "Joe Hill."

Students would stomp their feet and holler along to the songs that always carried messages about civil rights and social justice. These gatherings helped give me the feeling that I was part of a bigger movement. I was eager to take some more direct action.

My first action with the movement became the most impactful of my life. The March for Jobs and Freedom showed the strength of our movement and built momentum for the passage of the proposed Civil Rights Act. The march was organized by a coalition of groups called the Big Six, which included Dr. King. The goal was to build public pressure to pass civil rights legislation. The legislation would end Jim Crow laws still prevalent in the South.

President Kennedy helped by advocating for the legislation, but it had stalled in Congress. Dr. King and the rest of the Big Six invited hundreds of thousands of people to march on Washington to show support for that legislation. My classmates and I did simple things to publicize the march: we hung posters, campaigned door-to-door, and held discussions with seminarians and leaders of other faiths.

"Education is not the filling of a pail but the lighting of a fire," said Yeats, paraphrasing Plutarch. Dr. King's voice was the spark that became a clarion call to my generation. He lit the fire for human rights advocacy in me.

On the morning of August 28, 1963, our group of Franciscans, dressed in black suits rather than our usual robes, began the three-mile trek to the National Mall and the March on Washington for Jobs and Freedom. We were about a mile away when we hit the tail end of the crowd. It was a deeply moving sight. There were thousands of people standing shoulder-to-shoulder, walking arm-in-arm, together. Blacks, whites, men, women, children—friends, neighbors, and strangers all pressing as close as possible to the steps of the Lincoln Memorial. As we walked by the White House, we wondered how the president would respond to the March.

As we headed to a better vantage point closer to the Lincoln Memorial, I spotted a young Jesse Jackson. He was about my age. "Got to get going, Jack," I thought. On the marble steps of the Lincoln Memorial, Joan Baez was singing about peace, love, forgiveness, and overcoming. John Lewis, the youngest speaker of the day, said, "By the forces of our demands, our determination, and our numbers, we shall send a desegregated South into a thousand pieces, put them together in the image of God and Democracy. We must say, 'Wake up, America, wake up!' For we cannot stop, and we will not and cannot be patient."

Next, Bob Dylan strummed his guitar and told us to take the hand of the person next to us. Then they all stepped off the stage. The sun was beating down and people passed around water and cigarettes. There was lots of good-natured jostling as we all moved closer to those white marble steps.

Then Dr. King was there, about halfway up the stairs, standing in front of the Marines and next to John Lewis, raising his arms as he stepped to the microphone. He did not smile as he looked out at the thousands of us gathered there. The crowd fell silent. He began to speak, and his voice seemed to thunder from heaven itself.

Dr. King spoke to all of us and to each one of us. "The marvelous new militancy which has engulfed the Negro community must not lead us to distrust all white people, for many of our white brothers, as evidenced by their presence here today, have come to realize that their destiny is tied up with our destiny and their freedom is inextricably bound to our freedom. We cannot walk alone," he said. "Let us not wallow in the valley of despair."

When he told us about his dream, it was as if the dream itself was in front of us, within reach. We could believe that Black children and white children could grow up to share our country. We shouted our agreement with Dr. King from the crowd and from all over the country: "Thank God almighty! Free at last."

I knew I had attended a moment of history when the promise of hope had been firmly planted on American soil. My years at Catholic University (1962-1966) went beyond my expectations. I felt lucky to be living in an exciting time. The country was in a good place during these years. We had John Kennedy as our President. We had Dr. King working on civil rights. We Catholics had John XXIII as Pope.

I was learning about the changes sweeping the country and my church and was beginning to participate in them, if only in a minor way. My classmates and I were no longer isolated. We walked everywhere because we had no money for buses. We tutored at Kelly Miller Middle School, visited patients at the Washington Hospital Center, went to courts to hear criminal trials, visited Congress, sat in on Supreme Court cases, and participated in debates on campus. I was slowly testing my wings. There was a large gap between what we were saying and what we were doing, or more precisely, not doing. The frustration continued as constant background noise until November 22, 1963. Walter Cronkite delivered the news that the President of the United States had been assassinated. He had died while riding in the back of a convertible in Dallas on a beautiful, sunny day.

JFK was not supposed to die. He was the president for whom we had all been waiting. He was the young, handsome Irish Catholic who we thought would change our country for the better. Our faith for the future had rested on him. Then Lyndon Johnson was sworn in as president on Air Force One. Jackie Kennedy in bloodstained clothes. Caroline and John had no father. The future we had hoped for was shattered. The university was silent the night of the assassination. The cafeteria was desolate. The city itself was silent; we were all in shock. The assassination and the funeral were all that we could think about. On Friday, the day of the funeral, the Superior got up at breakfast and instructed us, in no uncertain terms, not to attend the funeral. We were to stay within the walls of the monastery and pray. The entire monastery was devastated. Later, some of us took advantage of the lunch rush to slip out the back door. We were walking down North Capitol Street, joining the crowd of thousands and thousands of people in black, when a classmate wondered aloud what our punishment would be. "Are you out of your damn mind, worrying about that right now?" said Joe, a Canadian. "Haven't you been paying attention? JFK is dead."

The feeling of isolation and of existing in an alternate universe got worse after JFK's death. It reminded me of the days during the Cuban missile crisis when every sixty seconds, you heard a jet fly over Washington, D.C. Fear dominated the atmosphere. I thought that the country was falling apart, and all I knew to do was to get through the next few steps, get ordained as a priest, and then try to be an active participant in change. Following Kennedy's assassination, the country refused to wait for civil rights legislation any longer. Activists mounted a vigil at the Lincoln Memorial twenty-four hours a day, every day, until the Civil Rights Act was passed. I participated in the vigil, along with many of my fellow seminarians and Protestant and Jewish faith leaders. We usually took the night shift because it was our only chance to get away. Among the many people who joined us was Jim Carroll, a former Paulist and writer. He later referenced the vigil in one of his books. We also had the dubious pleasure of the company of a crazy Nazi who would stop by to tell us about the Irish girls he hit on.

I surprised even myself at how quickly I could explode. One morning in my second year of theological study, I was upset about something or nothing. I tossed my bowl of milk at Joe MacDonald at breakfast. He returned the honor, and we were off, almost flipping the table over as we wrestled, upending the other monks' places and spewing cereal and milk all over. Joe sat across the table from me for all those years. Maybe, we were just tired of looking at each other. We grappled and fought while forty other monks sat in stunned silence. Afterward, Joe protected me from the Superior by saying he had provoked the fight by repeatedly kicking me, a lie that cemented our friendship. For a week after that, I ate my meals on my knees, in silence, on the hard-stone floor of the dining room.

I was sent to see a psychiatrist. I thought it was nonsense, but it was required to move beyond the incident. I told the shrink that I did not know why I had reacted violently. I still do not know why. I do remember his observation: "There is something wrong with your monastery," he said. Those words gave me great relief. I was not crazy after all. It was so refreshing to hear someone mirror my own thoughts. I loved the seminary. The fathers understood my dyslexia and gave me a solid education. I learned to pray. I was a social creature. I needed room. I was simply not built to be silent. My frustration stemmed from the internal conflict between love and honor for the Church, my mother, and my own personality.

Education is the Lighting of a Fire Not the Pouring in of Information

Chapter 4

Priesthood

1965-1968

The last step in ordination as a Catholic priest is to say Mass in your home church. My first Mass would take place at St. Bernards, a few blocks from my home. It was October 30, 1965, and I had been in the seminary for thirteen years. St. Bernards Church was full that day, but I barely noticed. I was focused on walking my mother to her pew in the front, so that she could see her son say his first Mass. She wrapped her shaking hands in a shawl.

Parkinson's disease had struck her a few years earlier, and she could barely hold her rosary beads in her hands. When I stood at the front of the sanctuary and offered communion to the assembled congregation, she walked to the front by herself to kneel and accept the body and the blood of Christ.

I became a priest for myself as well as for my mother. I have never known which motivation was stronger. I will always be proud that I lifted her spirits during her long wait for me to be ordained. As usual, she was quiet, serene, and simply present for me. No words, no pats. Just truth and love. My mother did not thrive on big congratulations. She simply said, "You set out to become a priest and you did it." She preferred delivery over promise.

• • • • • • • • • •

My first posting was in the Catholic diocese of Baltimore in western Maryland. I was a novice Master for brothers and a chaplain for the new Newman Center to be created at Frostburg State College in Maryland during the 1966/67 school year. Frostburg State had 3,000 students, most of them from nearby Cumberland. My boss in the monastery was Father James, my old mentor who had started me along the process years before. At the Newman Center, I was under the jurisdiction of Cardinal Lawrence Shehan of Baltimore.

I did not have a church. What I had was a small conference room with whitewashed walls and a sign on the door informing visitors that they were entering the ecumenical center where different faiths held religious services. It was a perfect complement to my style: simple, easy, plain.

Before I was assigned to the college, Catholic students at Frostburg State had never held a Mass or been offered communion at school. I was the first priest at the college, and the college was the first place I was a priest. They had no idea what to expect, which was good, as I had absolutely no idea what I was doing.

The first thing I did was to put up a paper sign: "First Catholic Mass, Sunday September 18, 1966."

As I stood at the front of that small room on my first Sunday, watching all of twelve people file in, it occurred to me that I might have underestimated the effort it would take to develop a Newman Center at Frostburg. The sermons that I had learned as a seminarian were irrelevant. What had I been thinking in planning to quote the Old Testament to these people? These were college students.

Whenever I speak in public I always pretend to have a written speech, but using written material to speak from is not an option for me. I cannot see the print with my eyes, and my dyslexia would make me jump from the page to my own thoughts anyway.

So, I gave that first sermon simply from my heart. I spoke about Christ, about what it meant to be a follower or a peacemaker.

I said that faith could be practiced in many ways: sitting at a lunch counter, riding a bus in the seat of your choice, or marching across a bridge that others tried to stop you from crossing. These actions, I said, were among the best examples of what it meant to follow Christ. I had hidden my talent for speaking from the Order; I do not know why I did that, but I had. My first sermon at the Newman Center showed me that God had given me a talent. Years later, Sting, lead singer of the Police, said: "Jack has a tear in his voice. And I am jealous of that."

The tiny group of students in front of me became, in my imagination, throngs of people gathered on the Mall in Washington, D.C., listening to me speak on the steps of the Lincoln Memorial while Joan Baez sang behind me, inspiring us all to walk together, holding hands. Then, abruptly, I realized where I was, and that everyone was staring. One girl had her mouth hanging open. A young man looked pale, shocked.

I stopped in the middle of a sentence about the fire hoses that had been turned on the children in Selma. A sermon on civil rights had not been within the expectations of the few students who attended Mass that day in that small, conservative college.

The silence lasted about forty seconds, an eternity as I stood alone at the front of the room. To my surprise, those twelve students seated on old cafeteria benches started clapping. It was an amazing day. Father James sent some of the monks to play guitars and drums. Some students could sing, and they joined the monks. It became a hootenanny/folk Mass.

The next week thirty students came, and then fifty the next. People came who were not Catholic and had never listened to the Gospel of John but had heard of John Lewis and the movements for workers' rights and civil rights. Then the next week, locals were crowding in around the students on the plastic cafeteria benches, and people had to stand in the back. My isolation, along with its silence, its eerie disconnect from the world, was slowly evaporating.

To fit our growing congregation, we soon rented half of a duplex for the Newman Center, right off campus. The first brochure we created for the center still says it best: "The Center provides a place where statements such as 'if the Church is going to be Christian, it must be willing to accept identification with the world in which it finds itself situated' can be freely discussed and practiced."

On April 4, 1967, I carried a radio instead of a pretend sermon into the Ecumenical Center. By the time people found seats or places to stand in the back of the room, Dr. King had begun his "Beyond Vietnam" speech.

> "As I have walked among the desperate, rejected, and angry young men, I have told them that Molotov cocktails and rifles would not solve their problems. I have tried to offer them my deepest compassion while maintaining my conviction that social change comes most meaningfully through nonviolent action. But they ask—and rightly so—what about Vietnam? They ask if our own nation wasn't using massive doses of violence to solve its problems, to bring about the changes it wanted. Their questions hit home, and I knew that I could never again raise my voice against the violence of the oppressed in the ghettos without having first spoken clearly to the greatest purveyor of violence in the world today—my own government."

It was not the first time that the Civil Rights Movement and the war in Vietnam had been contrasted. It was hypocritical to demand freedom for our own citizens, while our government was using napalm and bombs to deprive the Vietnamese of their freedom and their lives. Dr. King's speech made me realize that the two movements were so deeply intertwined that I could not be involved in either to the exclusion of the other.

The students, town residents, and I started talking about the war. We learned about the Gulf of Tonkin Resolution that had authorized the U.S. to attack North Vietnam and its leader, Ho Chi Minh, without further congressional action. He had committed the ultimate crime by using phrases such as "redistribution of wealth" and "neutrality in the Cold War." We talked about many of the serious issues of the time, including civil rights, Vietnam, women's rights, and drug use. These discussions took place in the Newman Center, in the Ecumenical Center, in clergy meetings, and in Father James' office when I stopped by most nights for a drink.

The talks were an important step, but I did not want discussions to substitute for active participation. The split between the church and action was beginning to resolve itself within me.

The Newman Center became a center for activism. The student leadership of Frostburg State responded. People like the Kenneys, the Boyles, the Sullivans, and others joined and eventually we had an active chapter of the Newman Center that was quickly and powerfully alert.

· · · · · · · · · ·

"Are you boys here to be social movement tourists or are you going to make yourselves useful?" Father Joe, Father Stan, and I had just gotten out of the car after a twelve-hour drive from Maryland. We stood there like idiots, blinking in the late afternoon Milwaukee sun. Father Stan started to speak, but before he could, Father Groppi rolled his eyes, announced that the copy machine was in the back of the church, and stalked off. "Copy machine?" Father Joe asked under his breath. That welcome was Groppi's way of telling us that if we wanted to be idle machines, we should move to the back of the room.

Like many northern cities, Milwaukee was a segregated town. Although the rules written into neighborhood covenants in Milwaukee claimed that all races were welcome to purchase a home in the neighborhood, home ownership in many neighborhoods was often impossible for Black people. Black men and women were thwarted in the process of getting a loan to purchase a house. The banks simply denied housing loans to any family of the wrong color who attempted to buy a home in a white neighborhood. This "redlining" reinforced an apartheid line.

For about five years, City Council member Val Phillips, from a largely African American neighborhood on the north side of town, introduced a bill to end redlining. Redlining was a discrimination tactic used to keep minorities out of white neighborhoods by blocking access to mortgages. She introduced the bill three times, and the bill was defeated each time. The 18-1 vote matched the racial make-up of the council.

Father Groppi was one of the few Catholic priests in Milwaukee who actively supported the Civil Rights Movement. As such, he had grown close to the NAACP membership. The NAACP youth commandos and Father Groppi organized protest walks in response to the repeated rejection of Val Phillips's proposal to outlaw redlining. Father Groppi had marched with Dr. Martin Luther King, Jr. in the South; was a close friend of Fannie Lou Hamer of the Mississippi Freedom Democratic Party; and was one of the early proponents of bringing the fight for civil rights north.

In the North, racism was seldom codified, but was no less virulent. Many Northerners who spoke out against racial discrimination in the South ignored the Black ghettos and gross discrimination in their own towns.

Milwaukee, a northern and supposedly integrated city, watched the battle on the 6 o'clock news along with the rest of the country. Father Groppi and the NAACP were using their moment in the spotlight to tackle the issue of fair housing in a major way. Father Groppi was threatened by phone and in person many times.

We attended Father Groppi's Mass and were shocked by the format. The entire parish stood in a circle around the altar and took turns reading from the Bible. We passed the chalice cup from person to person. Fannie Lou Hamer led the community in song. It was my first experience with an alternative style of Mass, and it was the first time I met this great woman of the Civil Rights Movement.

After Mass, the commandos would go to the baptistry to plan the march. Then we joined Father Groppi and his congregation on the streets of Milwaukee, singing our songs of freedom. We followed Dick Gregory, the activist and comedian, who walked with Father Groppi and led us down the streets of the white neighborhoods and the Black neighborhoods to the bridge, now named after Father Groppi, that crossed the river.

We ignored the police who surrounded our group of two or three hundred. We walked together: priests, nuns, and lay people, Black and white, men and women. There was safety in numbers and we were relieved because the NAACP commandos walked between the marchers and the police. We thought that the more of us who were present, the less likely it was that Milwaukee reactionaries would attack.

Groppi and Val Phillips won the battle against redlining, mainly because Milwaukee could not afford police coverage for the constant marches. The battle in Milwaukee also marked the beginning of my life-changing relationships with my mentors, Father Groppi, Fannie Lou Hamer, and Dick Gregory.

Around the same time, I started shooting with Father Pete. He loved skeet shooting and generally aiming his gun at different objects, dead or alive. I went along with Father Pete because he was fun and one of the younger priests in my area. One day Pete suggested I learn to practice self-protection. That was not my style, but I agreed, figuring that I was not going to harm anyone.

Pete drove us to a small, isolated field up against a hill. When he went to get guns out of the truck he brought out a Thompson submachine gun. Pete said, "It is an antique." I asked where it had come from.

"From the confessional," Pete told me. "Last winter, a guy comes into the confessional and says he killed someone. I was shocked, and all I could think to ask was, 'Why did you do that?' The guy said he did it as a living. I told him that I could not offer him forgiveness unless he gave up killing and his lifestyle. We went back and forth. He finally said, 'Okay, I will stop.' I told him I needed a real sign of his decision. It was so damn serious. I could not stand it. Finally, he said, 'Okay, Father, I will give you the gun.' I told him that was a good sign and appropriate. I expected a pistol, but he pushed through the old red curtains, and he gave me this gun." We had fun aiming the Thompson at targets, but neither of us pulled the trigger.

It occurred to me that we had an untenable situation in Frostburg. We made this whole trip to Milwaukee to advocate for civil rights, and then we returned to Frostburg where there were only four Blacks in the entire student body: two from the Caribbean and two who had been recruited to play football. There was no official policy at Frostburg against accepting Black students, just as there was no official segregation in Milwaukee. The dean claimed the admissions board was color-blind. However, every applicant had to submit a photograph along with an essay, which gave admissions the ability to select the race of its incoming class. We needed some direct action at our own college to confront the admissions department.

We wanted Frostburg to integrate its student population. Dennis Kuhn and Professor Robert Gilligan had been coming to Mass since my first week at Frostburg, and they wanted to plan a rally. We invited people prominent in the Civil Rights Movement to speak, to help us shame the hell out of the supposedly color-blind Administration.

Frostburg State had never hosted a conference like the Black Backlash Conference we planned in May 1968. We wanted the rally to be large and inclusive. We raised funds with the help of the entire parish, friends, and some of the professors like Bob Gilligan. We had bake sales, car washes, and everything else, and we plastered the entire campus with posters about the event.

We invited Rev. Braxton Boyd, a Washington minister who worked in Mississippi and Alabama with Dr. King; Dan Gant of the Congress of Racial Equality; Robert Jackson, assistant director of the Neighborhood Youth Program and a community organizer of Southeast Washington; Rev. Walter Lubarski, a sociology professor at Virginia Union College; Rev. Goodwin Douglas, president of the Cumberland NAACP; and Nelson P. Guild, dean of the College at Frostburg. Speakers came in from Chicago, Cumberland, and Washington, D.C. Stan Lubarski spoke, as did Dennis Kuhn and Professor Gilligan, as well as a Protestant pastor from D.C. Student representatives came from Bowie State College, Coppin State College, Morgan State College, Salisbury State College, University of Maryland, Catholic University, American University, George Washington University, Howard University, Virginia Union College, and Mary Washington College of the University of Virginia.

We managed to secure the necessary funds and a space on campus to hold the rally, and for a moment I thought that the rally might go smoothly. Then, the night before the event, as I was sitting in my little single room, puzzling out the order of the speakers, there was a knock on my door. It was Father James. He was pale and shaky, twisting a handkerchief as he stood in the hallway.

My mother had died, he told me. Her Parkinson's disease had become worse in the past few months, but I had somehow thought she was going to be fine. She had always been fine; she was my mother. It had been quick and relatively painless, Father James said. I slumped down and sat motionless in the doorway. This was not unexpected, but it was still difficult to believe.

Father James was saying that I should return to Pittsburgh and prepare for the funeral. I left early the next morning and picked up my brothers Joe and Mike on the way. We drove home without saying a word.

The funeral Mass was to be held at St. Bernards. I could stand and say the words of the Father and the Son and the Holy Ghost, but my mother would not be there in the front row. Instead, she would be lying before us in a mahogany coffin, covered in linen embroidered with the sign of the cross, just as she would have wanted. Because she would not be there, I asked Rev. John Petruha, my oldest friend from the seminary, to give the sermon.

John delivered a beautiful sermon in the church my mother had worshiped in every single Sunday. Even though it was awful, it was also beautiful. It was exactly how it should have been, with all of us there, and my mother finally completely at peace. But eleven of us sat there devastated. We knew what we had lost.

The Frostburg rally had gone on without me and brought state attention to the racial disparities at the school. By the next year, Maryland Gov. Marvin Mandel had appointed Pansye S. Atkinson to change admissions policies. Pansye Atkinson was the first to hold the new position of Coordinator of Integration, a position that quickly became Director of Minority Affairs. The governor mandated that the same position be created at all six state colleges in Maryland.

Ordination with (l-r) Mary Healey, me, my sister Elaine Manning with her two children, LJ and Elaine Manning, and Aunt Betty.

Saying Mass at Frostburg State.

Meeting with a student at Frostburg State.

Frostburg students and Brother Hillary playing at Sunday Mass.

Father Healey

Chapter 5

Awakening

I was heckled during Mass one day. "Father Healey lies! Don't believe him when he tells you everyone can reach the Kingdom of Heaven. Only Catholics can reach the Kingdom of Heaven. Only baptized Catholics." While Father Montgomery was right that I did not think the gates of heaven were open only to Catholics, I was furious that he had picked my Sunday Mass to make a public display of our theological differences.

Maybe Father Montgomery did not approve of the mixing of Jesus and John Lewis, of Ho Chi Minh and David, or maybe it was simply that many in his congregation had started attending my Mass instead of his own. I was sure that he did not approve of the reforms that had recently been instituted by the Vatican.

The reforms had been intended to make the Church more accessible by giving Mass in the language of the community's population. The church also removed the altar rails that had separated the priest from his congregation and suggested priests dress in more casual clothing for day-to-day work. The visionary Pope John XXIII was not admired by most priests in western Maryland who had little interest in the Church joining the twentieth century. Father Montgomery just happened to hit his breaking point toward the end of my Sunday morning Mass on Parents' Day weekend. He was standing in the back of the room with his face red and his starched white collar dripping with sweat. He bellowed at me as I began the final blessing. Shocked, the congregation turned around and stared at the balding, middle-aged priest who had committed the unheard-of sin of interrupting another priest's Mass.

I waited at the altar for him to finish. When he finally fell silent, I finished the blessings. After Mass, I considered my options. There was, of course, the violent route with a quick uppercut to the nose that would probably solve the problem. Or, more reasonably, I could call Cardinal Shehan, head of the Baltimore Diocese, and lodge a formal complaint. For once, I chose the latter. I called the cardinal and explained what happened and told him that if Father Montgomery pulled a stunt like that again, I would have no choice but to kill him.

At seventy-years-old, Cardinal Shehan was as sharp as ever. He cleared his throat and said, "May I remind you, Father Healey, that you are opposed to the death penalty?" In 1967, Father James and I had led a successful campaign to stop the execution of Gary Miller, a sixteen-year-old who had been convicted of murdering a young girl, Judy Lee Ziegler.

Two judges paid us a visit to challenge our position and asked us to look at pictures of the dead girl. "If you also look at the photos of the last people you hanged, I'll look at your photos." They left in a huff, the hanging judges of western Maryland. Spiro Agnew, then governor of Maryland, ultimately granted a reprieve because Gary Miller was a minor. The growing problem in the Church was bigger than just sour old Father Montgomery. The Vatican II reforms were hitting some of the priests hard, shaking up their routines and undermining values they had learned in seminary. For the Church, change was necessary to remain relevant in the 1960s. The Church could not allow itself to be extraneous. Television increased popular awareness of other cultures, and much of the world was becoming more urban and sophisticated.

Latin America had once been an unofficial laboratory for the Church's expansion of conservative policies. By the 1960s though, "liberation theology" was gaining ground and, among other things, it urged direct action for the poor. Many priests, especially in Latin America, believed such action was a prerequisite to being a good Catholic. Liberation theology, the priest worker movement of France, and Dorothy Day's work kept me involved with the Church. To the extent that I had a Catholic tradition, this was it.

As the superior of the monastery, Father James oversaw implementing the welcome changes. At our monthly priestly community meeting, we discussed how we were implementing the recent reforms. We shared reforms we had begun, how our congregations had reacted, and what we had learned that might help our priests. The meetings resembled a social hour. We would drink and talk freely. Franciscan monks held friendship with one another as an indispensable part of the life. In that isolated, airless environment, the men around you were your friends and your family. They were the only ones who understand the precise, quirky nature of the world in which we reside.

However, our Order was not isolated from the ideological battles splitting families apart all over the country. The split between old and new was just as vitriolic, if not more so, within the wood-paneled walls of our monasteries and churches. Father Guy, Father Montgomery, and other older, more conservative priests hated Vatican II. They grumbled at the suggestions of new liturgy, rolled their eyes at the idea of connecting with younger parishioners, and finally, at one particularly tense meeting, Father Montgomery outright laughed at Father James's suggestion of mixing Old Testament stories with parallel stories from contemporary politics. Father James turned crimson but kept talking to retain control of the situation. I leaned over to Father Montgomery and poked him. "Act your age," I told him, perhaps a little too loudly. Father James stopped talking, and the entire room looked at me. Father Guy narrowed his eyes. "Decorum, Father Jack," he said, shaking his head at the priest across from us.

Within a few weeks of that meeting, the conservative clergy simply stopped attending the sessions. Their open hostility and complete lack of fellowship went against every Franciscan principle.

Maybe Father James had always been a drinker. But now he drank nightly in the community room where monks visited each evening.

I generally joined him after the others had gone to bed. They did not like either of us. We were progressive. The old forty-five turntable spun an endless loop of "The Impossible Dream" while we discussed the pros and cons of the changes coming from Rome. We must have heard that song 10,000 times, night after night, as Father James gulped from a heavy glass tumbler of dark liquor. He would fill his glass again and again as the night wore on. I sat with him and watched as he moved the record player's needle back to the beginning again. It was not an inspiring experience for a young priest. Andy Williams and cheap whiskey were the soundtrack to our deep confusion and disappointment with the failure of the Church to stand up for Vatican II.

Father James was my mentor, and he was deteriorating in front of me. He reminded me of my late professor, Father Dan, and I was worried. I watched in sadness, feeling helpless to lift the weight of disappointment magnified by alcohol. I was torn between loyalty to him, our joint cause, and the others. He was in decline, and I did not want to follow his trajectory down. I wanted to continue for both of us, for my mother, and for the nation. By 1968, the United States was tearing itself apart. On the night of April 4, 1968, Father James was watching television when the news broke. Dr. King was dead.

We had plans to eat dinner in the cafeteria together, so he came looking for me. We both were in Washington, D.C. on a visit. He found me sitting in the garden. It was spring, and cherry blossom season in Washington was in full bloom. Father James looked pale.

"It's Dr. King," he said. We decided to go to the soup kitchen of a mutual friend. We served sandwiches, because we did not know what else to do and because it seemed to make sense. We worked in silence. There was nothing to say. It was one year to the day since I had carried that beat-up radio into the Newman Center so the students could listen to Dr. King's "Beyond Vietnam" speech.

While we served soup, a few miles away on East Capitol Street,

Stokely Carmichael, head of the Student Non-Violent Coordinating Committee, was leading a spontaneous walk, asking stores to shut down for the day in a show of respect for Dr. King. Tensions were high, and by the time the marchers hit the crossing of 14th and U Street, someone had thrown a garbage can through a window. Stokely had brought a gun in the hope of discouraging rioting. He pulled it out, threatened the assembled crowd, and told them to go home before people got hurt. He asked them to respect the memory of the fallen leader of the non-violent movement.

We heard the story later that day on the radio. The marchers had not listened to Stokely and had started to vent their anger. They threw bottles, stones, and anything else they could find. Washington was not the only city descending into lawlessness, fear, and violence. Rioting spread across the country. By that night, entire city blocks had gone up in flames, and the mayor of Washington, D.C. went on the radio, imploring residents to stay in their homes and lock their doors. Father James and I decided to spend the night in the rectory. We were setting up makeshift beds with the television murmuring in the background.

Father James burst out: "Tanks!" he said. "Tanks in the middle of Washington, D.C.!" Tanks were rolling down 14th Street, past the bars and restaurants, the clothing stores, the markets. They were followed by swarms of National Guard troops, nearly 13,000 of them. Tear gas blanketed the city by nightfall, and from the Church we could hear the occasional smattering of gunfire, too far away to know whether the National Guard had killed Americans on our own streets. The next morning a haze hung over the city. Despite perfect spring weather, it felt as though a storm was coming. When I risked leaving the Church for coffee, two young Black guys standing in the door grabbed me and slammed me up against the wall. "Go home. Get the hell out of here. This is our time," they yelled.

Back in Cumberland, miles from D.C. at a mostly white Catholic school, Father Birne, a local priest, was standing at the front of his classroom, trying to find the right way to break the news about Dr. King to his students. He wanted to talk about an American hero who had been shot and why large parts of the country were exploding with violence. He began by saying that Dr. King had been shot and killed. The room of high-school boys stared at him, and then in the back of the room, somebody spoke up.

"Is he dead?

"Finally!" someone yelled. Chaos ensued. Some of the boys were slapping hands and cheering while others were telling them to shut up. Father Birne was shocked by the divisive reaction. He walked quickly out of the room, found a trash can, and threw up. He called me to help him calm down. He wanted them to understand the tragedy of the violent death of a leader who advocated non-violence and social justice. I did not know what to say.

One of the worst effects of the assassination of Dr. King was the way it split the country along racial lines. The divide was also between long-haired kids and short-haired kids. Military and non-military. Red and blue states emerged. Catholics split over the pill. These schisms have never healed. In cities, the already existing racial rifts expanded, fracturing the tenuous connections that Dr. King had worked so hard to create. It was as if Dr. King had never spoken; the divide he had worked so hard to narrow still existed, and his message of nonviolence seemed lost.

After the assassination, we continued as before with civil rights speakers and marches. There was an increasing feeling of urgency but also of hopelessness. We were afraid we had lost, that we were soldiers standing on a battlefield shooting at shadows in the bushes long after the enemy had won the war and gone home.

Dr. King's last project had been the development of an "economic bill of rights." The Southern Christian Leadership Conference (SCLC) continued the project after his death. The document was intended to function as a statement of principle, establishing the right to housing, food, and education as a necessary precondition for the exercise of civil rights. Some Americans already had full access to these economic rights, but clearly, others did not.

The proposal for such a document was not new; in fact, it was first proposed by FDR, our Healey family hero. After Dr. King's death, the SCLC convinced 7,000 people to come to Washington, set up tents around the Capitol, to demand the passage of an economic bill of rights. They built a shanty town called Resurrection City and lived there despite the pouring rain and thunderstorms that marked the summer of 1968. Rivers of mud seeped into sleeping bags and food, but people would not leave Resurrection City until an economic bill of rights was enacted.

We found housing for two busloads of people headed to Resurrection City. Father Groppi arrived in Resurrection City and helped put up tents and maintain order. He and I often met at Mr. Henry's, a bar and restaurant in the heart of Capitol Hill, and he spoke to me of the drama of 7,000 people living in such close quarters in Resurrection City. I told him about the monastery and the division with the conservative priests who took the separation so far that they had stopped saying hello. I also told him that Father James was going through a full bottle of booze every day or two.

My mentor, Father Groppi, was facing a similar divide in Milwaukee. The conservatives there had called the Archbishop of Milwaukee, demanding that the civil rights work halt and that Father Groppi go back to his regular duties and cease his unbecoming behavior. Father Groppi responded that he found it more unbecoming to support a system that deprived a certain portion of the nation of life, liberty, and the pursuit of happiness purely because of the color of their skin. But he was not calling the Archbishop to complain, now, was he?

• • • • • • • • • •

One night I confided in him. I was considering leaving the priesthood and the Franciscans. I felt we were not helping anyone while stuck in the monastery, with our careful prayers and our quiet meals, watching the country collapse around us.

He spoke slowly, measuring his words carefully. "Here's the thing, Jack," he said. "You have a choice here. Do you want to spend your time fighting other priests, or fighting this messed up system?"

—65—

Leaving the priesthood required a lot of discussions. It had taken me more than twelve years to be ordained as a Catholic priest, and it would take me over a year to finalize my decision.

When I told my superiors in the summer of 1968, they asked me to pray about my decision for six months before leaving. I sought advice from friends in the priesthood. At the end of six months, I went to see the dean. He listened to me and said, "Father, you can really preach, and you are a good priest. Stay and work it out."

Then he squirmed, "That said, I guess I better confess something to you." He tugged at his collar. "I feel rather hypocritical because on Monday I will be leaving the priesthood to become an insurance agent."

The next thing I knew, we were laughing so hard that we could barely breathe. It was just time to go. I left the priesthood on Christmas Day, 1968, with nothing but gratitude toward the Franciscan Order and hope for the future.

I did not mind praying, meditating, going to bed early, and waking up early, but I wanted to expand beyond the walls of the Church. I wanted to see our big world and the people in it. I knew I was good in a fight, and now I was ready to take on some non-violent ones.

Cardinal Shehan, Monsignor Frank Murphy, and me at Newman Center.

Chapter 6

Baby Steps

For reasons that remain mysterious, my sister Naomi decided the first thing I had to do upon leaving the monastery was to go skiing. Naomi is the kind of person with whom it is useless to disagree once she has made up her mind.

Naomi always played the role of surrogate mother to me and watched out for me from the age of two until well into adulthood. She kept me out of trouble and would often grab me by the ear and drag me out of the local pool hall. She was my watcher. So, it was no surprise to see her face on the Christmas Day I left the priesthood. I had nowhere to live, no source of income, no savings, and no job prospects. But I did have a loving sister.

"We are going skiing," Naomi announced when she and my brother Mike came to pick me up from the monastery. We tossed my beat-up suitcase into the back of her Ford and drove off the monastery grounds for the last time. After the endless conversations I had been having that year, it did not seem possible I could just get in a car and leave, but the Order simply said goodbye. Money had never been a part of that life. I left without a penny.

Mike, who had spent the years that I was in seminary developing a successful career in marketing, made enough to buy a cabin in

Western Pennsylvania. So off to Pennsylvania we went.

I had never skied in my life, so Mike gave me my first ski lesson. I use the word "lesson" here loosely. Mike, despite being my favorite brother in nearly every other way, essentially strapped the skis on me and pushed. Also, I was twenty-nine years old, and pointing the skis toward the bottom and letting go was exciting.

It was a little less exciting when I found myself lying face up on the snow, leg bent beneath me at a sickening angle, hearing the voices of other, more judicious skiers, all around me: "Whoa, did you see him hit the tree?" "He just went right at the thing." Next thing I knew, Mike was in the back of an ambulance with me, looking nauseated, as we sped down the mountain toward the hospital, where I was treated for a broken leg. The cause of the injury, printed in big block letters on my chart, "Out of control skiing."

The broken leg landed me on Naomi's couch for the next few weeks. I slept and tried to figure out my life. I had never had a paying job (except summer jobs), done laundry, cooked my own food, or paid rent. I felt like one of those prisoners who are released after decades only to find out that people now have machines that allow them to type words on a screen. I had acquired plenty of practical skills at the monastery: carpentry, plumbing, laying tile, and shoe-making among them. Jobs in those fields just did not interest me.

• • • • • • • • • •

As I was driving down Connecticut Avenue in northwest Washington, I spotted the brick house across the park from the National Zoo where a lot of ex-priests lived. Cardinal O'Boyle fired about sixty priests on August 18, 1968, after the priests signed a petition demanding the Church change its position on birth control for Catholic women. Jane Briggs Hart, the wife of Michigan Senator Philip Hart, believed in what the priests had done. She rented a building for them to live in, buying them the time to start new lives.

I found an apartment on the other side of the zoo on upper

Wisconsin Avenue. My first home outside the seminary was a nice place with a rooftop pool. I figured all the fired priests would not fit in the Hart house, and more ex-priests were coming to town every day to look for government or teaching jobs. I hoped I could find tenants from among these ex-priests and use their rent money to keep me in groceries.

On one of those days when the rent had not covered the cost of scrambled eggs and day-old bread, I went to a soup kitchen with a friend. It was a nice evening, and we strolled through Lafayette Park across from the White House.

In the middle of the park, sitting in a big circle on the grass, was a gathering of people. It was a motley group, some in business suits, some in flowery dresses, some who looked like drifters, and some who appeared to be barely out of high school. It was an anti-war meeting organized in part by Sam Brown, who would later head the ACTION agency under Jimmy Carter. Sam and a few of his friends would devise a plan for a protest, a walk, a demonstration, or even a party, and the group would make it happen.

Although the group agreed that the war in Vietnam needed to end quickly, to stop the napalm, the body bags, and the dying children, the ragtag coalition sitting on the blankets often disagreed about everything else.

Some, the men in suits, wanted the war to end, and for business as usual to return to the United States. Others, the men in the ragged T-shirts, hoped a Trotskyite revolution might spring from these evenings in Lafayette Park. Everybody somehow agreed, to the extent that the protests happened, the walks took place, and the demonstrations resulted in action. For those equally committed to partying, someone always brought weed and beer for a party afterward.

Elizabeth was the center of attention at one of those parties. Dressed in bell-bottom jeans, John Lennon glasses, and with flowers braided into her long, black hair, she was stunning. A friend of hers had thrown the party, concerned that Elizabeth had met no one new in the months since she left her husband. That night, I watched as Elizabeth poured drinks for journalists, activists, and politicians. As she turned around from the record player, we locked eyes for just a moment. Then we stared a little longer, and she made her way over to me.

It was a little like Marcie all over again. I was talking to the beautiful girl in jeans as the other guys in the room shot me dirty looks. Those looks got nastier when Elizabeth pulled a piece of notepaper from the pocket of a nearby journalist and wrote her number on it. She handed it to me, smiled slightly, and slipped away among a bunch of guys arguing about Mao.

I called—how could I not have called—the following Tuesday. Tuesday seemed eager but not over-eager, I thought. After our date, I was sitting on her couch, talking about her three kids she was raising on her own. And then we were kissing, and all I could think about was that I had not kissed anyone since the ninth grade and I had no idea what I was doing. Fortunately, she did. Then she was unbuttoning her long, flowery shirt, and I felt so lucky I had left the seminary.

Elizabeth did not care that I was just learning how to live. I did not know how to hail a cab, order take-out, or date. Everything she did fascinated me, from the way she did her hair, to how she slept in some mornings until 11:00, or made dinner reservations and then canceled them. I was excited every time she called, and I never said no to dinner, drinks, or a party. All I could think about when I was with her was what it might be like to do this for the rest of our lives.

One day Elizabeth called and invited me to coffee in Dupont Circle at one of our favorite little cafés. As usual, I was early and ordered her a cappuccino and imagined we might go for lunch later. Elizabeth finally arrived and told me she and her ex-husband were getting back together. She was calm and direct about our breakup. She just recently divorced, and she was not prepared to jump into a serious relationship. I had to have known that, right?

I had not. She spoke about her husband and said he was moving back in with her. I could not listen. The only thing I could do was pay for the iced tea and the damn cappuccino and walk out of the café.

There was a pounding on my door late that afternoon. "What is going on, Jack?" It was Sam, an ex-priest friend of mine.

I told him that Elizabeth and I were not moving in together, and we would no longer be seeing one another. Sam and I sat on our wooden floor, Sam drinking a pop and explaining that this happened, at least once, to everyone. He patted my shoulder.

As he was getting up to go to work, he said, "I'd give it about a year." "Give what a year?" I wanted to know. "What could possibly take a year?" He smiled, "Getting over Elizabeth. I would give it about a year." "What the hell, Sam?"

That evening I went to see my friend Bob Gilligan. When Bob and I worked together at Frostburg State, he always knew what to say. He was often found calming the nerves of anxious college students, so I thought he could help me in my situation. Bob and Barb, his new wife, were kind about my misery. This happens to everyone, he proclaimed, absolutely everyone. Bob was a psychologist.

As I left, he said, "It's probably going to take you about a year to get over it." My friends confirmed what Sam had told me the day before. They looked after me for quite a while, and they were right… it took about a year. In that year, I was still trying to find myself when I came across the words of Malcolm X who said, "If you must ask whites for your freedom, they will always have the power to take it away from you."

Malcolm X, with his great eloquence, managed to express the sentiments of an entire movement in a single sentence. Many Black civil rights activists believed that collaborating with white activists was no longer the right way to equality. I respected their beliefs but that meant there no longer was a place in the civil rights movement for a white ex-priest, and that work was all I knew.

I briefly considered working for the government in the Office of Economic Opportunity that President Lyndon Johnson had created as part of his Great Society. I thought about working in a drug counseling program. Nixon was president and he was eliminating every job I might have been interested in. I did some paperwork to get a civil service rating in case I was hired for a government gig. My rating was low until an ex-priest challenged the process and we ex-priests ended up with a GS14 rating, way above where we were first placed.

Then one afternoon Sam and I were again sitting on the kitchen floor drinking pop—we never sat at the table—and Sam told me he got me a job interview. I had been unemployed for nine months. I was tired of having other ex-priests in my place. He said the job had something to do with walking around the world to end hunger.

Movements
Need Movement

Chapter 7

Students Become My Teachers

1969-1973

I interviewed the next morning for the job at the American Freedom from Hunger Foundation (AFFHF) that Sam had considered and rejected. He was headed to Peru to marry a mountain woman and has lived there ever since.

It was September 1969. I was wearing the ill-fitting suit I borrowed from Sam, and I had no idea how to answer an interview question. The aide to the executive director of AFFHF, former Congressman Leonard Wolf, asked why I wanted to work there. I told her I had experience with organizing students and had overseen the Newman Center at Frostburg State. The interviewer said she did not give a damn about the Newman Center. At AFFHF, I would be expected to nationalize the youth movement. She told me I could start work the next day, and I better be on time. Then she yelled into the other room: "Bryce Hamilton, get in here. We have a new staffer who doesn't know what the hell is going on." Bryce was leaving to work on a new effort called Earth Day. Congressman Len Wolf, with his shock of black hair and red tie, ambled in. "Son," he said, "you're going to need a passport and a suitcase."

Hunger was and is a pervasive crisis in the United States and around the world. Lester Brown published *Man, Land and Food* in 1964, and *U.S. News & World Report* picked up on the urgency of the issue. Brown predicted drastic world hunger by the end of the century. Drought, famine, and overpopulation were all issues that needed to be addressed. In the United States, people like Bobby Kennedy shined a light on conditions of hunger, especially in the inner cities, the South, on migrant farm workers, and on the many children going to bed hungry.

In 1968, when Len Wolf took over AFFHF, it was a small non-profit that served as the United States affiliate of the Food and Agricultural Organization (FAO) in Rome. The goal of AFFHF was to reduce hunger across the world. The youth arm of this organization was called Young World Development (YWD), and its focus was on raising awareness of the issue of hunger in the United States and around the world. High school and college students joined the movement and organized events, such as walks, to raise money and educate people about the food crisis at home and abroad. YWD had chapters in a few high schools in the Midwest.

The chapters organized hikes in which young people would walk up to thirty miles and ask people to donate a fixed amount of money for each mile walked. At the time, it was a new idea and it ignited interest. The chapter that organized the walk could decide where to donate the proceeds. The Congressman's only rules were that, after an allowance of 15% to fund AFFHF operations, the money raised had to go to organizations fighting hunger; half would fund projects abroad and half would stay in the States. Local decision-making and control could make the program work. The students learned about factors that caused hunger: war, drought, and corrupt governments. They learned how to analyze projects, organize large events, and communicate with city councils, radio and television station managers, school administrators, journalists and editorial boards, business leaders, and politicians of all stripes.

• • • • • • • • • •

Today the fight against hunger—to eradicate starvation, malnutrition, and food insecurity—is somewhat apolitical. The basic ideal of feeding the world's children is an idea that we can all support despite our differing political leanings. In the 1970s, the fight against hunger was inextricably linked to the ideological battle of the century. We couldn't seem to discuss global hunger without arguing whether communist or capitalist offered the best solution. It was a life-and-death battle both for those who struggled with hunger and those who were engaged in the fight against it, many of whom risked their lives to be a part of the conversation. My first assignment was to attend the annual YWD meeting at FAO headquarters in Rome. The goal of the meeting was to get young people who were working in the fight against hunger together in one room to share ideas and garner emotional support.

Rome was meaningful to me for many reasons. The Vatican and St. Peter's Basilica are the spiritual, physical, and political center of the Roman Catholic Church. The Order that had been my life for over fifteen years originated in Rome. There were buildings built before the birth of Jesus Christ. It was also a city where the bars stayed open all night and where people casually started a night out at midnight and stayed out until 5 a.m. I did not understand the exchange rate and aggressively overpaid my cab drivers. Everything, even the magnificent old architecture, was new to me.

Sitting in a conference room around a large table in the middle of the ancient city, we heard from young people, speaking in different languages, about hunger and food production. They spoke about land monopolization in Latin America, white minority rule in Africa and its control of resources. They told of unequal wealth distribution in Asia, starving children in Argentina, and governments that used food distribution as a means to maintain power, Stalin-style. The attendees came from so many places I had to run out at lunchtime and buy a map to locate them.

We discussed different models of development. These were extremely important issues to many of the participants, and because of the political situations from which they came, the conversation had to be held in complete confidence. Discussions of land reform had led to executions in some South American states. A young woman in a blue pinstripe suit quietly entered the room and slipped me a note. It read, "This meeting is being recorded and broadcast throughout the building." I stood up in the middle of testimony about the Brazilian government illegally seizing land from Indian tribes. I said, "This meeting needs to

—77—

stop, now." I announced that the conference was being broadcast throughout the building. Mr. Judd, the British parliamentarian who was moderating the conference, was apoplectic at my highly unprecedented interruption. He exclaimed, "You're out of line, Mr. Healey."

I agreed without apologizing. For a moment, nobody said anything. Then everyone was moving, whispering, and talking at once. The Brazilian student who had been talking about the seizures in his hometown calmly took the microphone. Running a hand through his black, curly hair, he said if his government were made aware of his remarks at this meeting, he might be shot. Land reform protective of Indians in Brazil, as in most of Latin America, was a dangerous topic. His blood, he said, would be on the hands of the FAO, because they had broadcast the conference without consent instead of keeping the meeting closed as promised. Brazil was run by the military at the time and recorded political sessions were not a promising way to stay alive.

Mr. Judd approached the microphone. Banging his gavel, he attempted to be heard above the din that had broken out in the elegant room. He placed the meeting on hold until we received an official reaction from the top. As he was making his announcement the door opened, and in came Mr. Boerma, the Director-General of the FAO. Very quietly, as though he hoped no one would hear him, he confirmed that the meeting was being broadcast and monitored in just this building. As he stammered through an apology, I could only look at the Brazilian student, standing there calmly next to the girl from Malawi. He was listening, politely, to the leader of this conference. The Brazilian student did not look surprised. That someone could die for expressing an opinion at a conference was a door into a new reality for me.

• • • • • • • • • •

My first year at YWD was surprisingly successful given my inexperience. We held Walks in cities such as Fargo, North Dakota; Minneapolis, Minnesota; and Madison and Beaver Dam, Wisconsin. I spoke to high school students from 9:00 a.m. to 6:00 p.m. every day. The high school approach worked, thanks to the great young people who joined YWD and organized marches against hunger in their hometowns and schools. The first group of kids that I met with was from Madison. They ran their office better than the office of any organization I have worked in before or since. Their local Walk for Development chapter was extremely efficient. Their phones were always answered; there was always paper in the copier, and nobody left for cigarette breaks and returned three hours later.

Over a cup of coffee at the neighborhood bistro, five YWD workers talked to me about their recruitment efforts in the neighboring towns and in the local schools. They told me the Walk, scheduled for the following week, had been organized over the course of six months. They had been aiming for 50,000 students but were pleased with the 30,000 who signed up. The student organizers were confident all 30,000 would show up. They had planned their route with a great media strategy to maximize the impact.

They had one big concern. "We have heard that Father Groppi, the dangerous radical, is coming to town this weekend. What if he sabotages the march?" Groppi was taking on the Wisconsin legislature as part of his civil rights work. Four of the five of them looked grave. Milwaukee's conservative papers had portrayed Groppi as a dangerous radical, hell-bent on disrupting and undermining white communities. I told them Groppi was an old friend of mine, and I knew he would support what they were doing. I suggested we have coffee with him the next day. When we did, Groppi ordered an iced tea instead and asked them about their project. At the age of fifteen, Bob Peterson had proven himself to be a brilliant organizer. Waving his constantly active hands as he talked, he got into the planning details and flushed with pleasure when Groppi admired their recruitment process.

Then it was the boys' turn to show admiration as Groppi described marching with Dr. King in the South and the disregard for physical danger the marchers had displayed. He recounted facing police shooting tear gas in Milwaukee. Bob told Groppi the Madison Walk would help two major causes: Freedom Farm Co-op, run by Fannie Lou Hamer in Mississippi, and the liberation of

Portuguese East Africa (now Mozambique). The Madison Walk in 1969 was a total success. The battles for civil rights and economic rights blended, as they maybe always should, as Groppi proudly joined the march, and walked with those 30,000 high school students the thirty miles and raised tens of thousands of dollars.

From Madison, I went to Chicago, where thirteen students had planned and superbly executed a Walk in the western suburbs in May 1969 that attracted 40,000 marchers and plenty of press. The event was planned without any organizational hierarchy, a fact that Len Wolf could barely absorb. The students created a process so effective that we wanted one of them to write a Walk manual we in the DC office could distribute to groups who wanted to coordinate a Walk for the 1971 International Walk Day.

I spent Christmas of 1970 in Chicago, where on a single day in May of that year, six separate highly successful thirty-mile Walks had been held. A key leader of the Walk organizers was Maryknoll College senior Bill Kokontis. Those six Walks had been so successful, YWD education director, Joe Kimmins, asked Bill to document the process for us at AFFHF's DC headquarters. Bill drafted the *YWD Walk Manual*. After Bill, Joe, and I polished it, we distributed it to every Walk group nationwide, no doubt contributing mightily to the success of International Walk Day, 1971.

The manual, together with the experience of organizing a Walk, served as a *master class* in project management, grant management, and public speaking for the organizers. The students planned every detail of their Walks from the selection and permitting of Walk routes to deciding which projects would receive funding locally and internationally. Sixteen-year-old Perry Muckerheide not only organized the Milwaukee Walk, but he also produced the film that became the Walk hallmark. It was set in a church and on city streets and rallied students to the fight to end hunger.

Anselm Rothschild and Laurie Ferber in Buffalo, N.Y., chose a Walk route designed to pass the maximum number of homes and businesses. The Buffalo team and Project 70, the North Suburban Illinois (Niles/Skokie) organizing team, each aspired to be the nation's largest Walk in 1971 (each drew roughly 100,000 walkers).

By 1971, there were twelve separate Walks in the greater Chicago area and six more in downstate Illinois. The Walks were organized by mostly high school students, although many Maryknoll College students did extraordinary work for the Chicago Walks, not least Chris Reynolds and Mike Donoghue.

Those students in Minneapolis, Madison, Milwaukee, Buffalo, Chicago, and elsewhere around the country taught us to keep things non-hierarchical but efficient. They had each person on their team pick a job and stay with it, holding themselves responsible and nudging along team members who proved less focused.

Bob Peterson and Debbie Sweet in Madison combed the manual again and developed an improved strategy for getting maximum press attention. Mike McCoy and Sue Forsythe led the work in Minneapolis; Pat Hughes in Boston; Bill Brieger in Chapel Hill, N.C.; Janis Goldstein in Miami; Jerry Schmitz in San Diego; Schlossberg and Lutz led Walks in Fargo and Bill Kokontis and Chris Reynolds led the Walks in the State of Illinois in 1971. Mike Seltzer was East Coast Regional director. Martha Fritts ran the Midwest office and Rosemary Rapp and Moira Sher ran the West Coast regional offices.

A plan that led to invaluable free publicity for the eighteen Illinois Walks was devised by Chicago Walk leaders Bill Kokontis and Chris Reynolds in February of 1971. Before the creation of the Internet, personal computers, and cellphones, teenagers learned about the latest music and news mainly from AM radio (not FM). The two most popular rock music broadcasters in Chicago were WLS and WCFL, each with a multi-state reach.

Montini High School senior Gloria Ciaccio had been the Chicago Interwalk publicity lead for the six 1970 Walks. She had convinced numerous Chicago AM and FM stations, including WLS and WCFL, to provide public service announcements (PSAs). Because of the success of the 1970 Walks, these two radio stations were eager to become the official Walk station, provided they were given an exclusive. Bill and Chris wanted to play the two stations against each other, with each station outbidding its rival to offer the greatest benefits to the Walks. They wanted the stations to agree to announce the Walk telephone number after every two or three songs during the three months prior to International Walk Day.

The climax came with Bill meeting with Robert E. Lee, the station manager at WCFL, while Chris was simultaneously meeting at WLS with its station manager Jim Stagg. After determining each manager's maximum offer, the two Walk leaders called each other using the respective manager's desk telephones and, using coded language, communicated the stations' respective final offers. Because Robert E. Lee offered to broadcast the main Walk phone number every ten minutes from 8:00 am to midnight for three months, provide helicopter-borne news coverage of the actual Walks, and volunteered to have major national celebrities record public service announcements promoting the Walks for months before Walk Day, they clinched the deal. WCFL became the primary Walk radio station. WCFL agreed to the Walks' requests even after Bill and Chris explained that the station could not have an exclusive. WCFL *would* be allowed to call itself the "official" radio sponsor of the Walks, however. In the end, every rock station in Chicago carried the Walk PSAs.

WCFL more than delivered on its promises regarding the celebrity PSAs and the frequency of broadcasting them. For example, Bill Kokontis remembers meeting Jose Feliciano at WCFL's studios two weeks after the deal was struck. The singer was recording a song which he had written for the Walks at WCFL's request. The extra publicity helped the Chicago Walks to collectively net $1.4 million in donations from Walk Day in May 1971.

• • • • • • • • • •

In 1970, the six Walks held around Chicago selected Fannie Lou Hamer's Freedom Farm co-op in Ruleville, Mississippi as one of their domestic grant recipients. One of the key Walk organizers in that 1969-70 school year was Gloria Ciaccio, who as a high school senior did extraordinary work as the de facto publicity director for the Chicago Walks. Gloria obtained invaluable commitments from radio and television stations to broadcast PSAs promoting the Walks. She was also a liaison with newspaper publishers large and small. The enormous success of the six 1970 walks was attributable in no small measure to Gloria's brilliant and diligent PR work. It is no surprise that she went on to have a brilliant career in public relations in Chicago. The largest single beneficiary of all that Walk organizing and fund-raising was Freedom Farm.

A year later, in May 1971, there were twelve Chicago area Walks, and they agreed to fund Freedom Farm again. Fannie Lou visited Chicago and attended the Interwalk meetings multiple times in 1970 and 1971, reporting to the student Walk volunteers in detail about the work she was doing with Freedom Farm. She pledged to return to Chicago on May 9, 1971 to visit multiple Walks.

Gloria had headed off to college in Wisconsin for the 1970-71 school year, but returned to Chicago that May 9. Stationed at the North Suburban Illinois Walk—the largest in Illinois, if not the nation—Gloria met up with Fannie Lou standing on the Interstate 94 overpass. Below them, stretching to the horizon, marched an unstoppable tide of 100,000 Walkers of all ages, mostly high school and college students. Gloria shared with me her poignant account of the conversation that ensued:

As Fannie and I stood on that overpass, she looked at me in wonder, "Is this for me?"

"Yes, it is, Fannie, it is," I assured her.

We both sighed, and as I put my arm around her shoulder and she laid her head on my shoulder, we both began to cry.

It was a brief moment, but the impact has lasted me a lifetime. It's a moment I will never forget…this incredible woman who had told the 1964 Democratic National Convention that she was "sick and tired of being sick and tired"…this indomitable woman who improved thousands of lives, whose "little farm" was the big farm that not only could, but did.

I'm honored and humbled to this day to have had her head on my shoulder, to share this moment with this peerless icon.

• • • • • • • • • • •

In a way, unbeknownst to the two co-conspirators or me, this broadcasting of music and endorsements by many of the most famous rock singers of the time foreshadowed how national and international rock concerts I would organize for Amnesty International many years later would harness the power of music for furthering the cause of human rights.

By the end of my first year at Freedom from Hunger, we had held more than three hundred Walks organized by deeply committed kids in high schools and colleges from across the United States. The second year there was a walk in almost every state.

Sister Corita Kent, made famous by her anti-war posters, made posters for the Walks, with words like HOPE, LOVE, and POWER filling colorful canvases. We printed her designs and pasted them like wallpaper across schools and storefronts. They covered every conference room where we sat with high school students and helped make their school's plans, and wondrously, the plans were implemented. These successes made me see the country as connected, open to possible change.

When I started two years earlier, AFFHF was $300,000 in debt and struggling to survive. Now it was at the forefront of a nationwide movement. We added Joe Kimmins, Kathy Desmond, and Mary Anne Mason as education officers. We had two people to oversee projects—Harvey Silver and Dave Landry. The money poured in, and we earned $12.5 million that year. Our slogan was, "Development is the New Word for Peace."

We were fighting for economic security as a necessary, not a secondary, precondition for peace and a basic human right. More importantly, we were raising money and funding initiatives that provided food and food production. The Walks were the means; food security was the goal. It was up to the young people who worked so hard to plan each Walk to choose which local and international charities would receive support. That was part of the task. Because each Walk picked its own grantees, a wide variety of projects spanning the political spectrum were funded. Greg Darnieder's St.

—84—

Louis group bought a bus and drove it to an agricultural cooperative in Honduras. Another donated to the American Indian Movement; still another chose Catholic Relief Services. Local organizers were often told that they were the toughest project analysts many non-profits had ever seen. They grilled applicants: "Exactly what does your budget cover? What are your outcomes? Show us the proof of your effectiveness over the past five years. We demand that every penny gets to its intended recipients." When the press asked me a question at the Chicago press conference, I stepped aside to let high school junior Steve Rabin field the questions. They were finding their voices. For International Walk Day 1971, we chose as our co-chairs legendary civil rights leader Fannie Lou Hamer for her Freedom Farm Co-op work and Mike McCoy, a sixteen-year-old organizer from Minnesota.

The full impact of this movement went beyond the approximately $15 million raised for anti-hunger projects. Many of the young people went on to lead lives marked by activism and service. They were the leaders of the movement. My first job became my best training. Greg Darnieder, who ran the St. Louis Walks, later became a mentor to thousands of young people living in Chicago's Cabrini Green public housing project and served in the Department of Education during the Obama Administration. Laurie Ferber became a Wall Street financier. Bill Brieger went into international health and was a part of the team fighting the 2014 Ebola crisis. AFFHF staffers Cathy Smith and Gerry Connolly married, and Gerry now represents northern Virginia in the U.S. House of Representatives.

One organizer recently shared a letter she had written to one of her friends in another school. She provided step-by-step instructions on how to organize a Walk: "Reach out to businesses. Have them supply water trucks, medical supplies, and the ingredients needed for thousands of peanut butter sandwiches." Next, she shared the message. "Development is the new word for peace. Tell the students we have to end hunger." The letter then seamlessly switched to teen talk of her most recent boy crush before ending with the news that she had spoken to Presidential candidate George McGovern earlier in the day and he had thanked the students for all their work to end hunger. They were normal teenagers, and also passionate young people who found their voices. Twenty years later, the friend returned the cherished and preserved letter. Letters like this spread the urgency for action across the country.

• • • • • • • • • •

I didn't notice Beckie Weiss when she first started working for Freedom from Hunger as a part-time accountant. When she joined our group after work for drinks, I was drawn to her beauty and grace. One Tuesday I walked with Beckie after happy hour at McFadden's, and she leaned over and kissed my cheek. She suggested we get a drink. I can remember staring at the plastic necklace she was wearing, at her short red hair, opening my mouth to say "No" (so far I had dated a grand total of one person, if you don't count Marcie Stinner), but instead said "Yes."

My year of grieving was officially over. We went out for drinks, then dinner, and began seeing each other every day. She was smart, good-looking, and kind. We talked about everything: our lives, our work, and our goals for the future. We went to parties where people had to shout over the din to announce the location of the next street demonstration and where we would all discuss the best place to buy cheap bread and cheese because none of us had much money. We would walk downtown holding hands for blocks and blocks and kiss next to the monuments.

And then, we were standing together at our wedding. Beckie was wearing a yellow sundress. I was wearing a suit, another one that I borrowed from Sam. Her father and mother sat together, the latter dabbing her eyes, mostly out of disappointment at the utter lack of niceties at the ceremony, and we were married. We rented a cute house a few blocks from the Capitol. It was a new life added to my new life at AFFHF.

• • • • • • • • • •

The Walks for Development were not a radical form of protest or agitation for change. They were not extreme or revolutionary, especially in comparison to the more violent protests of the time, such as killing little girls by detonating bombs in churches in Selma or destroying buildings on campuses. The mainstream nature of our organization was what prompted the recognition we received from President Richard Nixon. Before his name became synonymous with the Watergate scandal, he was a symbol of the endless war that was spreading death throughout the jungles of Vietnam and much of Southeast Asia.

The Administration was trying to reconnect with Americans—especially young Americans. In the aftermath of the wildly successful Madison Walk for Development planned by Debbie Sweet, the Administration sent her a letter of congratulations and invited her to a ceremony at the White House to receive the Young American Medal for Service. She asked me to accompany her and her parents.

Nixon, I thought, did not know what he was getting himself into with Debbie. Presumably, he thought Debbie would be thrilled to receive the medal. She was young and from the Midwest; she appeared harmless. Debbie and I made a pact in the car on the way to the White House that we would behave ourselves. Her parents liked the idea of the award. The ceremony was also important to the FAO and to Robert Nathan, chair of our foundation. We agreed Debbie could burn the photo afterwards, give away the medal or throw them straight at 1600 Pennsylvania Avenue. The plan was to get in and get out of the ceremony with dignity.

The President entered the room, said a few words about how pleased he was to be there, and started pinning medals on the recipients. Nixon stopped as he reached Debbie and paused to say, "The good kids are in here and the bad kids are out on the street." That was too much for Debbie, who had behaved with perfect decorum until then. As Nixon started to pin on her medal, Debbie said, "Mr. President, I simply cannot trust you until you end the war in Vietnam."

The President stepped back; his dark eyebrows shot up. The leader of the free world glared at Debbie, opened his mouth, and nothing came out. He turned and walked out, followed by a bevy of anxious-looking White House staffers, cabinet members, and members of Congress, including Sen. Tom Dodd and Sen. Strom Thurmond, J. Edgar Hoover, Richard Gordon, and Richard Kleindienst—juxtaposed with a principled sixteen-year-old. I thought, "If you cannot handle one anti-war teenager, how can you run a war?" Debbie walked out to a massive press conference and when she landed in Madison, a cheering crowd met her. Debbie used her voice to speak truth to power.

• • • • • • • • • •

Part of my job at AFFHF was visiting funded projects to ensure money was being spent properly. By the time I got to Saigon in 1971, I had visited project sites in several countries. They were beginning to run together in my mind—a blur of project managers, cheap hotel rooms, and amazing spicy food. Saigon was different— so different that I can still remember exactly what it felt like to stand in the middle of its hot, sticky and windy streets, so crowded that the motorbikes could barely make their way through. I remember the feeling of walking into a bar and seeing young American GIs raising shot glasses and blowing kisses to petite Vietnamese women dancing on tables, young women wearing too much makeup and selling anything for a few dollars. American helicopters generated background noise that drowned out all other sounds even on a busy street in the middle of the day. The first few times I heard the helicopters and saw them blowing up dust, I stopped and looked up. Then I realized I was the only one looking; no one else noticed the helicopters anymore.

I was in Vietnam to close a chapter of the International Volunteer Service (IVS) because Vietnam was expelling it. IVS volunteers had signed a petition calling for the ouster of South Vietnam's president, Nguyen Van Thieu. IVS's policy was that projects could not be involved in politics. This line was hard not to cross when it was clear that the U.S. government's policy of propping up the regime was causing devastating poverty, hunger, and despair.

Because Nixon had given Thieu his "absolute assurance" and sworn to support Thieu's government against aggression by North Vietnam, an American nongovernmental organization calling for his ouster was, at the very least, embarrassing. Thieu was furious and demanded the immediate removal of the organization, and the Nixon Administration was more than happy to comply.

I showed up at Saigon's IVS headquarters not knowing what to expect. It was my task to tell a bunch of passionate and courageous American volunteers they had lost their jobs because they had signed a petition with which I agree. There was no doubt that Thieu's government was corrupt and that ordinary Vietnamese citizens were being denied access to food, jobs, and clean water at the hands of this government to which Nixon had given our "absolute assurance."

The office was small, hot, and humid. We sat on plastic chairs around a card table that overlooked a rice paddy. I felt awful about my mission. The volunteers already knew the Vietnam program had been canceled. They all would get air tickets home, and they would have to find jobs. They opened up to me, explaining why they thought it was crucial for them to sign the letter to Thieu.

Many volunteers stayed in Vietnam even without IVS support. Those who could speak Vietnamese, French, and English sometimes became journalists. Their goal was to ensure that accurate news made it home to the United States. Many of them had used their time at IVS to gather information on American war crimes in Vietnam, including the slaughter of civilians, rapes, and the burning of homes. They were passing most of the information to reporters, saving some of it hoping that when they got back to the US, they would be able to get the news into the mainstream press. After explaining their true mission, they asked me what to do with all the leftover equipment. There were thousands of dollars worth of medical supplies that AFFHF had bought in addition to home building tools and agricultural supplies. I smiled. "Give it away to people who can use it," I said. They looked happy to hear this. We shook hands, and I walked out, past the rice paddy and onto the potholed street. I have no idea where all that equipment ended up.

I had a few days left in Vietnam after that meeting, and I wandered the streets of Saigon, chatting with vegetable vendors and eating pho. I was in a pho shop when I met a couple of U.S. soldiers from Texas and California who had been in Vietnam for more than a year. When I told them the organization I worked for, they asked me if I knew anything about the anti-war movement. In retrospect, it may not have been the most judicious move to identify myself as an anti-war activist while chatting with a couple of American boys risking their lives in the war effort I opposed, but we were all happily eating pho, and I had not spoken to any Americans in a few days. We bought each other colas and kept talking.

Another American soldier walked by and asked if it were true that some hippies tried to levitate the Pentagon. I explained that I had, in fact, been there when the crowd of thousands of people surrounded the Pentagon, linked hands, and tried to translate collective thought into action. This young soldier found it hilarious, but he finally stopped laughing long enough to buy another round and join us. He suggested that I visit the local GI hangout with them and explain this hippie talk to his buddies.

This was not a set up. It was simply a group of American GIs who wanted to talk about the war they were fighting. We walked the few blocks to their hangout, a large, open room with giant ceiling fans and throw pillows all over the floor. It had once been a tea shop, explained my new friend, as we picked our way through soldiers sitting on the big, plush pillows. I started coughing. There was so much smoke in the room rising from the glass bongs being passed around, that I got high just from breathing. I felt reassured. I was confident that most of them were so high they would not notice our little parade.

My friend stood at the front of the room and waved his arms to get everyone's attention. A few guys looked up sleepily. Someone at the back of the room started laughing as he gave me a little push, nudging me to the front of the room. "This dude is going to talk about the anti-war movement going on at home," he said. A few people sat up and looked at me blearily. I talked about how the anti-war movement had begun as a "hippie movement" and was rapidly spreading across the country and into the mainstream. Marches and demonstrations had occurred in almost every city. College campuses were often on strike. I told them that after the National Guard killed four student protesters at Kent State on May

4, 1970, more people had joined the movement. "*Ohio*," the Crosby, Stills, Nash and Young song about the egregious abuse of power had gone to No. 1 on the charts ("Tin soldiers and Nixon coming/ four dead in Ohio" by Neil Young). I spoke about the release of the Pentagon Papers by *The New York Times* and *The Washington Post* that had disclosed U.S. involvement in Vietnam since 1945 and proved that the White House had repeatedly lied about the nature of U.S. actions in Vietnam. Kent State, the Pentagon Papers, and a general war-weariness had convinced much of the U.S. that it was time to leave Vietnam.

I told them of the polls that showed the clear majority of South Vietnamese civilians wanted the U.S. out of Vietnam. The Vietnamese wanted to be left alone to sort out their own affairs. They were tired of being used as a pawn in a global struggle for hegemony. I expressed to them the anti-war movement was not an anti-military movement. I relayed my own family's service history in World War II and explained that most protesters recognized that the soldiers were also unwitting pawns of Nixon's policies. They knew, and I knew, that this was not always the case back home.

I asked if they had any questions for me. Initially the weed smoke-filled room was silent, the stillness broken only by the click of lighters and an occasional smoker's hack. Then a guy in the back of the room tentatively raised his hand. "Are all anti-war protesters Maoists?" He had heard we were planning a communist takeover of the world and wondered why I believed Maoism was the way of the future. I told him that was just nonsense. Somebody else raised his hand, and then two more. By the end of the afternoon, my voice was hoarse and there were no more questions. They stood and applauded as I left. I was grateful for the warm exchange.

I walked out onto the street, got a taxi, and climbed in. I sat and thought about the afternoon's conversation. It was tragic that those men had so little information about their own country and the war they were fighting. This same awareness has followed me through too many wars over more than 50 years. Our brave soldiers rarely know the full story of why they risk their lives. I was so lost in thought that I did not notice the police car pulling up alongside the car. Their car cut in front of us and stopped abruptly, forcing the taxi driver to slam on the brakes. Four Vietnamese officers got out of their car and approached the taxi. They gestured for the driver to roll down the window. My driver, an American, turned around and said, "Let's switch passports." When the police officer asked for my passport, I handed him the driver's passport. The police officers stood with their hands on their guns demanding something. The driver reached into the glove compartment and handed them a document. They glanced at it and then the driver shoved some bills out the window. They continued to stand there, so he offered more bills. Finally, one of the officers shrugged and said something in a low voice to his companions. They returned to their police car, which was still holding up traffic in the middle of the street.

The cab driver rolled up the window and cautiously put the car into gear. I asked him, letting out a breath that I did not realize I had been holding, what had just happened. "They wanted to know about your talk back there," he said, laughing. "They were not so pleased about it." He had saved me time and who knows what unpleasantness. He gave me back my passport and said he could get another one. I never found out the name of the man who got me safely back to my hotel. When I got out of the cab, I gave him all the money I had on me and thanked him again. My guardian angel waved me off, smiling, and sped away down the narrow street.

I left Vietnam with a renewed conviction that the U.S. had to stop its part in the war and leave this battered land. It was crazy to use U.S. money to feed people when money from the same source was used to kill so many of the same people. The U.S. was dropping thousands of tons of bombs, more than all sides had dropped in both theaters during WWII. The war was causing malnutrition and starvation, and the chemicals the U.S. dropped were killing, burning, and maiming the population. In addition, we had destroyed vast crop fields and destabilized Laos and Cambodia.

My trip continued on to Kenya, Zaire, Nigeria, and Algeria. In Kenya, I met under trees with the Maasai and discussed projects with them. In Kenya, I saw the Serengeti Plain with all its beautiful animals. But none of it was as compelling to me as Vietnam.

• • • • • • • • • •

After I returned, Groppi and I decided to go spend time with Fannie Lou Hamer at her Freedom Farm in Ruleville, Mississippi. Fannie Lou was a pioneer and soldier of the Civil Rights Movement. When she finally could register to vote, after countless attempts, she returned home only to find that she and her husband had lost their sharecropper jobs and their home because they had registered to vote. She endured jail, beatings, and hatred in her battle for civil rights. In 1964, as she was fighting unsuccessfully to get an integrated delegation from Mississippi seated at the Democratic National Convention, she authored the memorable line, "I am sick and tired of being sick and tired."

That summer of 1973, the Freedom Farm was a busy place. Hamer's project had gone from being a subsistence farm to a profitable organization. The farm had been partially funded by many of the Walks for Development. Profits were returned to the community through donations to food charities, scholarships for local children, and funds to create affordable housing. The goal was to make the farm blossom into a charitable community of wooden houses, vegetable patches, and arable land.

Mrs. Hamer lived in a small, neat brick house set on cinder blocks. I felt an affinity with her because she was one of thirteen children, and I was the last of eleven. Her home was always brimming with people coming and going, eating, drinking, and talking. It reminded me of my mother's home, when my mother never seemed to leave the kitchen and people were always at the table. Fannie Lou put Groppi and me in the spare room and announced that while it was lovely to see us, everyone who stayed at the farm had to work. On the first day, we worked in the vegetable patch near her house and met some of the other workers. It was late by the time we finished working and ate. About an hour after dinner, we heard a loud thud against the outside wall of the house. We did not pay much attention to it. Our muscles ached; it was probably not important.

The next morning, Groppi and I were standing in the walkway to her house admiring her small sitting porch, a popular feature in

Mississippi at the time, when Fannie Lou came out the front door. She walked over to a large, broken glass bottle. We examined it and found a long string wick inside and saw that the bottle had been recapped. Obviously, someone had thrown the bottle, and though it had broken, for some reason it had failed to explode. We were lucky, extremely lucky. The homemade bomb had been constructed so poorly that it merely flamed out, hurting the grass and nothing else. Fannie Lou had faced death threats before. She had known and worked with James Chaney, Andrew Goodman, and Michael Schwerner, all killed while working to register Black Mississippians to vote. She walked with a limp because when she was in jail overnight on trumped up charges, state troopers had forced two other prisoners to beat her so severely that they damaged her leg and her kidneys. She displayed no surprise at the glass bottle and the charred grass.

As Groppi and I were examining the bottle, a large white car pulled up. Two men in stiff black suits and sunglasses got out and approached us. "Mrs. Hamer, we are FBI agents, and we heard there was a bomb thrown here last night," one of them said. The second nodded, pushed his sunglasses onto his forehead, and arranged his features in a show of concern. Fannie Lou stood back from the bottle and crossed her arms against her chest, in unconscious self-protection. She told them that no one had called the police, "So that was probably you." And with that, she turned and walked calmly back into the house, pulling the screen door shut behind her.

Visiting her reminded me of the strength and bravery of the people in the civil rights movement. These people had been attacked physically, financially, and psychologically, but refused to give up their vision.

I left the farm, went back to D.C., and told AFFHF that I was quitting. It was time for my next project.

*Fannie Lou Hamer
at the Democratic
National Convention
in 1964.*

*Photograph by Warren
K Leffler from Library
of Congress archives.*

*Jack, John Hannah,
Administrator
of US Agency
for International
Development
(USAID), David
Brown, head of
AFFHF, and
Irwin Hedges,
Deputy Assistant
Administrator of
USAID admire Sister
Corita's artwork.*

World Food Conference, planning session for the U.S. delegation, 1970.

Some Young World Development leaders at a conference in Aspen.

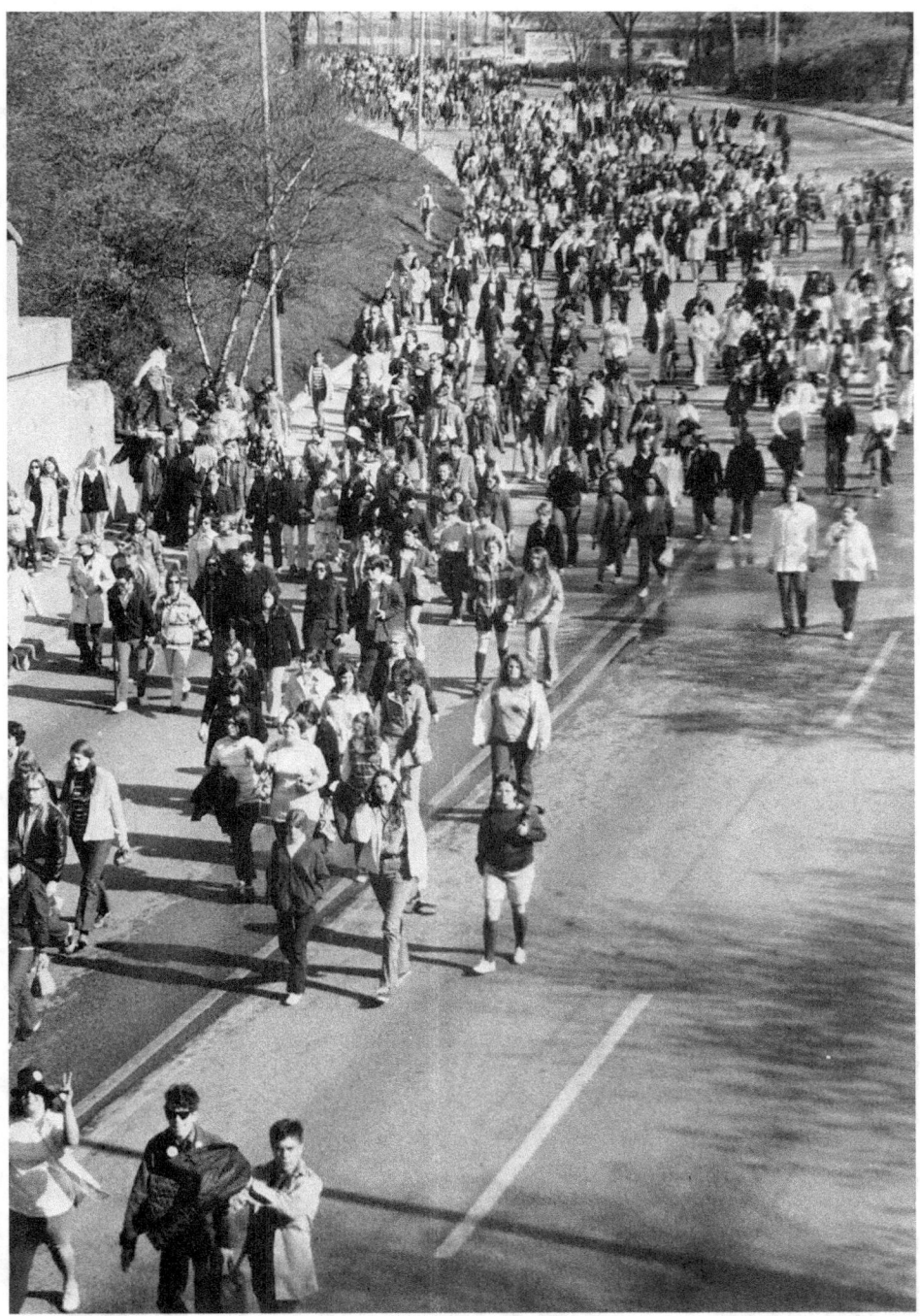

Walkers at the start of the 1971 North Suburban Illinois Walk for Development. The Walk coordinators were Debbie Gorenstein and Terry Cosgrove. They and the rest of the team were part of a student group at Niles West High School called Project 70.

Walking with Madison Walk organizers

Indian Nation visit and fast in Nebraska with Barbara Body , 1972.

Mike McCoy and Mark Stillman, two of the organizers of the Twin Cities Walk for Development. Mike became the 1971 International Walk Day coordinator with Fannie Lou Hamer. Photo from Mark Stillman.

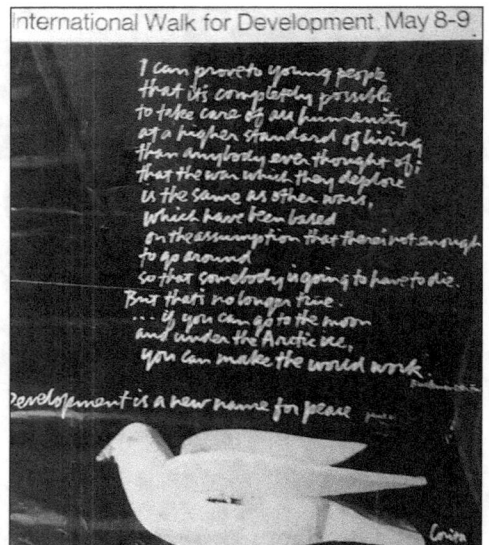

I can prove to young people that it's completely possible to take care of all humanity at a higher standard of living than anybody ever thought of; that the war which they deplore is the same as other wars, which have been based on the assumption that there is not enough to go around so that somebody is going to have to die. But that's no longer true ... if you can go to the moon and under the Arctic ice, you can make the world work.

Development is a new name for peace.

Sister Corita created the poster for
International Walk Day in 1970.

DEVELOPMENT: This symbol for development and change, adopted recently by Young World Development, is based on the Greek delta which stands for change and is comparable to the Arabic 'D' for Development. It is also based on an equilateral triangle which is the strongest geometric unit and indicates equality in terms of the three worlds. Together those three worlds make up one unity which is a circle.

THE NEW WORD FOR PEACE

The Freedom From Hunger
Foundation logo.

Bridge To Peace

We are very happy to announce that you may obtain *Development: Bridge To Peace*, by Kathy Desmond, from the Foundation. It is a 27-page booklet with appendices that suggests how development can be taught. It is designed to be a flexible curriculum unit for use in community seminars or in classrooms. It contains lists of films, books, activities, and discussion questions pertaining to global development.

YWD, civic and church groups are encouraged to use it to create a discussion series; High school or university teachers could use it for an "Introduction to Development" course of about 4-10 weeks' duration.

The unit is designed more to raise questions than to provide answers, to stimulate discussion and inquiry rather than to "dictate" what development is all about.

Copies of "Bridge To Peace" may be ordered ($1.00/copy) from the Foundation. Payment must accompany all orders.

GARY JOHNSON, Walk Coordinator in Cleveland, Ohio, suggests that all YWD groups:

DO:

1. Always have a well-organized core committee.
2. Divide responsibility among core members: do not take on all the work yourself.
3. Make sure that Walk Checkpoints are well organized long before Walk Day.
4. Be sure to plan the route early to leave time for legal problems which may arise.
5. Have three or more good adult advisors who know about banking and law.

DON'T:

1. Leave the total responsibility to the committee chairmen. Always make periodic checks on their progress.
2. Release information until it is completely planned and established. (This stops rumors.)
3. Try to keep all names, dates, and messages in your head; keep records and use secretaries.
4. Make exaggerated predictions about your projects.
5. Let anything go until the last three weeks. Have everything done early because problems **will** develop.

AFFHF staffer Kathy Desmond wrote
a booklet, Bridge to Peace.

Tips from a Walk organizer
Gary Johnson in Cleveland.

Chapter 8

Next Steps

1974-1976

Once again, I had no idea what I would do next. Washington, once the vibrant center of social progress, felt stagnant. The promises of the 1950s and the 1960s, including the social programs and safety nets that had sustained my childhood, were disappearing.

Slowly, and without much notice, progressive income taxes were being repealed, the programs developed during FDR's New Deal and LBJ's Great Society were being chipped away, and idealism was fading. High school students who ten years earlier had boycotted their proms and donated the money to charity were taking limos to country clubs in tuxedos and fancy dresses. I did not know whether the Civil Rights Movement would continue, whether we would ever leave Vietnam, nor what I could do about either. I began to question my own role and place in the movement for social justice and peace.

It was in that weird, nebulous state that I first got to know Dick Gregory, although I had seen him years earlier during Groppi's marches in Milwaukee. Dick was a huge celebrity, and I never expected to meet him in person. Dick was ironic, clever, and funny. He worked as a comedian and had been doing a stand-up routine in nightclubs all over Chicago. As a Black man, he had only worked in Black clubs until Billy Eckstine told Dick to get over to the new club owned by Hugh Hefner, called the Playboy Club. Dick was so nervous he got off the subway a stop too early, but once on stage, he lit up the crowd.

Hugh Hefner was not easy to impress, but that night he laughed so hard he cried. He decided to retain Gregory as the first Black comedian to perform regularly at the Playboy Club. After that start, he played his uniquely bold routines to mixed audiences; appeared on the Jack Paar show and was the first Black person to be invited to sit with Paar after a routine; and wrote his autobiography, *Nigger*, in 1964.

A year and a half after he appeared at the Playboy Club, Dick's annual income had risen from $1,800 to more than $3,000,000. Dick said he had decided that if he was making $3,000,000 a year, it was time to make a difference in the Civil Rights Movement.

His activism was obvious from the nature of his comedy, but it did not stop on the stage. Dick was one of Dr. King's closest confidants; he marched alongside Dr. King in Birmingham, Alabama and spent five days in a jail cell next to him after they were arrested.

He chartered a plane with the Student Nonviolent Coordinating Committee and flew to Mississippi to deliver food and water to the residents of a county who had been denied welfare checks in retaliation for registering to vote. Even though he was several years past his prime as a college athlete—where he set records—Dick ran the entire distance from Detroit to Washington to raise awareness of the importance of a good diet and adequate nutrition.

I met him at the end of that run at a small park in D.C. On my first afternoon with Dick in 1973, I was reminded that he was a good friend of Father Groppi's. We started talking about Groppi, what he had been doing lately, and how hard he had been working. At the end of the night, Dick scrawled his phone number on a piece of paper and suggested we get together sometime soon.

We developed a close friendship. Dick was a frequent visitor to our townhouse and stayed with us when he was in town. One morning over coffee at the kitchen table, he threw his newspaper down.

"Across the country," he said as if we had been having a conversation. I looked at him blankly. "I am going to run across this country to end world hunger," he said. And with that declaration, he resumed reading *The Washington Post.*

I said, "Let's steal the Bicentennial with a *Dick Gregory World Hunger Run* across the country." We decided that his run would end in New York on July 4th, coinciding with New York's Bicentennial Independence Day celebration. A highlight of New York's holiday was the arrival of the Tall Ships in New York Harbor. Some of the ships were intended to represent ships on which immigrant settlers from Europe had sailed to North America.

Dick pointed out that one of the ships, the Esmeralda, was from Chile, and one of its prior uses had included serving as a prison where political prisoners were tortured after a military coup overthrew President Salvador Allende in 1973. Some of the ships were replicas of the slavers which had sailed to North America with hundreds of thousands of kidnapped Africans taken away from their homes and families, shackled in the hulls of the ships to die on the rough seas, or to be sold into slavery and a life of backbreaking work.

Dick's goal for his run was to stop and visit every mayor, governor, church, synagogue, school, and politician along the route, as well as soup kitchens and programs of people feeding people. The kickoff date was April 23, 1976, at Mayor Tom Bradley's office in LA.

Among Dick Gregory's good friends was Charles Mingus, African American jazz musician, civil rights activist, and arguably the best bass player of all time. He played with many big bands and premier jazz acts, including Louis Armstrong, Charlie Parker, and Duke Ellington before forming his own record company and jazz ensemble.

It was not uncommon for Mingus to visit Dick's immense, beautiful house in Plymouth, Massachusetts, and stay for a couple of days. Usually, these trips were prompted by Mingus' desire to gain control over his eating habits. Dick would advise Mingus on nutrition and get him back on the right track. Then Mingus would go back to bingeing. In the summer of 1975, I was staying at Dick's house, working on the plans for his bicentennial run, when Mingus and his wife Sue arrived. Mingus was down in the dumps and needed cheering up.

Mingus said, "Dick, tell me every joke you know—especially the anti-white ones." Dick expressed his sympathy and agreed to entertain Mingus.

Dick offered to have his driver, Big Mike, drive Sue back to the airport. Dick added to Mingus, "Why don't you jump in the front seat there, and see her off to the airport. The ride's on me."

Mingus said he thought that was probably a good idea. As Mingus was about to sit back in the car, Dick hollered: "You'll take anything for free!" Mingus bolted out of the car in anger. As I and everyone else looked on in shock, Mingus' temper was obviously about to boil over. Then he saw that Dick was laughing. Dick could pull a line out of even the direst of situations. The tension broke, and we all laughed.

Dick sent Mingus and me down to his large boathouse on a beautiful inlet. After the previous scene outside, I did not know what to say. Finally, after a long silence and some uncomfortable tiptoeing around Mingus' volatile personality, I asked him, "What do you do, Mr. Mingus?"

I had been so sheltered in the seminary. I wasn't even sure what instrument he played. Mingus turned on the radio, "You hear that? That bum-bum-bum-bum? That's what I do. I have a whole orchestra in my head." I said I was not quite sure I had anything in my head.

Mingus said, "Yeah, and when you were born you thought you were better than me, too."

Surprisingly, this started a conversation. We talked on and on about mortality, philosophy, and human rights as we ate dinner. By the end of our meal, Dick still had not shown up. Nobody was surprised because he was often late. We decided to call it a night and went to bed.

In the middle of the night, Dick woke us up. Dick sat Mingus in the chair and told me to stand in the corner and watch. I understood. It was Mingus' night.

Dick turned on some of Mingus' music and began a monologue that lasted until dawn: "I am going to run for the presidency. I am going to win the presidency. And I am going to paint that White House." And it went on from there. Dick went through his entire repertoire that night.

Finally, the sun came up, and Dick finished. Mingus said, "Thank you, Dick. I am ready to die." It was an incredibly moving scene, shared by two of the most talented men of the 20th century: Dick Gregory and Charles Mingus.

Dick knew everybody. He called Stevie Wonder from Beckie's office. He asked Stevie to set up a concert in New York City and perform on July 4th. Dick planned to have Stevie Wonder close the concert just as he ran into the stadium. "While they have that tight-ass party in Manhattan, with their thousand-dollar fireworks, we'll be dancing in Giants Stadium," Dick said to me, grinning as he put down the phone.

I did advance work for the run, and my friends Bill Davis and Danny Sheehan from the Jesuits and Margie Tabankin of D.C.-based Youth Project helped me raise over $90,000 to start. Oxfam, through its representative, Nathan Grey, worked with Dick as well. We needed money for events Dick planned to have in each city he ran through. The money that we raised during the run would be donated to organizations working to end food insecurity and hunger in America.

At one point, Dick asked me to go over to Richard Pryor's house and get seventy-five from him. I picked up the check for $75 and gave it to Dick, who looked at it incredulously. "$75,000, Jack, I asked for $75,000!" When I returned to Richard Pryor's place, he had a $75,000 check for me and a huge grin. "I thought I was going to get away with saving some money," he said.

Every comedian in LA showed up at Mayor Bradley's office for the kickoff, including Richard Pryor, Soupy Sales, Shecky Greene, and Redd Foxx. Foxx rode up in a dune buggy sporting a bright red velour running suit.

Olympian Tommie Smith, who had made the famous clenched fist salute during the Mexico City Olympics, and Big Mike, Dick's go-to guy and driver, were there. The *Los Angeles Times* and *San Francisco Chronicle* covered the kickoff. They all stood around the mayor's office and watched Dick do jumping jacks and stretch. Dick chatted with the photographers as though he was preparing for a casual five-mile loop around the neighborhood.

Dick pointed his feet in the direction of New York and started running. In every city, he visited the local high school, stopped by the offices of a few nonprofits, and talked with the local politicians. He publicized the fact that hundreds of thousands of Americans were suffering from malnutrition and food insecurity. Some lacked access to enough food to keep their families going. A country was not truly free if people were starving or living hand to mouth and thus falling ill, he proclaimed.

At first, there were photographers and journalists in every city along the route. Students lined the sidewalks alongside mothers with babies and men in business suits. Well into the run, somewhere around New Mexico, attention started waning. Americans had other things to worry about.

Dick called me from a coffee shop where he was drinking his usual giant glass of water. His diet for the run was limited to water, fruit juice, and a vitamin-enhanced drink he had developed. I had just been on the phone with the press. They were not interested in where he was going next. I was worried—seriously worried.

I heard him take a gulp of water. "Go see Muhammad," he

said. "Muhammad always helps me out when things get like this."

I was surprised. Dick knew my background.

"I'm Catholic," I said jokingly, "and I pray to Jesus. And I don't think Jesus does publicity runs."

Dick laughed. "Jack. Muhammad Ali. Go and see Muhammad Ali before his fight with Jimmy Young in Landover, Maryland," he told me. It was April 30, 1976.

"Just go over. I will send George O'Hara from Chicago to help you. When Muhammad wins, he will speak on national television about the run. Get him to run with me for part of the run and announce it on national TV," he said, planning out loud.

I said, "If Ali is fighting Jimmy Young I can never get in." When Ali was on TV after winning a fight, he was the biggest event going. He was at the top of his game. This was a big deal. I had no idea who Jimmy Young was or whether he could fight, but I had to hope Ali would win so he would get the mic after the fight. Ali spoke to the world, not just the United States.

"Don't worry, man. He'll win," Dick assured me, clearly amused. Because it was Dick and because he was usually right, I agreed to go and try to see Muhammad Ali, king of boxing and one of the most well-known faces on the planet.

Lil Gregory, Dick's wife, had called ahead to set it up for us as she always did. I picked up actor George O'Hara at the airport, and we went to Ali's hotel. It was a madhouse, but we went in.

George and I managed to make our way into Ali's suite about six hours before the fight. He was sitting at an ornate desk at the front of a large room. He was wearing black silk pajamas, through which you could see the outline of his muscular shoulders and powerful forearms.

He was declaring: "I am the greatest and I will destroy Jimmy Young tonight."

There was a very long line of people waiting to see him:

reporters, photographers, fans, and assorted others. I slipped into line behind someone with an enormous camera. Nobody seemed to notice. The atmosphere in the room was interesting. Around the champion it was quiet, while everywhere else it was madness.

Ali saw me and immediately came over and reached for my hand. He graciously welcomed us to the room and to the fight.

"You're with Dick Gregory," Ali said. He waited politely for me to say something. I was completely tongue-tied for what seemed like minutes.

"I am here, Mr. Ali, to ask if you would consider joining Dick Gregory on his run across the country to raise awareness of the problem of hunger in the U.S. and around the world. We need you in New Mexico to get us an extra kick of publicity." I blurted this out all at once. Behind us, a photographer stamped his foot impatiently.

Ali said, "You want me to pee blood for two weeks, fly out at my own expense, and go running in the desert?"

I stammered, "Yes, sir." Ali smiled.

"Okay," he said.

That night, Ali beat Jimmy Young after 15 contentious rounds. Surrounded by hordes of sports reporters and TV cameras from all the major networks, he simply ignored the reporters' questions about the fight and looked straight into the camera.

"I'm headed to New Mexico," he said. "I'm going to join Dick Gregory on his run across the country to fight hunger in this country and the world." This was a moment that was watched by millions, and it is impossible to overstate its impact. Thanks to Ali, the nation rediscovered the run.

With Ali on the run, we were back on the front pages. The two of them made quite a sight as they ran into a city. Dick was in his beat-up running suit while Ali ran in tennis shoes, which he refused to exchange for running shoes, no matter how many companies offered to make him personalized shoes. The run was once again filling city blocks with people, drawing out high school students, businesspeople, and local political types.

I felt like I was fourteen again, standing in that courtroom with Charlie Maloney. All we had to do was ask, and someone stepped up and threw themselves wholeheartedly into the cause. A few months after the run, Dick Gregory called me. He asked me to be his representative at a luncheon in Virginia organized by Chip Carter, son of the new president, Jimmy Carter. The lunch was designed to bring together people and organizations working to alleviate world hunger. Singer Harry Chapin was there along with representatives from several organizations. Don Greene represented Sam Brown, the new head of ACTION, which included agencies for seniors, volunteers, and the Peace Corps. I asked Don to arrange a meeting for Dick and me to meet with Sam.

At the meeting, Dick said he wanted to secure a good position for civil rights leader John Lewis. Sam assured Dick that John was already his deputy.

Sam was eager to learn Dick's opinion about what ACTION could do for the country. On our way out, Sam asked me to join him at ACTION. I knew that I could not work in political Washington and said, "No, Sam, I am no bureaucrat."

I told him that I would take a posting for the Peace Corps if it were Lesotho. Lesotho was an independent country entirely surrounded by South Africa. My friend Jerry Brady had told me about Lesotho and how much potential influence the Peace Corps could have there. I wanted Lesotho because of its location inside the apartheid beast, South Africa. A few interviews later, I was offered the post. Dick Gregory, Mary King, John Lewis, Sam Brown, and I went out to celebrate.

Giving the opening speech for Dick Gregory with Tommy Smith for the World Hunger Run, outside of Los Angeles Mayor Tom Bradley's office in 1976.

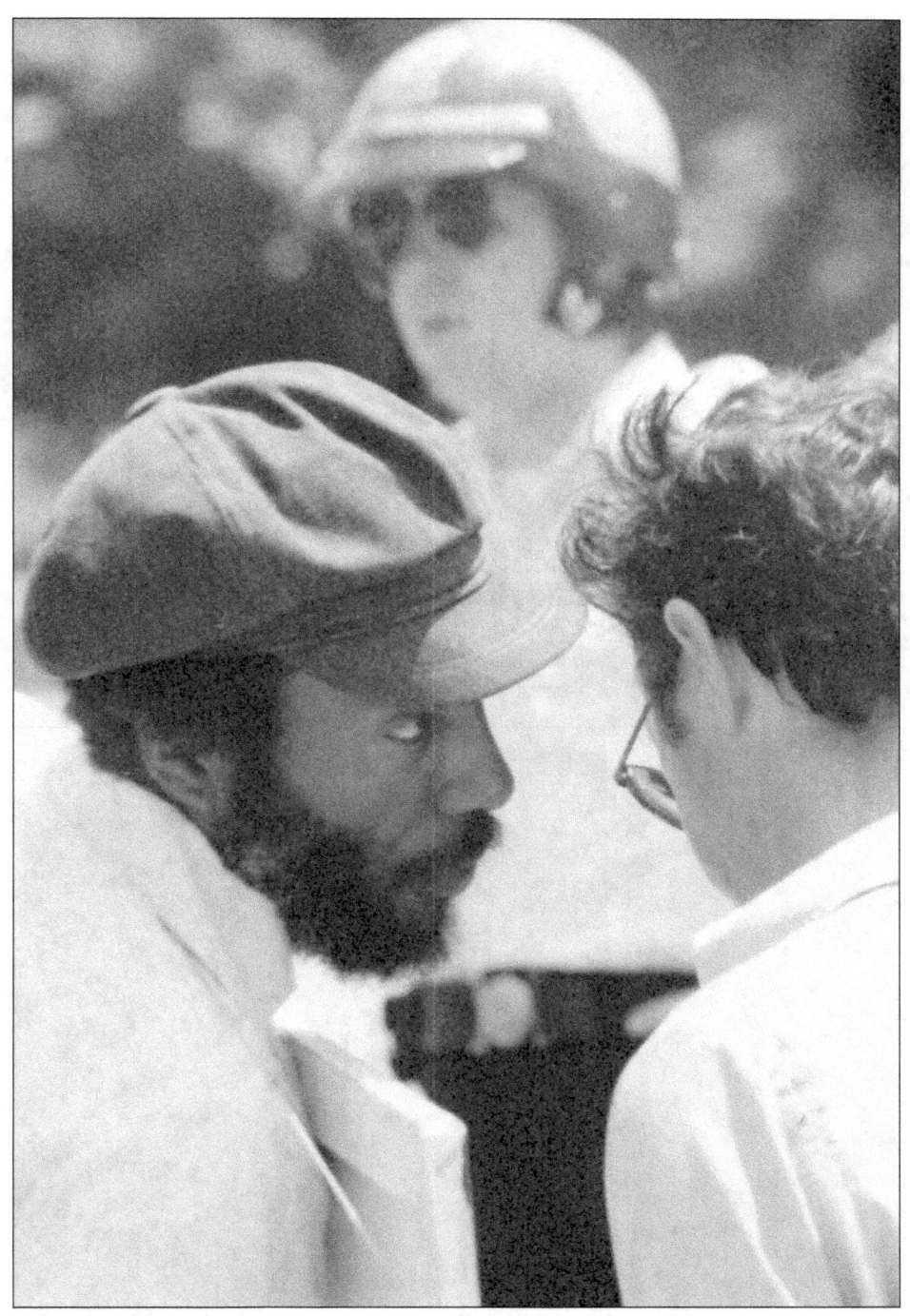

Dick Gregory leaned into me and said, "Jack, you better call Danny Sheehan, my lawyer. I think that guy is about to arrest me." Family Photo.

George O'Hara, Muhammad Ali, and me on the day of the Jimmy Young fight outside of D.C. Dick Gregory suggested that I ask Ali to join him on his national run for hunger. Ali did join the run.

Dick Gregory and I protested at the White House to demand a reopening of the investigations into the assassinations of both Kennedys and Martin Luther King.

Chapter 9

The Peace Corps Years

1977-1981

Once I accepted the Peace Corps posting, I devoted myself to learning everything I could about the political situation in Lesotho and South Africa. Father De Soto, a Jesuit priest, stopped by to help me pack, and he told me that Julius Nyerere, then president of Tanzania, would be giving a lecture in D.C. the following week. The lecture would cover different issues in Africa, but its true focus would be apartheid.

The talk was not only about the effects of apartheid on South Africa but its harmful effects on the region in general. Nyerere wanted support for the fight against apartheid from the United States. The lecture was surprisingly informal and personal and not at all the speech I had expected. When he finished, Nyerere stayed to chat with the attendees. I told him I had just been appointed director of the Peace Corps in Lesotho. He squeezed my shoulder. "You, my friend," he said in his low, lilting voice. "You are going into the belly of the beast itself. Be sure to give them some indigestion over there."

My first day representing the Peace Corps in Africa was September 25, 1977. That was the day Stephen Biko, anti-apartheid activist and hero of the Black consciousness movement, was buried. Biko was among the principal organizers of the massive and powerful Soweto uprising in 1976, for which the South African police arrested him. He was a member of the Xhosa tribe who had popularized the phrase "Black is Beautiful." By the fall of 1977, in South Africa, it was a radical statement.

Biko's death was officially attributed to his prison hunger strike. The beatings with clubs were not recorded on his death certificate. The true cause of his death was revealed much later: he died in a police van due to police brutality and neglect.

Thousands of people, including leaders from all over the globe, showed up in South Africa for Biko's funeral. His coffin was passed from person to person in the streets as mourners shoved their fists in the air, singing, marching, crying, and chanting.

Years later, Biko's words were combined with the music of Peter Gabriel to become one of the most moving parts of the concerts I did for Amnesty International. Biko said, "We have set on a quest for true humanity, and somewhere on the distant horizon we can see the glittering prize."

I entered the Peace Corps with waves of other Americans who had been active in social movements since the fifties, sixties, and seventies. My colleague Reg Petty, director of the Peace Corps in Swaziland, had spent a year in Mississippi registering voters with the Student Nonviolent Coordinating Committee. Norman and Elsa Rush, who directed Peace Corps Botswana, spent some time in federal prison for refusing to fight in the Korean War. The first time the four of us met was amazing. I remember this energy in the room, a feeling of hope that I remembered from my days marching for civil rights. We were there to continue the struggle for justice for all that we had started at home. This goal never changed, but we would soon find out that our methods had to be altered.

When Beckie and I arrived in Lesotho, our books, clothes, and chipped dishware were moved into the Peace Corps house reserved for the director in Maseru. Beckie set up her office to work as a freelance accountant. Although we lived and worked in Lesotho, we were directly across the river from South Africa. The only fertile region in Lesotho, and the area where most Basotho lived, was on the border with South Africa. This proximity meant that most people crossed the border frequently to get the many necessities that were unavailable in Lesotho. Traveling on the roads of Lesotho was extremely dangerous. There were a lot of accidents and no ambulances. You stayed close to home when you could.

My first effort was to post a "Boycott RSA" (Republic of South Africa) sign on the volunteers' message board. I asked them not to spend money there if they could avoid it. The volunteers, of course, were free to go where they wanted, but I wanted them to be conscious of apartheid as a system that damaged everyone it touched. Within twenty-four hours, the chief of security from Bloemfontein, the heart of the Boer farming power structure, met me as I was on my way to the local store in Lesotho to pick up the newspaper. He identified himself and welcomed me to South Africa. He told me the volunteers were still welcome in South Africa even if I did not want them there.

My Peace Corps directors and I were not naive about conditions in Africa but our knowledge was spotty. We were left with more desire than ability to help effect change. We decided to focus more on preparing Peace Corps volunteers for their time in South Africa. Tactics that were effective in the U.S. were unsuitable to Africa.

There was a 'line from hell' at the border between South Africa and Lesotho. As a white man, my ability to travel out of Lesotho was easy. I would drive up to the window of the concrete building and hand the border agent my passport. The gates would open, and I would drive our little VW across to South Africa. Basotho entering South Africa had a different experience. They could not drive up to the building as I did. They were forced to stand in a separate line for Blacks—women shopping and miners trying to find work. Moving through this line could take a full day as the white South African border guards took coffee breaks, cigarette breaks, and lunch breaks while others slowly and casually examined the passport of each Black person who went through. I had seen the tactic of civil disobedience work in the U.S., and I wanted to try the same strategy. So, leaving Lesotho for my first visit to Pretoria, I joined the Black line at the border crossing. After about three hours, I reached the window and approached the guard who was engrossed in lighting a cigarette. He saw me, reached up, and slammed the window shut. He shouted into a megaphone that the border was closed for the rest of the day. "Get out of our line," someone shouted from behind me. It echoed again and again, up and down the line, which stretched for hundreds of people.

The miners behind me were enraged. My efforts had left them with no income for the day and I had in no way improved their status. The kind of civil disobedience that I was familiar with was not going to work in South Africa.

Minority volunteers, whether Black, brown, or Asian, were at serious risk if they ever needed medical attention in that part of the world. Lesotho had a reasonable hospital for minor emergencies but people with serious illnesses or injuries were sent to South African hospitals for trauma level care. However, about 15% of our volunteers were minorities.

If one of these volunteers needed care we would be faced with choosing among three terrible options. One was to try entering one of the "whites-only" hospitals in South Africa. Even if admitted under pressure from me or the ambassador, these patients would likely be ignored or mistreated. Or we could take our chances at one of the deeply inferior Black hospitals and pray for the best, like the Blacks in South Africa had to do every day. The third bad option was to hope an American jet could fly from Frankfurt, Germany and transport the patient back in time to save his or her life. I was fortunate not to face this dilemma during my tenure, but it weighed heavily on me every day.

These challenges became topics of discussion at Fat Alice's Restaurant. Fat Alice's was an Israeli-run African deli where diamond dealers met mercenaries and U.S. Peace Corps volunteers met volunteers from other countries. Issues were argued, events were planned, and ideas were explored over supper at Fat Alice's. The great anti-apartheid and religious leader Archbishop Desmond Tutu frequented the restaurant. He'd smile when we called him "Macaw" because of the colorful clothes he wore while dining with his wife. It was a spot to meet — a kind of African salon.

The ideas we bounced off one another over coffee at Fat Alice's soon germinated into a proposal we could share with David Levine, who led Peace Corps training in Washington. David's backyard in D.C. had become as much a gathering place for Peace Corps leaders as Fat Alice's had been in Lesotho, so it was fitting that at one such gathering, we began to restructure the Peace Corps training program.

In addition to our own difficulties with apartheid, we realized that in some ways our work inadvertently supported apartheid. We provided volunteer teachers to South African villages, brought agricultural experts to struggling farmers, and expanded medical care outside of the townships. None of these activities threatened apartheid.

The American government actively supported the Republic of South Africa and therefore supported the country's ability to maintain the apartheid system. The U.S. government paid our salaries and set our mission while simultaneously supporting an apartheid government politically and financially.

We were functioning in a gray area. We were complicit, but we were trying not to be. The Basotho parents wanted the Peace Corps volunteers to teach their kids math and science in the schools. This was some of our most valuable work. The boys who learned math and science could go get jobs in South Africa. Girls learned the same math and science but still became domestic workers. We were trying to do the right thing by educating students in Lesotho, but young graduates went to find paying jobs in South Africa and in a sense, were economically supporting apartheid.

Lesotho's largest export was human blood taken from the miners as they came and went through Lesotho. The mission the Peace Corps had given me was Development. "Development" can mean many things, but to us, it meant trying to make the communities we worked in a little better. Non-governmental agencies joined with the United Nations and tried to implement improvements for Lesotho. We were rarely effective. Countries like Lesotho were accustomed to Western nations coming in and changing agendas every few years. Our mission during the Carter years was to provide for basic human needs. Despite our resources, money, personnel, and experts, we were ill-equipped to effectuate real change. American aid could bring in tractors and build roads and dams. Inevitably, a few years later, there would be no gas for the tractor, no road upkeep and the dam would leak. There was no point in funding development unless provision could be made for the future.

At times, the aid agencies failed to understand the people they purported to help. That was the case with the construction of rondavels—the historic thatched roof homes of the Basotho. A few mountains and valleys away from our home in Maseru was the small, isolated town of Thaba-Tseka. Thaba-Tseka was made up of many small rondavels where families lived with four or five people in a room. If you kept driving through Thaba-Tseka and up the bumpy dirt road for a few minutes, there were a few beautiful, thatched-roof homes with no one in them. I asked Sam, my Peace Corps driver, why nobody lived in these rondavels.

"That home has a window that is too high," he said. I looked at him blankly. It turned out that no one, including the Canadian engineer who built the rondavels, or the NGO funding the project, had bothered to ask the Basotho whether they wanted a high window.

I learned that the height issue was about the children. "They would climb up and hurt themselves, and there are no doctors around," Sam told me. "We Basotho hate lightning. It kills us all the time. We do not want to look up in that big window the Canadians put in. None of us will live there. I know they meant well, and they thought to provide heat because a big bucket in that window will absorb heat and warm us at night. But the children might fall, and we cannot take that risk," he said.

The misguided attempts at helping were not a reflection on the volunteers. My respect for the Peace Corps volunteers was enormous as I watched how they interacted with the people, endured separation from loved ones, and struggled with new cultures and languages. As in all my previous work, I saw young people as the hope of the world. These young people came to another world to give of themselves. The people they worked with were grateful, and I was proud of the volunteers in Lesotho.

Across the border in South Africa, with a clear vision of what they wanted, some were fighting hard to end the apartheid system. People like Nelson Mandela, in charge of the African National Congress (ANC) and its armed wing, Spear of the Nation (MK), were constantly and unflinchingly challenging white supremacist rule in South Africa. Unlike the Civil Rights Movement back home, where nonviolence and dignified struggle were the keywords, the anti-apartheid movement was violent. It was a world of AK-47s and homemade bombs and kissing your wife or your husband goodbye every single time you left home, even to go around the corner to buy a jug of milk because you knew you might die that day.

The ANC practiced civil disobedience, but it was disobedience bolstered by guns. The slogan, chanted at rallies and whispered by Black families, was simple. The goal was to "make the country ungovernable," and keep it ungovernable until Africans of all colors won equal rights and equal treatment under the law.

In retaliation for their work, Mandela and many other leaders of the ANC were locked in small, cold cells in a prison on Robben Island, a small rocky island off the coast of Cape Town. Mandela's home was an isolated, desolate place surrounded by an ocean that was home to great white sharks on all sides of the island.

Despite the absence of many of its leaders, or perhaps because of anger at the injustice of depriving the movement of its greatest minds, the anti-apartheid movement continued to grow both in size and power.

• • • • • • • • • •

In 1993, years after I had moved from Lesotho, I had the opportunity to meet Nelson Mandela. President Carter, and U.S. philanthropist Dominique de Menil, a lovely woman who had worked in the Carter Administration, presented the Carter-Menil Human Rights Prize to Nelson Mandela. I was invited to the award ceremony.

The rush and commotion around this hero of the world made it difficult to converse with him. I did get a photo with him; one of the many he graciously permitted. A camera crew had set up right outside the entrance to the bathroom, so Mandela and I had to wait together. I tried my minimal Sesotho on him and told him I had been in his hometown in the Transkei. He nodded kindly.

I asked him, "What would you have done if there were no apartheid?" His answer was quick and easy: "I would have been a boxer." I smiled and left him alone with his thoughts.

• • • • • • • • • •

Archbishop Desmond Tutu lived in Lesotho during my tenure at the Peace Corps. As the Episcopal bishop, he walked a fine line neatly and skillfully. Tutu spoke at Episcopal churches around the region, some built with brick and marble and others with a cross under a thatched roof and open-air seating on the reddish dirt. He told his congregations that they could not lose hope. He told them the struggle was succeeding and they needed to keep at it. It was written not in sand but in stone, he said, that the Blacks would succeed. I met with Archbishop Tutu regularly to place Peace Corps volunteers in the Episcopal school system in Lesotho.

Another great anti-apartheid leader living in Maseru was Chris Hani, who oversaw the military operations (MK) of the ANC. Chris had been trained in the Soviet Union. His 30-ish face was like a teenager's, youthful and full of energy.

He was well educated, and we talked about Gilbert Chesterton, the lay theologian; and Hilaire Belloc and John Henry Cardinal Newman, which gave away his Catholic background. Anti-apartheid activist Phyllis Naidoo and I met with Chris Hani at small, closed events. I wanted to learn from both about their movement. Phyllis approached the apartheid issue as a mother and activist. Hani came at it like the philosopher-soldier he had become. Not angry, but steady and sure. Sadly, Hani was assassinated on April 10, 1993, right after Mandela was released from jail. His funeral was one of the largest in African history.

At one point, I needed to hire a lawyer to deal with a hiring dispute within the Corps. I had no understanding of the legal system in Lesotho, and I asked Chris Hani for a reference. He referred me to Khalaki Sello, a radical anti-apartheid fighter and a brilliant attorney. Sello was wanted for murder in South Africa. His cellmate in South Africa had been Joe Quobo who was executed by the South African secret police in Zimbabwe.

The legal system in Lesotho was modeled after England's, so we needed a barrister as well as an attorney. Khalaki called Denis Kuny to be our barrister. Kuny had defended everyone in the movement from local activists to Nelson Mandela. Mandela, facing the death penalty for sabotage and conspiracy, stood in the courtroom and bravely proclaimed that the establishment of a multi-racial democracy, "The ideal and democratic free society," was an idea "for which I am prepared to die."

Kuny, as a young barrister, was part of the team led by George Bozos who defended Mandela. The lawyers' eloquent arguments and evidence underscored the David and Goliath nature of the struggle. Mandela was convicted as had been preordained by the government, but he was spared the death penalty. I was honored that Denis would represent me. He and Sello thought it highly amusing to be paid by the U.S. government.

Denis often held dinners in his home for me with anti-apartheid poets, journalists, and activists. Phyllis Naidoo worked with the MK in South Africa until she received so many death threats that she escaped to Lesotho. She introduced me to Father John, an Episcopal priest, who was both a political radical and a reliable and devout priest. Phyllis recruited me to help with the work. She was the heart and soul of the work. Phyllis, Father John, and I made a habit of sitting outside chatting and enjoying the cool African nights. Denis introduced me to his favorite habit: eating lychee nuts. Denis spoke about the legal issues of the ANC and the MK and the endless uphill struggle against apartheid. David McAdams of the United Nations Development Program often joined us for card games at the home of the chief justice—we would play all night.

I was with people who were among the best and bravest human rights activists ever. For me, this was the equivalent of Paris in the twenties for American artists. We had fun and serious talks, lots of laughter intermingled with moments of sadness. The air was heavy with unfulfilled expectations. There was just so much to hear and to be aware of every day. As the Persians say, I fell back in the honey. These folks helped me get a layman's Ph.D. in South African politics.

Father John always maintained his composure during our long, rambling conversations. One night, he uncharacteristically quieted a heated discussion about the role of third-party governments in supplying weapons to rebels. He was frustrated and was showing it.

"Jack," Father John said, "You can't do much to help here. It is not your fight; you know that. All that you can do is to support the people the fight belongs to and, for heaven's sake, listen to those people when they tell you what to do." He was right, and I vowed to follow his advice.

• • • • • • • • • •

To avoid mistakes others had made, I decided to ask the refugees from South Africa what we could best do to help. One thing they wanted was help with hospital visits. Hospitals in Lesotho did not provide patients with nutritious food. It was up to family and friends to supply food to their jailed loved ones. The hospitals were under the constant watch of the South African Defense Forces who had a nasty habit of picking up family and friends of hospitalized ANC members and making them disappear into a labyrinth of jail cells. My Peace Corps friends and I began delivering food to injured ANC members.

Phyllis Naidoo and Father John ran an organization that supplied blankets and clothes to political refugees from South Africa. The clothes and the blankets were primarily from East Germany, sent in packages decorated with exotic stamps.

One afternoon Phyllis and Father John were sitting in

Phyllis' rondavel, which also functioned as their organization's headquarters and mail room. Father John picked up a small, brown package like any other, complete with German stamps and duct tape. Phyllis was standing behind him folding blankets into a neat pile. She did not see Father John cut the cord that set off the bomb.

By the time Peace Corps nurse Faith Mareck-Kuhn arrived at the scene, Father John was unconscious. Phyllis had pieces of metal shrapnel lodged in her lower back. The folded blankets and the furniture were stained red with her blood. Phyllis' eardrum was permanently damaged. Father John's hands were dripping with blood, there was shrapnel in his chest, and a testicle had been blown off. Faith stabilized them both as best as she could. She helped Father John, who was white and British, into her car so he could get to health care. They drove him to the nearest good hospital, twenty miles across the border in South Africa.

Phyllis could not go to South Africa for treatment without risking arrest. No decent hospital was available to her.

Faith found an IV needle, and in the dusty, blood-spattered office, put Phyllis on a morphine drip. Then, working slowly and carefully, she pulled the shrapnel out of her back and cleaned and bandaged her wounds. We crossed our fingers and prayed for Phyllis, Father John, and Faith.

When both patients, thank God, recovered fully, we thanked the universe for Faith's healing hands. Years later, when Phyllis joined us for the Amnesty International concert in Zimbabwe, I prayed the audience understood what a hero they had in their presence. Later, Phyllis turned down political jobs to pursue her anti-death penalty work in South Africa.

Chris Hani and Phyllis Naidoo led the anti-apartheid movement in Lesotho. Going to Lesotho was the fastest and easiest way out of South Africa for those under threat for being members of the African National Congress. Many refugees came, some damaged already from torture. These folks, along with Chris and Phyllis, had to change lodging almost nightly in Maseru, Lesotho's capital. Quite often the raids by South African forces hit the wrong rondavels in these illegal, cross-border incursions, and citizens of Lesotho were killed as well as the ANC members from South Africa.

Lesotho's government was at times as tough on their dissidents as the South African raiders. Citizens of Lesotho were often found dead along the highway. Lawyers Khalaki Sello and Denis Kuny discovered one victim's cause of death: he had been shot on the top of his head, and the wound had been covered up to disguise how he had died. No one knew how many people died or who killed them. The raids by the South African police were not challenged by the Basotho police so we assumed there was cooperation for getting in and out of Lesotho. Lesotho would blame South Africa and vice versa. Finding the truth of who killed whom was impossible for us expats.

Phyllis Naidoo was the mother figure; she took care of people. She held their hands and solicited and received clothing for the incoming refugees and donations for medical care. Phyllis was South Africa's Fannie Lou Hamer.

Many years later, Naidoo became the officially designated representative to the 1988 Human Rights Now tour in Zimbabwe. In that role, she thanked Bruce Springsteen and Sting for their contributions. However, much like Fannie Lou Hamer, Phyllis was largely forgotten by her movement.

Bombs were not dropped every day, but they were not infrequent. Many of them were aimed at Chris and Phyllis. I remember one at the German embassy and another where Chris aided a dying man who was probably the maker of the bomb. Another bomb went off when I was having supper with Joe Lelyveld of *The New York Times* and author Allister Sparks. We went to the scene of the bombing and got as close as we could. We were questioned and detained for a brief time.

Getting information from the police was impossible. Phyllis Naidoo was the source to go to for any real evaluation. Chris Hani's job was to make South Africa ungovernable. Naidoo and Hani did their jobs and survived the apartheid state—memorable people for sure. I got a call from the Peace Corps asking me to go to Sudan to attend a meeting about Africa. Crossing into South Africa from Lesotho on a Sunday required police consent. Boers were forbidden to travel on Sundays. I stopped in a small town in the Orange Free State and went to the police station to ask permission to buy petrol.

"No, we will not permit you to buy petrol," was the answer. The police officer in charge thought President Gaafar Nimeiry of the Sudan was a communist. It took me two hours to convince him that Nimeiry was not a communist. He figured because Sudan was in another part of Africa, it had to be communist.

My plane took me from Lesotho to Mauritius to Dar es Salaam to Sudan. It was a slow trip, but beautiful. I knew that civil rights icon, John Lewis—*Saint John* as we called him—was to be there as well. He was one of the "Big Six" who had organized the 1963 March on Washington. The presence of this living monument to decency and the power of an individual to effect change made me so happy that I did not mind attending yet another conference.

Due to overbooking, I got to share a room with this legend. John and Dick Gregory had helped me get the Peace Corps job in Lesotho, so I had met John before, but I did not know him well. One of the best honors I have ever received was when John said "Okay" at the front desk when asked if he would be willing to share his room with me.

Over the next three days, I witnessed his love for his wife Lil. He called her frequently. I teased him about it while I admired his devotion. "Quit calling her. She doesn't want to hear from you all day. Leave Lil be." I don't remember much about the conference, but being with a legend was great fun. Later, in 1986, Lewis was elected as congressman from Georgia.

At the same time we struggled with apartheid in Lesotho, the anti-apartheid movement was gathering momentum in the United States. The movement in the U.S. started with the Trans Africa Forum, a small non-profit dedicated to fighting apartheid from within the U.S. The Forum had joined with the Congressional Black Caucus, and together, they were turning a national human rights struggle into an international one. Randall Robinson was the inspired dreamer and motivator of this enormous effort.

Desmond Tutu, who later served as Episcopal Archbishop of South Africa until 1996, spoke from the cathedral in Cape Town to ask for the world's help in fighting apartheid. He asked companies, wherever they were located, to oppose apartheid by refusing to do business with the South African regime. It was a grass-roots sanctions movement, and many people boycotted companies that continued to sell lumber, oil, food, and other products to the South African government. Protests and arrests at South African embassies increased regularly.

The U.S. government was obsessed with the notion that the ANC had ties to the South African communist party and to other leftist organizations. The U.S. continued hosting politicians from South Africa and sending them money and business to prevent South Africa from becoming a communist domino in the war of ideologies. American politicians used the ANC's communist affiliations to avoid taking a stance against apartheid. As my friends in the ANC were constantly reminding us, the best thing Americans in Africa could do was to convince our government to stop supporting the regime.

When my first term of two and a half years was up, I begged Peace Corps director Dick Celeste to let me stay in Lesotho. He made a special exception to the usual rules to allow me to stay. I was delighted.

• • • • • • • • • •

The State Department called during my third year in Lesotho. Sandy Berger, an old friend from D.C. and President Carter's deputy policy man in the State Department, and later National Security Advisor to President Bill Clinton, wanted to visit Lesotho on one of his trips to South Africa. I was asked to show him around. Sandy arrived dressed in khakis and a rumpled shirt. He proved willing to try anything. I liked Sandy enormously. He told me that he wanted to see the area up close, more of a native tour than an official visit. We drove around Maseru and to the mountains, including Thaba-Tseka, where Sandy laughed at the clean, empty, ill-advised rondavels.

I set up meeting after meeting for Sandy. The arrangements could be difficult because it was forbidden for me to set up a meeting between a U.S. government employee and an African National Congress (ANC) member. When I invited Sandy to Khalaki Sello's home to meet some young ANC members who might be seen as communist activists, I told Sandy only that they were active in the anti-apartheid movement, and that they could give him the real story of what had been happening in the jails of South Africa.

Sandy brought a few young Fellows who were about the same age as the ANC activists. The Americans listened intently to the young activists. One man made an emotional appeal that gave Sandy and the Fellows a feel for what went on in the torture chambers of South Africa. It riveted the young people. The activists spoke in detail against apartheid and what happened to them in torture chambers and how U.S. support for the South African regime was undermining their work. As they spoke of torture, one of the Fellows began to look ill, sweating heavily.

The young man's empathy was evident. He stood and said, "I can't, I can't.... As an American, I cannot work for the U.S. government when it is supporting this type of regime. This is wrong. I am not sure of my traveling now with this delegation."

The Fellow had been deeply rattled by what one of the ANC members had to say. Sandy and I were speechless. The fellow was right about the U.S. government. Sello asked the young man to step outside with him. Later, Sello told us that he had told the Fellow that "The ANC is multi-racial always," and "no one is permitted to insult Jack in his home. He is with us, and you should join us too. If you can do so, come on back into my home and the meeting." They entered together.

• • • • • • • • • •

With the help of Dick Celeste and David Levine in the D.C. office, Norm and Elsa Rush, co-directors in Botswana, Reg Petty, and I developed a training seminar for new Peace Corps recruits.

We held our training sessions at an international hotel. Our staffs were African and found places to make things easier for all of us. We taught the history of the region, its colonization, and specifically about apartheid. We compared it to the Jim Crow laws in the U.S., which our volunteers were familiar with through their high school texts.

We invited representatives from embassies, the U.N. and, of course, the anti-apartheid movement, to speak at seminars. We addressed directly the issues raised when Black and white volunteers were treated differently, and we warned them that this would happen. We also talked about what they could do to help, here in Lesotho or in Swaziland or Botswana. Sen. Jesse Helms of North Carolina challenged our program, as did some Peace Corps volunteers, but Dick Celeste and David Levine stood behind us, and we could continue the program.

After our initial correspondence from Helms, the first few letters were polite. They asked if we were hiring ANC "communists" to train our Peace Corps volunteers in violation of U.S. law.

We explained we were not, but the letters increased in number and became more strongly worded. First they asked us to change the training program, and then they accused us of being communist collaborators.

We were visiting the U.S. embassy on a regular basis to explain to our ambassador that we had no way of knowing who worked for the ANC, nor did we care, and that we needed the freedom to hire the best of the brightest to train our volunteers. We were lucky that we had friends at the State Department, beginning with Sandy. We were also lucky that the Carter Administration valued the Peace Corps and considered the organization an important part of its foreign policy. Dick Moose, the Assistant Secretary of State, was a supporter as well. But we became increasingly nervous. The political climate was complicated, and we could not be sure what was coming next, whether the Administration would support us or cut us loose. We were sitting around on my porch one night when Reg slammed down his beer, making all our glasses jump.

"I'm going to quit," he said. I started to protest. He explained: "I am going to quit if even one of you gets fired. If they want to fire one of us for what is going on and for what we are trying to do here, they are going to lose all of us."

We made a pact. Although Norman and Elsa Rush were not there that night, Reg and I figured the pact would sit fine with them. If the government fired one of us, we would all quit in protest.

Congress had passed a law forbidding Peace Corps employees from giving information to the Central Intelligence Agency. To avoid any potential conflicts of interest, I stopped visiting the embassy except to pick up cables and to attend the ambassador's requisite weekly meeting. The directors of Voice of America and USAID attended these meetings. I was present to report on the activities of the Peace Corps.

I kept in strict compliance with Peace Corps rules. My reports were meticulously bland, recording the number, background, education, and sex of new recruits. I would write about the number of schools that the Peace Corps was now operating in (and the number of classrooms and what color we had painted the new office) and in a sleep-inducing report, the budget. I could, I found, go on for as long as I needed to about the budget, and eventually everyone would stop paying attention.

What I did not answer in those endless meetings were questions about the demonstrations and bombings. "What is Phyllis Naidoo like?" "Why does the prime minister like you?" When I was out jogging, they noticed that Prime Minister Joseph Leabua Jonathan would stop his car and talk to me. "I think Leabua liked me because he found out about my family's history in coal mining."

The first ambassador I worked with, Ambassador Donald Norland, found my refusal to discuss politics merely irritating. He would ask about a bombing. I would ask to which bombing he was referring. He would bring up Phyllis. I would explain that I bumped into her occasionally. He would roll his eyes and get on with the agenda. Ambassador John Clingerman replaced Ambassador Norland in 1979, and he found my silence infuriating. One particularly unpleasant exchange was over a July 4th celebration at his home. I found out the embassy hired a South African caterer to cook the July 4th hot dogs. The prime minister always came to this event, so I told the ambassador that I was not going. He asked why, and I told him that the Basotho could cook hot dogs. I did not want a South African hot dog. I wanted a Basotho hot dog. He explained to me that July 4th was an important day to show that I was a part of the team. I went to the barbecue. The longer we spent in Lesotho, the more the political situation heated up.

● ● ● ● ● ● ● ● ● ●

My relationship with Beckie was affected by our life in Lesotho. Beckie had been an incredibly good sport about the move to Lesotho. She traded her job and the culture of a city for freelance work and tall mountains. Beckie and I took a trip to Southwest Africa, now Namibia, to see the lions, giraffes, springbok, and elephants, but we also were witness to the South African army at work against The South West African People's Organization (SWAPO). One day on the bus, we saw people from Latin America in SW Africa to celebrate Hitler's birthday. SWAPO later won, and Sam Nujoma took over as prime minister.

During my days at AFFHF, some of the Walks had funded a hospital for the Frelimo people in Mozambique. Sharfuddin Khan, who represented the Frelimo people and the project, spoke at one of our YWD conferences. Now that we were in Africa, Beckie and I were excited to visit him. Few Americans were permitted into the country at that time. After a short meeting, Mr. Khan excused himself. He was worried about being seen as "too Western" by being with us. My reaction was instant. If this is the left, I want no part of it.

● ● ● ● ● ● ● ● ● ●

For two years, Beckie and I had to learn what we could eat, with whom we could talk, and where we could go, and even where to buy blankets for the cool nights. Slowly, our relationship disintegrated.

She was tired of me being distant, distracted, and overly independent. I was away almost all the time, caught up in my life with the Peace Corps. When I was home, I spent the night entertaining and participating in conversations in which she was becoming less interested. She missed seeing or even being able to call her friends, her family, or her home.

This time there was no discussion over an ill-advised cappuccino, or locking myself in a bathroom, or even having Sam around to talk sense and laugh at me. The dry season came, and the wild grass turned brown, providing fuel for an occasional brush fire. I went home one day to find Beckie packing. She was crying. She did not have to explain; I understood. We did not talk about our marriage. We just packed.

After Beckie left, I started traveling to Johannesburg to spend time with Denis Kuny on the weekends. I went to the swamps of Botswana, where there were snakes, crocodiles, giant worms, and crayfish. I drove a Land Rover down the rocky South African coast. I almost drove it off a cliff once. I went to the long, wide beaches of Port St. John where I waded into the clear, blue ocean, which stayed shallow forever. I rode horses through the bright green mountains of Swaziland, camping, making fires, and sleeping under the stars. Beckie and I wrote to each other less and less often and the expensive phone calls became shorter and less frequent.

● ● ● ● ● ● ● ● ● ●

The political climate in the U.S. changed again. Jimmy Carter had failed to free the hostages in Iran, and soaring interest rates during his presidency undermined his domestic policy. He had not convinced Americans that the global fight for human rights was worth their attention or their tax dollars. His successor, Ronald Reagan, barely mentioned civil or economic rights in his campaign. Instead, phrases like "supply-side economics" and "competitiveness" in economic policy dominated the national rhetoric. Deregulation, once a dirty word in Washington, was being negotiated over coffee in neighborhood restaurants in Dupont Circle and Adams Morgan.

Reagan's presidency focused on cutting federal programs and easing regulations on large corporations. Reagan's policy toward South Africa was dubbed "constructive engagement." The White House expanded the financial and political ties between the South African regime and the U.S. I am certain that it was constructive for "supply side" economics and the diamond trade to strengthen trade relations and to export more goods to South Africa. In addition, Reagan could assure the Republicans in Congress and the American people that the godless communists—in this case, the African communists—were never going to win.

U.S. policy was less constructive for Reg, Norm, Elsa, and me. We did not buy into the portrayal of Nelson Mandela and the ANC, including Phyllis Naidoo, Khalaki Sello, and plenty of other people as "communists." My days on the porch in Maseru eating lychee nuts with Dennis Kuny were going to end, and probably very soon.

One afternoon, I was wandering through Lesotho's Peace Corps headquarters and noticed a flier stuck over somebody's desk. It pictured a burning candle surrounded by barbed wire, with the notice, "Amnesty International Seeking New Executive Leader."

I had been donating small amounts of money to Amnesty International for a while, but I did not know much about the organization.

My only prior exposure to Amnesty occurred one afternoon during my fourth year in Lesotho. I stopped by the Hilton Hotel and saw a line of South African and Lesotho men and women snaking out the doorway and around the block. They were waiting to talk to a man sitting at a table holding a notebook and pen. He was impressively dressed in a linen suit that defied the brown dust of Lesotho. He was very much the British gentleman.

It was a dangerous line for any South African or Basotho to be seen in. The man was David Soggot, and he was on a mission for Amnesty International. He had come from London to record individuals' stories of torture at the hands of the government. Just being in the line could easily bring about an arrest, a brutal interrogation, or death. And yet people waited patiently in the brutal heat, eager to share their stories despite the grave risk.

Soggot asked very thorough questions, took extensive notes, and then dabbed his forehead with a carefully folded handkerchief. Khalaki Sello and I invited him over to talk and see if we could help him. He surprised us that afternoon over tea. He knew a lot about South Africa and Lesotho and had a lot of information we did not know. Amnesty, I figured, must be doing something incredible back home. I was surprised to discover that whenever I talked about it to friends from home, the name and work of Amnesty International was unknown to them.

I stuck a copy of my resume in the mail to Amnesty's New York City office. Beckie called about three weeks later to tell me that Amnesty International had asked me to interview and they offered me transportation to the U.S. At that point I had not been home in a long while, and the free flight was an additional incentive to interview.

My interview took place in former U.S. Attorney General Ramsey Clark's office in Greenwich Village. The questions were difficult and made it obvious I did not know as much about Amnesty as I should have.

The questions were: Who are you? How would you improve the effectiveness of the organization? What is your background? What makes you qualified for this position?

My answers were basic: Son of Jesus Christ, John L. Lewis, and FDR; cut programs that are not working; Irish Catholic and poor; struggling against injustice in South Africa and the U.S.

After I answered a question, the eight interviewers seemed to be waiting for me to say more. When I was silent, they would glance at one another then write something down. I was unsure how the interview had gone, but I was relaxed, with an understanding that I would probably never see them again.

I went to see Beckie in Washington. We sat in the backyard and talked about the mortgage; the parts of the house that were falling apart, probably because we had traded beer and not dollars for home repairs; and the bills that we needed to pay. We discussed how Beckie could tell me if I got the Amnesty job. She could not just forward the letter because there was little chance that letter would reach Lesotho anytime in the next decade. We knew that the South African intelligence service listened in on our calls, and we did not want to give them or the Reagan Administration warning that I might be leaving the Peace Corps. My starting salary at Amnesty would be $34,000, a $20,000 decrease from my salary at Peace Corps.

Beckie suggested that if she called and told me that we were at war that would mean that I had gotten the job. If she called and said that we were not at war, it meant that I had not gotten the job. A few days later I packed my bags and returned to South Africa and Lesotho. I tried not to think about the last time that I landed in South Africa—when Beckie and I had gone together.

I got back to work with the Peace Corps volunteers who continued teaching and farming and building bridges. They followed the rules and treated their students with respect and showed up as required at our meetings. We had contributed grants and farming techniques and reliable teachers who taught English and math and were not abusive to students. I was proud of their achievements and happy that, as expats and volunteers in Lesotho, we had made things a little better for the Basotho.

Two of the volunteers had fallen in love and planned to get married in Lesotho, where they met. My house in Maseru West had a great backyard, maybe the best in town, so I offered to host a backyard wedding during the dry season.

The wedding was untraditional, messy, and lovely. Tons of people packed into the living room and onto the deck and spilled out into the backyard. Everyone made a speech about our time in Lesotho. The speeches grew longer and longer as the night went on, as more of the strong beer and South African wine disappeared. There was lots of food, and everyone was barefoot.

The party was still going on when I decided to go to bed. I grabbed a meal and a brownie from a tray and headed to my room.

Then, I was lying on the bed with no idea how I had gotten there. Everything was liquid, heavy, and slow. The ceiling was spinning around the fan. The fan was perfectly still. The patterns on the peeling paint were moving slowly around me, fascinating in their complexity, in their connection to one another, and to the rotating ceiling. It occurred to me, after about a half hour, or five minutes, or possibly two years, that maybe the brownies were pot brownies.

Eventually I realized that I was high, out of my mind, and I was totally losing it. I laughed and could not stop laughing. I was completely stoned.

I was slipping in and out of sleep, with dreams that were vividly colored and included lots of fabulous people, when the phone rang. It was Beckie, calling from Washington. "Jack," she said. "Jack, war!" Furious, I demanded to know who we had gone to war with, why I had not heard about it, what the hell was the Reagan Administration thinking involving us in yet another war, and what were we supposed to do in Lesotho? Then I realized that obviously, it was not Beckie on the phone. The phone had been tapped. The South African government was pretending to be Beckie to get to me. I had to hang up immediately or the house might be bombed. I threw the phone as if it were a poisonous snake and then I climbed safely back into bed and passed out.

The next day, after we had cleaned up from the wedding and thrown away all the baked goods, I called Beckie to ask about a mortgage payment. Beckie wanted to know why in the hell I had hung up on her on Saturday. She also wanted to know why I was turning down the position of executive director of Amnesty International. Had I lost my mind in Lesotho? I finally realized that it had been Beckie on the phone using our code for the job. I explained what happened with the brownies, and then both of us were laughing hysterically on the crackly long-distance call, maybe the only laugh we had shared in the prior two years.

As soon as Beckie and I hung up, I called Amnesty headquarters and formally accepted the job. I apologized, profusely, for not responding immediately, but did not explain this lapse in judgment.

Every Peace Corps director who leaves a posting is given a farewell party hosted by the U.S. ambassador. Among the volunteers and people in town that I invited were Khalaki Sello and Phyllis Naidoo. They found the idea of attending a fancy dinner at the U.S. embassy faintly ironic, but they agreed to come. After a lovely dinner with lots of fancy imported wine, the time came for toasts.

Khalaki stood and clinked his glass for attention. He spoke briefly about our friendship, our nights on the deck, meals at Fat Alice's restaurant, and the many volunteers he had met through me. Then he added: "I am a fan of Jack's. The thing that I'm not a fan of is the U.S. government's policy regarding apartheid, the greatest struggle of our time." He spoke eloquently of the horrors and the abuses of the apartheid regime. His voice was clear, spreading through the big room, commanding the attention of every single person. When he finally sat down, raising a fist in the air, the ambassador's sigh of relief was audible.

That night represented the jarring coming together of two sides of a contradiction that I contended with throughout my entire Peace Corps career. On the one side, my job was to promote understanding between peoples and provide skilled volunteer labor to countries that wanted it. On the other, I was the representative of a government that promoted policies that resulted in quite the opposite. Though my Peace Corps experience was invaluable, I knew the U.S. was the place I needed to be if I wanted to make large-scale change. I knew a single vote in Congress could go much further toward changing the wretched conditions that my friends in South Africa were forced to live in than all my efforts in Lesotho. It was frustrating to feel so far from where actual decision-making was taking place. I enjoyed my Peace Corps experience as well as my time with the volunteers. However, in my next role, I wanted to raise the consciousness of the American public to the perils of U.S. support for apartheid and other similarly restrictive systems at home and abroad.

No matter what the politics, Khalaki spoke eloquently of the horrors of the apartheid regime. When I left Africa, Khalaki Sello's strong voice went with me.

A few years later, I discovered that 2,400 shock batons had been sold to the Republic of South Africa by the Reagan Administration. I visited the manufacturer in Florida, and they told me they were cattle prods, not weapons of torture. In LA, I visited the chief of police, Darryl Gates, and suggested to him that he buy the prods for his work in LA. "I would not use such a thing on human beings," he said. This sale was hidden from Congress for a while. To me, it was a slap in the face of all the anti-apartheid folks I had met.

Friends Dick Gregory and John Lewis with me when I accepted the appointment to Peace Corps Lesotho.

With Nelson Mandela in 1993

In Lesotho, enjoying the Mountain Kingdom

Lesson Four

Once You Gain Awareness, Go Do Something about It

Chapter 10

Too Small to Win

1981-1994

I am uncomfortable in suits, but I was wearing one to meet with Assistant Secretary of State Elliott Abrams. My discomfort grew as sweat soaked my collar while I walked down humid Washington, D.C. streets. Once inside, I was cold and sticky in the stale air circulating through the State Department building. I kept thinking about what I was going to say when we got into our meeting. Distracted, I handed the guards my library card.

"Sir, this building requires a photo ID." "Right, right," I assured him as I searched my wallet for my driver's license. While I was fumbling with my wallet, Patricia, Amnesty's D.C. director, placed her ID on the desk and strolled through in one graceful motion. "That's why you run the Washington office, and I am up in New York," I joked.

I could tell she was fighting the urge to roll her eyes, but it did not matter. We had to have our game faces on because we were about to confront a very unsympathetic audience.

Assistant Secretary of State Elliott Abrams met us at his door. He had short hair, neatly parted to one side. We were there to talk to him about a soon-to-be-released Amnesty report on the human rights record of the Sandinista government in Nicaragua and the

U.S.-backed Contra rebels with whom they were at war. It was a sweeping document that we could have begun with the adoption of the Monroe Doctrine in 1823, which marked the official beginning of U.S. interference in the region, but Amnesty's style was to focus on more recent history.

Nicaragua in those days was violently transitioning after a revolution. Longtime U.S. ally General Anastasio Somoza, whose family had ruled Nicaragua for over forty years, had been overthrown in a popular coup by the Sandinistas. The Sandinistas pledged liberal benefits, multi-party elections, and an end to exploitative business contracts with the U.S. These contracts were unpopular in Nicaragua because they caused the over-mining of natural resources and depressed grain prices by dumping subsidized grain on Nicaraguan markets. Washington was divided between those who believed that the Sandinistas represented a Marxist takeover of Nicaragua that would adversely affect the balance of power and those who saw the Sandinistas as legitimate representatives of the Nicaraguan people.

President Carter sided with the latter group, and he did not want to intervene in Nicaragua. About three years after seizing power, the Sandinista government announced they would nationalize some mines owned by U.S. companies.

This was too much for U.S. business interests. In 1980, President Carter authorized the CIA to give "advice" to the Contras, and by the time Reagan took office in 1981, Washington had turned against the Sandinistas. They were viewed as an existential threat to the United States, its global standing, and its local and foreign markets.

Reagan sent U.S. military advisors to Nicaragua to train right-wing rebel groups to overthrow the Sandinistas. With the help of the experienced U.S. military, a mixed group of rebels morphed into a well-organized military group that became the Contras. The U.S. began sending guns, surface-to-air missiles, and ammunition to the Contras. Human rights did not appear to be a major objective in this effort. By all accounts, the Contras harmed anyone in their path.

The Contras waged a devastating war against the Sandinistas. The American public, uninformed about politics and developments in Latin America, paid little attention. *The New York Times* and a few other publications reported that the Contras were using tactics that included kidnapping, rape, and bombing schools.

As awareness of the war and its atrocities grew, pressure on the Administration to stop supporting the Contras grew with it. In 1982, and then again in 1984, a bipartisan majority in Congress passed the Boland Amendments (I and II), which barred the U.S. from providing any more weapons, money, or military training to the Contras. The Administration did not let anything as insignificant as the law interfere with its policies. Reagan treated the struggle against the Sandinistas as essential. No longer able to use taxpayer dollars directly for the Contras, a new plan was devised.

At that time, there was an arms embargo against Iran resulting from its 1979 capture of American diplomats. The arms embargo, originally designed to force Iran to free the American hostages, left Iran without the weapons it wanted and with no spare parts. The Reagan Administration entered a secret deal to sell weapons to Iran in exchange for cash. They were even able to overcharge for the weapons because Iran was restricted by the U.S. arms embargo. The influx of money from that sale gave the Administration money that Congress, and especially Rep. Edward Boland, did not control.

Cash from the sale of weapons slid into Nicaragua and into the hands of the Contras. The newly enriched Contras could continue running training camps and, once again, buying weapons for use on Nicaraguan citizens. The plan was partly the brainchild of Elliott Abrams, and when we met with him at the State Department, the whole arms for cash deal and America's covert support of the Contras were still secret.

Our meeting started out as banal as any other run-of-the-mill business meeting. We were all very cordial, breaking the ice with some pleasantries about the weather before jumping into discussion about the report. We went through it in detail. There was one aspect of the report that I wanted to make sure he would understand; it had to do with the report's focus. The first thirty-two pages dealt with the human rights abuses of the Sandinista government, but only four pages addressed the abuses of the Contras. The report was explicit as to why this was the case.

Amnesty International's policy was to condemn the killing or torture of captives both by government forces and those of opposition groups. However, Amnesty acted only with respect to governments because they are bound by the international legal standards that Amnesty International upholds.

I pushed this point to Mr. Abrams. Then I reiterated to him that the report's attention on the Sandinistas did not mean they were engaged in more human rights abuses than the Contras. It simply reflected Amnesty's focus on the human rights abuses of governments. I remember him nodding and telling me that he understood Amnesty's position.

I pushed more, asserting that all available evidence seemed to indicate that the Contras engaged in far more terrorist acts than the government and a harsh U.S. statement condemning the Contra violence could do a lot of good because of the Administration's ties. At this point I was expecting him to explode, but the anger never came. He simply restated to us the Administration's position on the matter, that while the Administration was concerned about the Contras, it was more concerned about the spread of Cuba-style communism.

I left with mixed feelings: somewhat satisfied that Abrams had listened to me, and slightly uneasy, feeling that little would change. I was not at all prepared for what happened next.

Elliott Abrams was discussing U.S. Latin American policy with some members of the press who had gathered in the hall by his office. Nicaragua's revolution was on everyone's minds. I watched him chat, hoping that our meeting had impacted his message. Any mention of the human rights abuses of the Contras would have been a victory. As allies of the United States, the Contras would surely take Washington's criticism to heart.

About halfway through the conference, Abrams turned to a reporter who pressed him about his vocal support for the Contras. He told the reporter that Amnesty International had released a report about the ongoing war in Nicaragua. I was eager to hear what he had to say next.

The report, he noted, had only four pages detailing the abuses of the Contras, while it contained over thirty pages on the Sandinistas. Nobody should question the severity of the communist threat or the valor of the anti-regime fighters.

I was completely shocked. Abrams had ignored what I said entirely and was using Amnesty's work to support his claims that the U.S. should continue to bolster the Contras. The idea that politicians spin stories to their own advantage was nothing new to me, but it was unnerving to experience it in such a direct way. Once an official with Abrams' stature makes such a comment, it can become hard to counter in the media. In newsrooms where fast turnaround is key, critiques of U.S. foreign policy are often viewed as too difficult to substantiate and not worth the time and money. Because of the need to get the news out quickly, U.S. government sources like the Pentagon and State Department are granted a certain benefit of the doubt that most organizations outside of the government are not.

I began to feel that lobbying the Administration on behalf of human rights was a waste of time. State Department officials knew what we knew—they were just looking for ways to use our work to advance their own arguments. The pressure for change had to come from an angry and informed citizenry. This would not be easy. Amnesty would have to find a way to be in the media as much as the government. That way, the human rights side of the story would get out just as strongly.

• • • • • • • • • •

How was I going to get Amnesty listened to with the same frequency as the institutions we were trying to critique? There was little to improve in terms of research standards. Our research department was already regarded as the gold standard by many of the world's top academics and policy members for its reporting on human rights abuses. What we lacked was people power. We had to turn our voices into thunder and turn our candles into bonfires so the government could not ignore us.

I had been at Amnesty for a while when the Abrams incident occurred. Initially my goal as executive director was to raise the profile of the organization and make it a familiar presence within the United States and around the world. After our encounter with Abrams, I knew we had to change the power balance in the media. The way to combat this type of information manipulation was to make Amnesty so well known that we did not need to use politicians to get information into the public forum.

$$\bullet \ \bullet \ \bullet \ \bullet \ \bullet \ \bullet \ \bullet \ \bullet \ \bullet \ \bullet$$

Amnesty was created in 1961. It was the brainchild of English barrister Peter Benenson, who had written an opinion piece in *The Times of London* about the illegitimate arrest of two Portuguese students in fascist Portugal. In his essay, Benenson appealed to the people of the world to not allow injustice to pass unnoticed.

He broke new ground in establishing the importance of people caring for people. This crucial work could not be left in the hands of governments: a rare man, a rare thought, and a rare action.

It was one of those welcome times when journalism inspired the community and became a catalyst for immediate and tangible change.

The essay sparked a rally in Tottenham Square in London that attracted activists and students. Maybe the first step in creating any type of social revolution is to find a proper town square. Those who gathered chanted a phrase that represented both idealism and realism. "It is better to light a candle than to curse the dark." It may not have been poetic or even original, but it sure as hell was powerful.

Amnesty had its origins in this initial small protest and began operations with a tiny, all-volunteer staff. Benenson began his fact-finding missions to uncover human rights abuses in Haiti and then expanded his research to much of the world. Amnesty International grew under his direction.

Twenty years later, Benenson's vision had been bureaucratized. Amnesty USA was stagnant and demoralized. The original founders had moved on to other jobs, and volunteers were few. Reports of human rights violations took six to nine months to produce. The volunteer board and the professional staff did not get along to the detriment of the entire organization. That conflict continued for decades.

At that time, the U.S. chapter of Amnesty had about 35,000 dues-paying members. The average member was over forty and the annual budget was about $3 million. There were ten staff members at the New York office, five in D.C., four in San Francisco, and one each in Chicago, New Orleans, and Los Angeles. The London office was responsible for research; our U.S. offices were supposed to focus entirely on increasing our influence in Washington, spreading the news of human rights abuses, and energizing and building the movement. Nobody knew, in or out of the organization, what Amnesty was trying to accomplish. Amnesty was making itself irrelevant in a time of need. Ronald Reagan, trickle-down economics, and military buildup were gaining momentum, and opposition was badly needed to counter their ill effects. Deaths under Central American dictatorships and military juntas had to be addressed, and apartheid needed to go.

· · · · · · · · · ·

It was time for Amnesty to undergo an overhaul. I dismissed the law firm, CPA, and fundraising firms that had been on retainer. I hired fund raising consultants Craver, Mathews, Smith & Company and a dynamic law firm, Hogan & Harston, where my friend Sandy Berger worked. These were two of the best decisions I made at Amnesty.

In prior years, Amnesty branches "adopted" a political prisoner. Members of an "adoption group" wrote letters of protest to the government holding that prisoner. The groups met once a month and sent a dozen letters to offending governments. This was a start, but letters for each prisoner were limited by the size of the branches that had adopted him or her.

We implemented a new campaign to increase the volume of mail. Once a month, each Amnesty donor received three pre-addressed letters in their mailbox. The letters were addressed to leaders of different countries, including India, Thailand, Yugoslavia (notably in Kosovo), and Iran. Each letter contained a description of a political prisoner with their name, personal information such as to whom they were married, the names of their children, and a detailed explanation of the facts behind their imprisonment. The letter had space for the Amnesty donors to write personal notes of protest to the governments that had imprisoned these individuals, demanding their immediate release and the restoration of their civil liberties. The result was a huge increase in the volume of mail about each prisoner. We hoped these letters would have some effect on the governments receiving them and keep Amnesty donors feeling involved in the human rights process.

A trade unionist in Guatemala had been in solitary confinement for years. After the first two hundred letters demanding his release arrived from around the world, the guards had given him back his shirt and pants. When the next two hundred arrived, the prison director came to visit him. Then when the next four hundred arrived, the prison director's superior came to visit his tiny cell. When the letters reached 3,000 and could no longer be contained by the mail bins at the prison, the president of Guatemala invited him to his office. How, the president asked him, how on earth could a trade union leader from a small town have so many friends all over the world?

● ● ● ● ● ● ● ● ● ●

I was in Washington for yet another Amnesty board meeting. I called Beckie, and we met for coffee at a place near our house. We sat and attempted to have the conversation we had avoided for the last three years. We left the coffee shop and stopped at a nearby bookstore. As we browsed through the books, Beckie stopped and held up a small, tattered book: *How to Get Divorced*.

Her sad gesture let me know that we had both accepted that our marriage was over. The book turned out to offer extremely good advice about ending a marriage and moving on with life. My salary at Amnesty was only $34,000 so we had little to split up. Beckie kept the house, and I bought an apartment in New York. We were both happy with this arrangement. I went to see a therapist, Dr. Philip Luloff, for three years, and I was grateful I did. It may have been he who let me know I made a better priest than husband.

• • • • • • • • • •

I was in Boston to speak on a panel at Harvard University on "the spread of democracy around the world." I would be appearing with, among others, a representative from Freedom House, a conservative organization that annually releases an index ranking countries based on the freedom level of their governments. The criteria for a country to be ranked as "free" were very narrow. White, Christian, European countries were continually ranked as the most "free," while no African nation had ever been ranked higher than a five, the lowest score. These criteria caused a lot of friction among human rights organizations.

I sought out social justice activist Noam Chomsky for support, and he kindly offered to have dinner with me. His ability to marshal facts and stories to bolster his cause was impressive. I resolved to acquire a similar ability. His invaluable advice to me both during the conference and during my tenure at Amnesty boiled down to this: pay attention to the research, stick to the facts, and you will be fine.

My draft conference speech would offer a few suggestions on how the criteria could be made more inclusive and it would go easy on what I thought was a nonsensical way to view the world. When their representative began the event by launching into a long monologue about the advantages of their ranking system, and the ways it could change the world, I decided I was not going to allow this philosophy to go unchallenged.

When it was my turn to talk, I asked the Freedom House guy what, exactly, he meant by freedom. "Does that term carry with it any cultural baggage? Why is it that only white middle-class countries seem to do well as judged by the organization's criteria?" The audience began paying attention. Comments, arguments, and time flew by. The Freedom House representative became noticeably angry. At the end, I asked him how dividing the world along racial and cultural lines was going to make it freer. The audience roared its approval, giving me a standing ovation.

Ginetta Sagan, one of the founders of Amnesty International USA, arranged a supper for me with Apple founder Steve Jobs in the fall of 1982. After the appropriate niceties, Steve let me know he did not like charities much. He said charity work was too inefficient and slow. The numerous board members guaranteed confusion and stagnation. I did my best to debate this highly intelligent man who did not like my line of work. I have never been a money chaser, and I was not there to solicit funds from Jobs. I wanted him to take a stand against human rights abuses around the world. I didn't care whether he donated to Amnesty. I was after memberships of young people at $25 each.

Depending upon the rich has never been my game, dating to when I was a priest refusing to raise funds for new churches. I knew clearly what my intention was: I would use membership funds to try to free political prisoners.

Money alone cannot solve human rights abuses. It takes people. Human rights without a constituency is a river without water.

A few years later, I was at a reception that Harry Kraut, Leonard Bernstein's manager, set up in the hall where Leonard had conducted the San Francisco Symphony. Steve came over and politely told me that he had not changed his thoughts about charity but was happy to see me and to come to the event. Years later, Steve and his public relations firm hired U2 as the poster child to sell a new iPod. Rob Schwartz, of the global advertising agency TBWA Worldwide, created the campaign that worked so successfully for Apple.

I never wrote Steve, but I was waiting to run into him again so I could say, "You paid a lot to use U2 at the turn of the century.

Amnesty International, our slow-moving, stagnated non-profit, had U2 in 1986 free of cost for two weeks." I kept myself entertained with that thought.

On the other hand, Steve made a good point about inefficiency. We had eleven chairs during my dozen years at Amnesty and went through more than 140 board members in that period. I once calculated that during my twelve years as director, I spent a full 365 days in board meetings.

• • • • • • • • • •

Human rights reports focus on incidents of torture or statistics about deprivation. It was my conviction that such slices of truth are not enough. To create a movement, you need something that captures people's aspirations. Music, especially live music, has the unique ability to inspire people, moving them physically, intellectually, and emotionally all at the same time.

When I had first arrived in South Africa with the Peace Corps, people were singing protest songs in the street. Long after I had forgotten other details, the music stayed with me. The music brought the crowds together, and the music carried their message with more strength than words could. I was intrigued by the power music could have and wondered how we could use it to advance human rights.

I am an Elvis fan. His songs and charity work awed me. When I was in my teens, he woke me up with his music. What struck me most was his energy. My epiphany was, "Music generates energy. If we attach music to our message, it will help create the interest and excitement that is necessary to move people out of inertia and into activism."

I realized that artists make the best activists. In every culture, it is the musicians, painters, and writers, not the politicians, who are the highly visible, prophetic leaders conveying the emotional state of society, and questioning what is right and what is wrong. Goya's *The Third of May 1808* or Picasso's *Guernica* are examples of artistic works that allow us to see with new eyes.

I was not the first to exploit the symbiotic relationship between music and message. The iconic Odetta Holmes—singer, songwriter, and human rights activist—was known as "The Voice of the Civil Rights Movement." Harry Belafonte, Bob Marley, John Lennon, Joe Strummer, Bob Dylan, Jackson Browne, Joan Baez, Pete Seeger and many others had harnessed music to serve the Civil Rights Movement. The songs that arose spontaneously from the crowd filling the National Mall on August 28, 1963 were as powerful as any of the speeches given. Activism followed the artist.

Desmond Tutu said upon accepting his Nobel Peace Prize, "Most of God's best collaborators and partners have been young people."

I committed to bringing young people into the work at Amnesty because in every struggle in the world, whether it is South Africa, Latin America, or Burma, it's the kids, the babies, who are in jail. The soldiers are babies. The demonstrators are young, as in the 1960 Sharpsville Massacre in South Africa. The young girls being raped are babies. They are ten, twelve, fifteen years old. They are seldom over twenty. I wanted to connect those who were struggling for justice overseas with those struggling for justice in the United States, because they are the same age. It is not for older people to save the young. It is for the young to save the young. The youth deserve to be supported by us. This was my belief and my intention.

I needed somehow to make it happen. I had to. Sello, Kuny, Hani, and Gandhi were in my ear.

The first opportunity to use music as a voice for human rights came with a concert in May 1983, featuring the Modern Jazz Quartet. Kita Taylor and John Morris coordinated the event. We took a risk, not knowing if there would be interest, if we could raise funds, or if musicians would even participate. The concert raised $10,000 for Amnesty. This early success bolstered my confidence that music could work for us.

Twice before, in the spring of 1982 and then again in 1983, Amnesty had sponsored concerts titled "The Secret Policeman's Ball" in London. Sting had performed as a young musician. The concerts received some airtime. Amnesty even made some money when Harvey Weinstein acquired the rights to sell the movie of The Secret Policeman's Ball for HBO.

Leonard Bernstein performed in San Francisco for a Bernstein fund in honor of his deceased wife. Cellist Yo-Yo Ma performed for Amnesty. Emanuel Ax performed in Chicago. The music was lovely, but nobody under the age of fifty paid much attention. I wanted to find the music that would draw young people to the fight.

I went to see concert promoter Barry Fey in Denver to get some ideas. One of our ideas was to create an anti-torture train to go across the U.S. flying the flags of nations that sanction torture. If a country stopped allowing torture, we would take their flag off the train. I would still like to do the train idea.

We did need something that would attract notoriety. We needed the type of music young people flocked to hear. I flew to San Francisco in late 1981 where I managed to set up a meeting with Bill Graham, a renowned promoter of the best talent in the rock business. He was a legend; he had represented major rock groups including the Rolling Stones and the Grateful Dead.

He was a German-Russian Jewish Holocaust survivor, an orphan because of the gas chambers of Auschwitz, and he owed his life to the networks of people who risked their lives to spirit Jewish children out of France and later, Germany.

In the 1960s, Graham managed a radical mime group who performed street theater and protested the Vietnam War by wearing fatigues and acting out scenes of soldiers attacking Vietnamese villagers. The sidewalks in the midst of the towering office buildings in San Francisco became their stage. They would put somebody in shackles and pretend to beat him, while men and women with briefcases hurried by on their way to work.

Eventually, some musicians joined the mime group. At first, there were just a few guitarists with the desire to protest the war. When the Grateful Dead joined, the performances moved from the dirty square in the middle of the business district to Golden Gate Park. Eventually, Bill started a new business organizing shows for people such as Allen Ginsberg and Jefferson Airplane through contacts he had made during mime shows in the square.

Bill's large, sunlit office was no longer in Golden Gate Park by the time I met him in December 1981. Bill knew about the original Amnesty protest but had not followed Amnesty. I told him about my plan to extend Amnesty's reach to thousands of people playing the kind of music you can dance to—an explosion of the Golden Gate Park idea for human rights. He was twirling his pen, nodding along, but he did not express any interest.

I thought about Charlie Maloney, the lawyer from my childhood who went to bat for me, so I said, "Come on, Bill. I know you care about this stuff. At least, you used to care. Now that you're here in this fancy high-rise office twirling your pen, you don't care, suddenly?"

"I mean, do you know what we are doing here? We are fighting for human rights. This is not some teenybopper concert where we can just sign up some talent and call it a day. We need you, Bill."

Graham kindly explained that he did not take orders from arrogant assholes even if they were the heads of human rights organizations. "Then prove me wrong, Bill."

That ticked him off. The staff gathered outside the thick mahogany door eavesdropping on what was quickly becoming a shouting match. Bill was pounding the desk.

"Fine. Fine. But Jack, I am not Superman. These things take work. You have to get the talent. If you can do that, I will run the damn show."

"Is that a deal? I need a contract," I pressed.

"Yes, okay, yes, Jack; that is a contract. It is a solid contract. Now get out of my office."

• • • • • • • • • •

Radio City Music Hall was gorgeous, with high ceilings and red carpet and recently reupholstered leather chairs arranged so that the stage was visible to the entire audience—no need for pushing, shoving, or crowd surfing. But the first time that U2, the Irish band led by Bono, played at Radio City, people climbed up on top of those chairs. They stood on those chairs, and fought to see the stage, and we thought that a mosh pit might break out.

I found myself at that concert on December 3, 1984, because of a $10,000 check Amnesty received from U2. The check was accompanied by two tickets to the show at Radio City Music Hall which I promptly passed off to my secretary, Claude Isakov, not having a clue who Bono or U2 were. Claude's friend could not make it at the last minute, and she burst into my office and told me I needed to go with her because she was simply not willing to miss U2 live. So, I went.

Two minutes into the song "Bloody Sunday," I was shouting along with the rest of the crowd. The lyrics were about truth and human rights, justice, freedom, and power to people who have been denied access to power. There was a picture of an American Indian and Dr. King on the back wall of the concert stage. That sealed it for me. I had found our band.

• • • • • • • • • •

I believed, and still do, that there are two causes that the United States must understand and come to grips with: the taking of land from Native Americans and the issue of slavery and racism in the United States. Bob Peterson, our Madison Walk coordinator, then sixteen, spoke at the World Food Summit in 1971. He said, "We stole the Black man to work the land we stole from the red man." Bob ultimately went on to become a union leader and educator in Wisconsin.

In 1985, when I headed to the annual worldwide Amnesty Conference in Finland, I flew through Dublin. I arrived in Dublin August 23 with the plan to recruit U2 and get the blessing of Sean

MacBride, the worldwide chair of Amnesty for its first thirteen years. We landed in Ireland just as the morning fog was lifting. Every time I land in Ireland, I am home.

Sean MacBride had been responsible for growing Amnesty beyond its small London office to the U.S. and other countries. At twelve, he had been tutored by Irish Nobel Prize winners in literature—Sean O'Casey, George Bernard Shaw, and W.B. Yeats, as well as Ezra Pound. The British executed his father in 1918 during the Irish War of Independence when Sean was thirteen. After that, he joined the Irish Republican Army (IRA), and eventually became head of the IRA. After he left the IRA, he became a successful barrister who freed numerous Irish political prisoners from British prisons. As foreign minister of Ireland, Sean brought Yeats' body back from Europe to be buried in his home turf. Sean was a recipient of both the Nobel Peace Prize and the Lenin Peace Prize.

I had no idea how to find Sean MacBride, so I decided to just check the phone book. His number was listed next to all the other MacBrides in Dublin. He answered on the third ring and invited me over. Sean was eighty-one years old in 1985, but he answered the door of his big old brick house himself. He was well-informed on world politics and on Amnesty. We had coffee in a large room with lots of paintings on the wall. He was pleased that I was Irish, and I asked him about the IRA and Irish history. We spoke of his mother, Maud Gonne—a giant of Irish theater, a great human rights worker, and the fantasy woman of Yeats' poetry. Sean and I discussed the need for a youth movement in the U.S. "Art," he said, "any type of art, which gets these people up, music and painting, these are the ways that we convince people of the importance of doing something other than sitting on their front steps and smoking cigarettes." U2 was a great way to do this. Then, being Sean, he got me to agree to help the Irish section of Amnesty if the concerts raised enough money. A year later, he was pleased when the Irish section received a check for $300,000.

Next, I took a cab to a small, hip office at Windmill Lane. At the top of a narrow flight of stairs, I knocked on a large wooden door on which someone had scratched his initials. U2's manager,

Paul McGuinness, let me in. Bono came over and shook my hand. At twenty-five, Bono already seemed quiet, much quieter than he later became.

I did not have a lot of time because of a connecting flight. I asked Bono, "Are you really Irish?" This rattled him for a minute. I said quickly, "Amnesty is struggling. We are failing to get people who matter involved enough to pay attention to the things that matter. We need help. I need your help to build a movement. We need the young with us."

Bono looked at Paul. Paul looked back. Bono said, "Sure." I asked Paul to write up the agreement right then because Bill Graham said it had to be in writing. We said goodbye, and then I tried to hug Paul, but he did not know how to hug. We all laughed, and then we all hugged. I was back in the cab with the signed agreement within eight minutes.

When I got to the Dublin airport, I went directly to the payphone and, emptying my pockets, called San Francisco. Bill answered, already irritated. I had awakened him or interrupted his breakfast or his mid-morning meeting or something. When I told him about the contract with U2, he started laughing, and then I was laughing too. "You crazy bastard. You did it."

*With Steve Jobs at the Leonard Bernstein event for
Amnesty International in San Francisco, 1983.*

Chapter 11

The Conspiracy of Hope

1985-1986

T he Conspiracy of Hope tour took place during the summer of 1986 in celebration of the 25th anniversary of the founding of the modern human rights effort by Peter Benenson. At Amnesty's meeting in Finland, I told anyone who would listen that Amnesty was evolving and that music would become our magical messenger. Music crosses borders. Music will give human rights a stage and explain Amnesty's work and goals. We are on a search for young people for the human rights movement.

Amnesty's chair, Professor Charles Henry of the University of California at Berkeley, supported the effort. We wanted a platform of some length so we could explain the mandate of Amnesty as well as recruit a new generation of activists. Amnesty would no longer be a well-kept secret in the U.S. We were 25 years old, and it was time to grow up.

With the smarts and friendships of Bill Graham, U2 manager Paul McGuinness, Miles Copeland, Herb Alpert, recording executive Jerry Moss, music and film executive Gil Friesen, record label executive Gary Gersh, musician John Sykes, entertainment industry executive Tom Freston, and MTV's president Bob Pittman, we began to make it happen. Bono recruited Peter Gabriel and Lou

Reed. Gil Friesen and I flew to Vancouver to see Bryan Adams. He agreed over supper. John Sykes and Mike Ovitz of CAA, one of Hollywood's top talent agencies, allowed me to hold meetings in their offices.

Norm Pattiz of Westwood One was on board to do the radio work for the shows. My staff at Amnesty USA was smart. My deputy, Curt Goering, held it together while I roamed around doing work out of the office. Mary Daly was our talented press secretary, and James Radner managed administrative operations with ease.

Mary and I met Sting for lunch at his apartment in SoHo. He agreed to join the tour and even agreed to reunite the Police for a concert if we kept it a secret. Bill Graham recruited Joan Baez, the Neville Brothers, and Jackson Browne to join us on the six-city tour.

· · · · · · · · · ·

The tour adopted six prisoners. Six was hopeful and was possible without overreaching. Selecting the prisoners was the most difficult part because it was hard to pick only six. We sat around, late into the night, shuffling through reports of dirty prison cells, no food, no clean water, diseases, and criminal charges for such "crimes" as distributing poetry. The six prisoners were the reason Bill Graham picked the name "Conspiracy of Hope" for the tour. We did our best to select a representative group of political prisoners. The ones we chose provided compelling cases:

1. Hugo de Leon Palacios was in a tiny cell in Guatemala, jailed because he had worked at a school known for grassroots organizing for anti-government politicians.

2. Thozamile Gqwetha sat in a crowded cell in South Africa because of his membership in the South African Allied Workers Union.

3. Lee Kwang-Ung was placed in solitary confinement in South Korea for distributing poetry attributed to a North Korean artist.

4. Riad al-Turk lived in a filthy cell in Syria because he had joined

the Syrian communist party, which was reviled by the Assad regime.

5. Tatyana Semyonova Osipova was jailed in the Soviet Union because she had been documenting stories of police brutality and beatings and rapes by soldiers. Tatyana was later freed and attended the Human Rights Now tour in 1988.

6. Nguyễn Chí Thiện was in prison in Vietnam accused of distributing literature deemed "political" in nature.

We posted each of their pictures behind us at all the press conferences. They were to be featured as often as possible. These six would help explain political imprisonment and provide the tour's strength and purpose. At each venue, Amnesty volunteers distributed sample cards and letters for new members to send to governments holding Prisoners of Conscience. Tens of thousands of such missives were eventually sent by these new members.

My "office" in LA was the office of A&M Records, home to the Police and Bryan Adams. Jerry Moss and Herb Alpert generously opened their offices for the venture. Bob Pittman, John Sykes, Tom Freston, and Jock McLean of MTV agreed to give us the entire eleven hours on their first major MTV Live show in addition to all the advertising revenues from the show. Meetings with Viacom produced a syndicated show from 7-11 p.m., giving us a national audience.

A board member from Los Angeles, Sandy Elster, met with me to see how he could help. He told me he knew the Pritzker family, owners of the Hyatt Hotels. Their grandfather had died in the Holocaust. Sandy thought that he could get the Hyatt to give us free rooms for the six-city tour. They generously agreed and saved us a lot of money. Bill Graham loved this touch.

In addition to publicizing the plight of the six prisoners, we wanted the tour to raise the profile of Amnesty. But we needed to figure out where we stood in the public eye before we could raise our profile. Who knew about Amnesty? How relevant were we to the ordinary person on the street?

Bill Fertik, an excellent filmmaker, decided to conduct an experiment. We stood next to a coffee shop beside a crowded subway stop in New York City. It was a hot, brutal summer in New York, but Bill was determined that we "set a baseline," as he called it. We stopped people at random as they left the coffee shop. We asked them what Amnesty International was, or what it did, and then recorded their answers.

Perhaps Amnesty was an organization that advocated for lower taxes, one man suggested. No, no, argued the woman we stopped next. Surely, Amnesty was an organization sponsored by Vietnam War draft dodgers. We ought to be arrested, or at the very least go back to Canada. The third was disappointed that our most recent record had not yet been released and was also upset that the long-haired drummer had left the band. How had we let that happen?

After fifty interviews, we gave up. We went to have a coffee, and Bill came up with solutions. He created the message: "Use your freedom for another's lack of freedom." And he developed a series of brilliant public service announcements that ran on television for years.

We shot for two days. All the actors volunteered their talent. Robin Williams told his hilarious jokes in perfect time for both thirty and sixty second spots.

John Huston came in a wheelchair guided by his daughter, Anjelica. John's lungs were giving out, and he had a breathing tube. I was so pleased that he came to do a spot for Amnesty and human rights. It took a while to get the shoot right. Others who were waiting to be filmed began to complain about the time we were taking until they heard it was John Huston. Robin Williams told them they had to be patient when "real" talent was working.

John Huston was an Irishman, like MacBride, Yeats, and my mother. He, his dad, and his children were all symbols of Irish talent and ability, and I loved them for that. When John finished his 30 and 60-second spots, I asked him if he would allow me to take a picture with him. He shrugged and said "sure." Bill Fertik, our brilliant director said, "I want in that photo."

The three of us mugged, and as the photographer got ready, John Huston said, "I am glad to have my picture taken with an ex-priest."

The Oscar-winner smiled the whole time we worked on the PSAs. After Anjelica wheeled him out, I asked Bill, "How does he know I am an ex-priest?" Bill said, "Jack, he doesn't know. He is a great casting director."

Adam Ant, Rosanna Arquette, Marissa Berenson, Stockard Channing, Elvis Costello, Jamie Lee Curtis, Tyne Daly, Richard Dreyfuss, Mike Farrell, Margaux Hemingway, Susan Lucci, Richard Pryor, Keith Richards, Carly Simon, Paul Simon, Meryl Streep, John Taylor (of Duran Duran), Marlo Thomas, and Sam Waterston all graciously made supporting spots for Amnesty. This ad campaign ran so long and successfully that Robin Williams' manager finally asked that we take the PSAs off the air because, he said, "Robin Williams does not look like that anymore."

A kick-off dinner and press party were held in New York on April 1, 1986. Mary Daly, Amnesty's PR specialist, set the event in motion. Jane Alexander, Tom Brokaw, Glenn Close, E. L. Doctorow, Bill Graham, Peter Jennings, Paul McGuinness, Inge Morath, Bayard Rustin, Rose Styron, and Sam Waterston were all there for us. Yelena Bonner, wife of Soviet dissident and human rights activist Andrei Sakharov, spoke at the dinner, calling for a new beginning for human rights. The dinner inspired a five-part series on NBC's Today Show that ran right before the concerts, and merited spots on Nightline and ABC News.

Michael Ahern joined the tour as manager, and Ken Regan became the official photographer. Both excelled at their jobs.

We set and met a goal of raising $3 million for Amnesty and adding 35,000 new members, each paying $25, thereby doubling Amnesty USA's membership. We sold 180,000 tickets at $36 apiece. In addition, we got 5,600 mentions in the press.

Our first concert was in Bill Graham's hometown of San Francisco, at the Cow Palace, an iconic 16,000 seat indoor arena. The doors opened at 7 p.m. Joan Baez was the opening act. She walked on stage without a guitar and began her set with her cover of Bob Dylan's *The Times They are a Changin'*. Because it was Joan, it was strong and moving, but there was almost nobody there to hear it. It was 7:30 when she finished her set, and there were about five hundred people in the stadium. It was much, much too quiet.

I found Bill and dragged him out to where I had been sneaking peeks from behind the curtain, pointed to the empty stadium, and described the headlines that were surely going to run tomorrow in the *San Francisco Chronicle*: "Political Prisoners Remain Jailed–Americans Do Not Care" and "Nobody Cares about Amnesty International."

Bill laughed. "Calm down, you big loser. This is how rock concerts go. Everyone's got to get up, smoke their weed, get over those hangovers, and get their asses down here. Wait for it. It will happen," Bill told me. "Wait till Gabriel hits the stage."

As usual, Bill was correct. By the time Peter Gabriel banged out "Sledgehammer," the stadium was packed. When he closed with "Biko," his tribute to Black consciousness and the anti-apartheid struggle, I was crying like an idiot, like most of the audience. After Peter finished, I got Sonny Venkatrathnam, a former prisoner of conscience from South Africa and we went backstage to see Peter and thank him. We were all weeping.

Then Peter asked, "Was I any good?" The answer was: "Peter, we got a tour."

As Bryan Adams held his guitar over his head following two encores and a standing ovation, Bill nudged me with his elbow. "Your turn, buddy. Remember to kiss the mic, okay?" he said with a big grin.

"What the hell are you talking about?" It was my turn to get on stage and remind the audience why we were there. This was not just a concert, even though everyone was energized and happy. There were six prisoners hoping that this concert would change their lives. We hoped the concert would help more people, but there were certainly six.

"Now. And if you're not better than U2, you'll never see that stage again," Bill said.

The crowd of 16,000 fell silent as I passed Bryan on my way onstage. He patted me sympathetically as I walked past. The crowd watched, perhaps afraid that I might try to sing or play the guitar. I closed my eyes and kissed the microphone.

"Do you support our campaign against torture? Do you support our campaign to end the death penalty? Do you support Amnesty International?"

The audience screamed its support. Bill was standing on the side of the stage, laughing. He hugged me and told me I'd done a great job, but he could not stop laughing.

"Jack," he said. "'Kiss the mic' is an expression to remind you to stand close to the mic. I didn't mean actually kiss the damn microphone. Rip Van Winkle over here." It was pretty funny.

U2 was the closing band that night. The level of talent on the tour was truly amazing to see, especially close to the stage. Bryan Adams was a stunner. Sting was not with the Police then (that reunion came later). His band of Branford Marsalis, Kenny Kirkland, and Darrell Jones was arguably unrivaled in talent and ability.

Sting was as brilliant on TV as he was on stage. Asked by a TV interviewer to describe Amnesty, Sting said, "It is great to have a dictator as a pen pal." It was the perfect nod to our letter-writing campaign.

At the press conference, one journalist tried to embarrass the artists by asking how much money they each made. Graham almost went down the guy's throat. Before Bill could do that, I introduced the six prisoners of conscience that we had adopted. That quieted the press. Their pictures hung behind us in the press room. That was the real purpose behind the tour.

Good Morning America interviewed both Sting and Bono during the first week. Guest host presenters helped on all six stages: Muhammad Ali, New Jersey Senator Bill Bradley, Robert De Niro,

Mia Farrow, Elliott Gould, Dick Gregory, New Jersey Governor Tom Kean, Madonna, Sean Penn, and Steve Reeve.

I gave a sixty-second energizer to the crowd each night. Our task was to introduce and attempt to free six political prisoners of conscience and to explain our four mandates: No Torture, No Executions, No Unfair Trials, and No Imprisonment based on color or creed.

The day after San Francisco, we flew to Los Angeles for the concert at the Forum. Celebratory pillow fights all the way. Those pillow fights were a constant on the tour, providing relaxation, tension release, and pure fun.

Time magazine met us at the Los Angeles airport for a photo that started our national coverage. We headed to a press conference organized by Brian Murphy, our promoter in LA, who had gathered a large press crowd. Each artist spoke of a political prisoner and a certain rhythm and excitement set in. You could feel it now.

One journalist asked if all the artists were against the death penalty. He was expecting at least one of them to give him a negative story to write about but got none. Everyone raised their hands to support abolition of the death penalty.

I got lucky when we went to lunch with my staff members Mary Daly and James Radner. We ate with Peter Gabriel and have been friends ever since.

Bill Graham added more talent to the performances: T-Bone Burnett, Bob Dylan, Bob Geldof, Heart, Don Henley, Maria McKee, Joni Mitchell, Tom Petty, Bonnie Raitt, Carlos Santana, Curt Smith, and Dave Stewart for the closing jam. The Forum was filled.

Madonna and Sean Penn spoke at the event.

Bono did something I will never forget. He climbed on the equipment with a blindfold on to show the vulnerability of a prisoner of conscience after an arrest. Later he grabbed me, and we did an Irish jig around the stage. U2 was bonding with Amnesty. This was the first time I ever saw backstage. It was a zoo of famous record people and friends.

Jack Nicholson asked me how he could help. He said, "I hear Amnesty is Huston country." I grinned, "Jack, we only take good talent."

My second one-minute blast on stage got a little easier, and I learned to just ride the wave. Robert Hilburn, music reporter for the *Los Angeles Times*, wrote a glowing review:

Amnesty International's nearly six-hour "A Conspiracy of Hope" concert Friday night at the sold-out 18,600-seat Forum was a dramatic demonstration of how we changed a political "benefit." Lighting and sound were state of the art, the pacing was brisk, and many of the artists were more inspiring than they were at their own paid concerts.

The Denver concert was only half sold. As soon as we landed, all the artists actively promoted the concert; they visited the local radio stations the morning of the show. They did not announce their arrival in advance; they just appeared at the stations. The morning DJs nearly fell over in shock when they arrived at work and found Bono or Sting sitting on the steps drinking coffee and offering to go on their show. The radio studios were elated to see them.

Scott Harrison of our Amnesty staff pitched in with vital help. We pumped it up. Graham had a previous commitment, and I wondered what that could be. The artists did not seem to mind; they played ball and roamed about the hotel. It was strange to me that tickets hadn't sold well given the amazing talent line-up, but I did not care because we had two successful concerts and ended on a high note in both cities. The reviews were great, and MTV was saying they were awaiting the next show with great anticipation.

Bill called me and said, "We are two up and one even." He explained how concerts were like meals: "The potatoes were just okay, but the salad and appetizers were terrific."

I had a long lunch and got to know Lou Reed a little. He took me from the Velvet Underground to where we were that day in Denver. It was a great learning experience. The concerts were building into a movement, and we all were feeling good. The T-shirts sold out again. Denver might have been the best musical night yet. We boarded our concert plane ready to hit Atlanta.

Alex Hodges was the promoter for the Atlanta concert, and he was ready for us. The concert had sold out the 16,000 seat Omni. REM was in the crowd and later credited the show as having been influential to them.

The musicians were eager to visit Dr. King's grave and meet Mrs. Coretta Scott King. U2 was especially eager because of their song about Dr. King. Aaron Neville sang "Amazing Grace." Peter Gabriel called on the governor of Georgia to stop an execution, and it worked for a short while. The biggest news was that The Police came back together for the Atlanta, Chicago, and New York concerts. The Police closed the concert in Atlanta. I was not told in advance they would be closing. This shook me as a producer. Not because they were anything less than great, but I felt strongly that it was my decision as the producer. I was not willing to cede my authority to potential power plays between managers more concerned about their individual groups than the tour. I knew how important it was to maintain strict protocol and lines of authority. I also was determined to honor all the commitments I had made to artists along the way.

Artists who play as the closing band pick up a buzz that stays with them. I felt strongly that this honor belonged to U2, to whom the tour owed its start.

Going into a meeting with the artists regarding these issues, Bill Graham told me: "I will block but I cannot tackle."

I said, "No problem, I can tackle." Bill replied: "You are crazier than me." That statement gave me pause and continues to do so. Miles Copeland and I eventually resolved most of our differences. But the closing band issue stayed around.

After the concert in Atlanta, all the talent took to the smallish stage at the hotel. Some of the best musicians in the world were just hanging around jamming, only to be kicked out at the witching hour. They all snake-danced out into the lobby.

Sting and I sat alone together on the plane to Chicago. I

explained the importance of the closing band issue. This was not an "Irish" thing, it was simply that U2 was the first band in, and I honored their early commitment. Sting's reaction was powerful, sincere, and wonderful: "Jack, do as you see fit. I am here for Amnesty, and you and I will do whatever is the best for this tour."

I went back to my seat thinking, "This guy is someone special." We kept our running order in Chicago. It was another night of great rock. Then Miles sent Sting's British manager, Kim Turner, to see me. We argued for an hour. Finally, I said, "You Brits have had your boot on our neck for seven hundred years. This will stop now."

I apologized later because my comment was over the top. Kim was a great guy, and they all accepted my apology. But I was still sticking to my guns on the running order.

Chicago was a sold-out gig produced by Arne Ginsher at the 17,500 seat Rosemont Horizon (named the Allstate Arena since 1999). Robin Williams did a 15-minute introduction for the Police. It was tremendously funny, and the crowd roared its appreciation.

Talking to an arena filled with thousands of people takes courage, especially in the middle of a rock show. Before we left Chicago, Bill asked me to address all the artists about the NYC gig on MTV. I did my best, but I wept a bit as I thanked them for their tremendous effort. By their rallying for human rights and Amnesty International, Amnesty was becoming the charity of choice, and the American people were getting the message of our four main goals: fair trials, no torture, no executions, and no political imprisonment.

Bill Graham; Bob Guccione of *Spin* magazine; and the artists wanted to highlight the successes that Amnesty had achieved. We asked Nigerian singer Fela Kuti to join in the Conspiracy of Hope. He was a constant critic of the Nigerian government, a freed prisoner of conscience, and his life had been devoted to human rights. He was a symbol of all we were working toward. Fela and his band arrived in time for the big press conference to discuss the upcoming 11-hour telethon of music and human rights.

The ticket price remained at $36. Best ticket ever for the price. The concert featured Bryan Adams; Joan Armatrading; Joan Baez;

Pat Benatar; Ruben Blades; Jackson Browne; Miles Davis; John Eddie; Peter Gabriel; the Hooters; Howard Jones; Stanley Jordan; Joni Mitchell; the Neville Brothers; Yoko Ono; Peter, Paul and Mary; Jamaican reggae fusion band Third World; Pete Townshend (when Pete's father fell ill, Pete left the tour. Joni Mitchell took his place); Paul Shaffer with the Police; and U2. The promoter, John Sher, did an amazing job.

At the beginning of the flight to New York someone asked Bill why it was so quiet. He answered, "The wives are here." The quiet was temporary; eventually the usual pillow fight broke out. The pillow fight kept the plane busy as we landed in Newark, but I felt the plane bounce and said, "too high!" Then slam! Two tires had blown. We got off where we landed, in the middle of the runway.

Shaken, we immediately went to the press conference. Fela's statement was that "We could never do this in Africa." He was referring to Nigerian rejection of human rights. But that put the idea into my head of producing an event in Africa someday.

• • • • • • • • • •

It was a beautiful day, with just enough afternoon rain to cool things off. All the VJs from MTV were ready: Bob Pittman, John Sykes, Jock McLean, and Tom Freston. Viacom would film from 7 a.m. to 11 p.m. The stadium opened at noon and young people raced across the field to get seats in front.

The New York show was insane from the start. John Sher, our New York promoter, had set things up to run smoothly. Michael Ahern did a superb job running the show. It was an amazing feat keeping all the acts running on time. It was MTV's first big live broadcast. I asked for an addition to the VJ lineup to allow Amnesty chair, Charles Henry, a chance to speak. The idea was rejected until Bill Graham threatened to cut all the TV lines by ax if Charles were not allowed to speak (Bill could tackle when it was needed).

Reporters were packed backstage. Amnesty had volunteers throughout the stadium. We sold 30,000 T-shirts that day. The public service announcements by Bill Fertik were running on MTV before, during, and after the concert.

Muhammad Ali, Senator Bill Bradley, Dick Gregory, Governor Thomas Kean, and Robert De Niro, spoke about Amnesty.

Robert De Niro came over to me. "I have no idea what I am supposed to say," he said flatly. I told him he could say what he wanted; if he mentioned the political prisoners or Amnesty, it was up to him. He looked at me blankly. I handed him a copy of one of our public service announcements and he walked onstage, in front of more than 50,000 people, pale, shaky, and sweaty.

He began, "I uh… I didn't really know much about Amnesty until… well, I am new to this, really." People in the crowd laughed as he stammered over his words. He looked back at me and glared.

"All right," he said, tossing aside the public service announcement and starting over.

"After 25 years, we at Amnesty know that a government, even one that commits unspeakable crimes against its people, can be affected by your opinion, what you do and what you say. You can stop torture. You can free prisoners. You can stay executions. Join us, here today. Get up out of your seat and join us. Because, what you need to remember, is that all that evil needs to succeed is for good men to do nothing. So, do not do nothing. Do something."

He received a standing ovation.

It was a great speech, and it was followed by equally memorable speeches by Dick Gregory and Mohammad Ali, who addressed bigotry against the Muslim faith and its followers.

When Little Steven of Bruce Springsteen's E Street Band went on stage with Bob Geldof, he devoted his song and album to Leonard Peltier, an American Indian leader who had been in federal prison since 1977.

Miles Davis, known for often playing concerts with his back to the audience so he could see his band, turned to face the audience during his segment.

A great moment of the show was when Sting graciously turned the stage over to U2 as if to say, "Now it is U2's turn."

All the bands were great that day, but U2 went from being a popular band to being acknowledged as one of the very top bands. It was great to see that happen to a band that had given so much to others. Sting's strong, quiet demeanor during this enhanced the respect I already had for him.

All the bands and dozens of former prisoners of conscience who were at the event did the closing jam on stage and sat for a picture later.

• • • • • • • • • •

The Conspiracy of Hope tour sold 138,000 tickets. A new generation struggling for human rights was awakened. Amnesty, and its call for human rights, became famous. We wanted to shine more light on the jails, the torture chambers, on death rows, and justice systems around the world. Rock and roll delivered the message and young people responded.

Peter Gabriel and Sting did twenty-three more concerts with Amnesty during my time, including Human Rights Now in 1988 and a Hug to a Hope in Chile in 1990. Those two artists got it and lived it.

Bill Graham more than lived up to his agreement with me, his family, his nation, and his world. He enriched the movement for human rights.

The day after the tour ended, I was working in the Amnesty office in New York. We counted our new members. In six weeks, we had more than doubled our membership from 40,000 to 90,000 and had an additional $3 million in our bank account. Amnesty chapters were opening in high schools and colleges all over the country. Six months after the tour, the U.S. section of Amnesty had tripled in size.

• • • • • • • • • •

A year later, I was in Los Angeles for a meeting. A young kid around ten or so kept following me around the office. Finally, I said to him, "Hi, I am Jack Healey of Amnesty."

He immediately shot back, "I am the President of Amnesty International in my school."

I felt that day that I was doing my job. Amnesty chapters had sprung up in thousands of high schools, colleges, and even grade schools. Young people had responded.

With Bill Fertik and John Huston. Bill produced and directed the public service announcements for Conspiracy of Hope; John Huston is one of my Irish heroes Photo by: Mitzi Trumbo.

From the left: Coretta Scott King, Aaron Neville, Joan Baez, me, Lee Shin Boom (a prisoner of conscience from South Korea), and Bono in Atlanta during COH, Atlanta, 1986. Photo by: © Ken Regan/Camera 5.

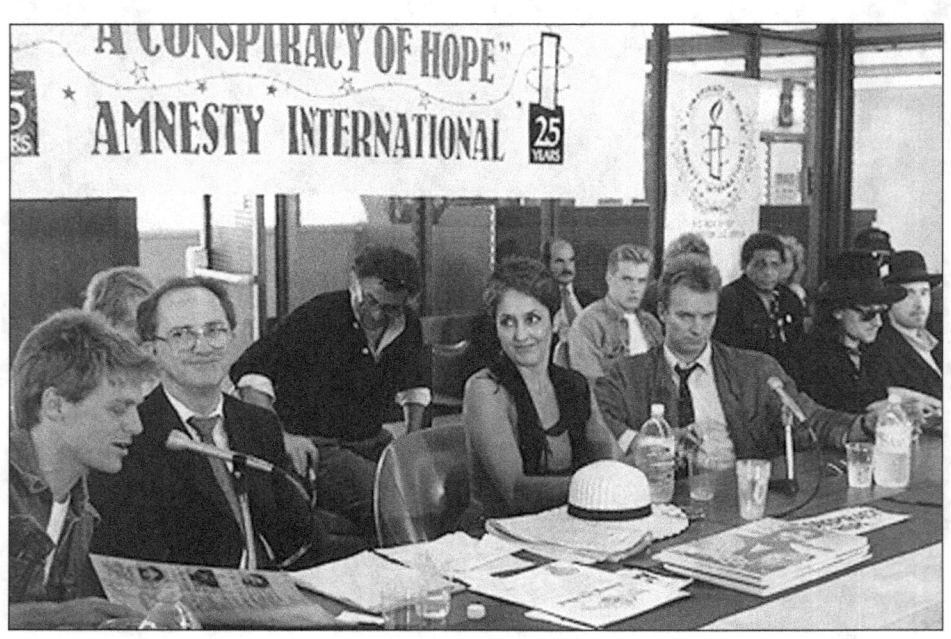

Press Conference for Conspiracy of Hope with Bryan Adams, me, Joan Baez, Sting, and Bono. Photo by © Ken Regan/Camera 5.

Aaron Neville, Joan Baez, and Keith Scott; Bono and me; Sting and Bryan Adams at Giants Stadium, 1986. I can't sing or dance, but it was great fun to be on stage with these talented artists.

Photo by: Ebet Roberts

Greeting Meryl Streep, a long-time supporter.

Muhammed Ali and me at the final Conspiracy of Hope concert.

Bono helped me celebrate my 50th birthday in Los Angeles, 1988.

The Conspiracy of Hope team at Giants Stadium, 1986. Every person in a white T-shirt, except me, is a former prisoner of conscience. Photo by: © Ken Regan/Camera 5.

Peter Gabriel and Joan Baez singing "Biko," written by Peter to honor and remember Biko, who was tortured and killed. Giants Stadium, 1986 Photo by © Ken Regan/ Camera 5.

Chapter 12

Feryal Gharahi

I met Feryal in Boston in 1982 at a reception hosted by Josh Rubenstein to welcome me as the new director of Amnesty. Feryal belonged to a local Amnesty chapter and was told she could speak freely for her group. Standing nearby was her seven-year-old son Aram. "What is your job at Amnesty?" she asked.

I murmured some silly response as I tried to hide how stunned I was by her intensity, directness, and her beauty. "That is not your job," she challenged. "Your job is to lower the pain level of the world. If you cannot do the job, resign now." I may have fallen in love right there. I am still in awe of that comment and those qualities.

Beautiful muse, devoted mother, a fierce defender of human rights, Feryal Gharahi was the love of my life. I hesitated to relay that to readers in the first edition of my memoir. Feryal was modest and shunned attention. Whenever I brought up including her story in my book, she would say: "Focus on the work, Jack. I don't need praise or adulation. The work is what matters." Out of respect, I agreed to largely omit her from the first edition of my book; but the truth is that my story is incomplete without relating at least a little of who she was and what she meant to my life and career.

So, it is with a bit of rebellion and a mountain of love that I share Feryal's story, here in the midst of my work for Amnesty because she was in the midst of my work. Her life was a gift to the next generation of women unwilling to stand down or back down. It is Aram's story of his mother's love. It is the story of the courage she showed while in grave danger and the promise of hope she offered to others by working to create a new future.

In addition to being a part of its inspiration, Feryal provided the title of this book, *Create Your Future*.

She did it herself. She created her future, working extremely hard to navigate a radically different culture from the one she had known a child, becoming well educated, learning multiple languages, and forging a career—all while raising a son, for the most part, on her own. From the first time Feryal held Aram in her arms until her final day, she was a devoted and loving mother.

For the greater part of my adult life, Feryal was the voice of encouragement in my ear. She was my muse and my partner in work and life. She was the elbow in my side if I became discouraged or had too small a vision. She would urge me, "Do more, Jack. Just do more." Feryal inspired and supported me with such grace that I discovered a happiness that I never thought possible. I was sharing my life with a superior mind. I felt as though I was a VW Bug next to a Ferrari. Her center of integrity was so clean and clear, it made an Irishman like me feel the need to go to confession.

Now she smiles at us in the eyes of our granddaughter Laila. They bring light and joy to my soul. Aram and his wife Julia Sara, through Laila, have proven that this irascible Irishman can melt as fast as any grandparent.

Feryal Gharahi was born November 19, 1954, to Mohammed Solemani Gharahi and Nostrat Erfanain Mahajer. The oldest of six children, she and her three sisters: Forooz, Fariba, and Firouzeh, and two brothers; Mostafa and Majeed, were all born in Roshtkhar, Iran. The family subsequently moved to Mashhad, Iran. As the oldest, she was often tasked with raising her younger siblings, ensuring they had the basics while their parents attended to various business interests.

Feryal was proud to be Iranian and loved the Iranian culture and its people. She knew the poetry of Rumi, Hafez and Ferdowsi by heart. Persian music regularly played on every device, in the car and at home. Often she would say, "I miss my language. My head hurts from translating all day."

When she was sixteen, she wrote a column for a local newspaper in Mashhad. Later in life, she would develop the eloquence and the power of a great speaker in English as well as in French. She read widely in several languages, learning new ones whenever a project or new interest would emerge in her life.

As a child, she was a true daddy's girl. He felt the same about her and thought, as radical as that may seem, that she should have run for political leadership in Iran. She might have done so, but understood more change was needed in the role of women and in freedom of expression before she could be taken seriously in an Islamic republic.

After living in the U.S. for more than three decades and becoming a U.S. citizen, she received word from family in Iran that her father had passed. As with most family losses, there was much to do in a short amount of time. Feryal quickly obtained a return visa, arranged with her two sisters to meet at Dulles Airport, and flew to Mashhad to gather with her family to grieve and help with the final arrangements. Despite family estrangement that comes with distance and the passage of time, she wanted to help in what ways she could. She was generous to a fault with her family, immediate and extended. She never skimped when it came to them. Mohammed Solemani' s death was a terrible blow. She never stopped missing him after he was gone.

School was easy for Feryal. She compensated for the lack of institutional challenge by reading books on her own whenever and wherever she could. Her father gave her a set of books of classical Persian literature; she finished them all by her 12th birthday.

Her books augmented a more practical education passed on by women she met and worshiped with at her mosque. Many of these women had nothing. She loved them, loved their storytelling and how they showed her Iranian culture through their eyes. These now nameless friends and mentors shared their wisdom, their proverbs, their recipes, and their life stories. Feryal listened to their successes and failures with wonder and empathy. Her books and these women fed her intelligence and her compassion.

When I wondered at her deep love of the poor and politically disadvantaged and her concern for their plight in life, she would remind me of these teachers.

A rarity at the time, Feryal was admitted to university in Peshawar, Pakistan. She was one of five female exchange students from Iran. While at university, Feryal met Nozar Jafarey. This was not a time or place where dating in the conventional, Western sense was allowed. They courted as best they could and married in a small ceremony in Rawalpindi, Pakistan. After Nozar's graduation, they immigrated to the United States in 1974 to further pursue their respective educations. Both enrolled at Oregon State University. Shortly after arriving in Oregon, she and Nozar had a son, Aram Jafarey.

Wanda Munn and Feryal were the first women to study nuclear engineering at OSU, and they became good friends. Wanda described Feryal as "Indomitable, ridiculously passionate, stubbornly opinionated, brilliant, instinctively generous, secretly unsure of herself, blindly compassionate, multi-talented, incredibly vulnerable, and loyal beyond belief. She was the most complicated person and probably the most beautiful woman I have ever known. She wove her vibrant history across my heart. We were important to each other. She was my friend."

Towards the end of their studies at OSU, Feryal and Nozar's marriage had become strained. They separated and eventually divorced.

Feryal earned a Bachelor of Science in Nuclear Engineering from OSU in 1979. After completing her degree, Feryal and Aram, who was five, moved to Boston, where she had been offered a job. She held several positions with nuclear power suppliers as a licensing and safety engineer.

Feryal's greatest gift to me was to allow me to know and love her son Aram. Like his mother, Aram is serious, intellectual and wise. Aram has taught me logic mixed with warmth. Much like her own education, Aram's early education was lived. Feryal made sure he joined us on trips, domestic and international. He met judges and political leaders and witnessed both the beauty and the hardships of many.

As a child, Aram sat on his mom's lap watching the nightly news. He spoke Farsi with her most of the time. After discussing current events for a while, Aram would ask for the schedule for the next day. She gave him the plan and he went to bed. He knew his mom was serious and he would entertain her as much as he could with language and tricks. During the time we lived Washington, D.C., Aram graduated from Gonzaga College High School, earned his B.A. from American University, and went on to Brooklyn Law School.

After Aram moved to New York for law school and pursued his career, he visited his mom at least monthly. Most times, he would arrive in D.C. by train on Saturday and return to New York on Sunday night. These visits were special for both him and Feryal.

The night before his visits, the cooking would start. Feryal shopped to find just the right herbs and ingredients. The mornings he'd arrive, four or five different pots of Persian food were simmering on the stove, baking, or cooling. The first time I saw this feast, I thought Aram was bringing his law school friends home with him. We had enough to feed a dozen people. "Who else is coming?" I asked. "No one but Aram," was her proud answer. She made everything perfect for Aram and every pot was filled to the brim with love.

By 1985, Feryal had grown tired of nuclear engineering. Her instincts pointed toward law and she began applying to schools. She was granted an interview with John Kramer, the Dean of Georgetown Law School. I waited for her in the car, hoping she would be able to apply. The interview lasted at most a half hour. She left the Dean's office and signaled for me to join her. She appeared neither elated nor disappointed. Concerned, I asked her how it went, and she replied, "Fine. I'm in."

Confused, I inquired further, "In what?" She answered, "I am going to Georgetown Law in the fall!"

Feryal earned her Juris Doctorate in 1988 and was admitted to the District of Columbia Bar Association, passing the bar exam on her first attempt after a summer of intensive study. After graduation, she established a private practice in Washington, DC.

Her primary practice was as a public defender in the Superior Court of the District of Columbia, but she also litigated civil cases. In the 1990's, defending people accused of crimes during a time of rampant drug use and high murder rates took its toll on Feryal. She stayed in her practice for about a decade before joining me at Human Rights Action Center.

● ● ● ● ● ● ● ● ● ●

In the late 1980's, with Jessica Neuwirth and Navi Pillay, former colleagues of mine at Amnesty International, Feryal started an organization that would be called Equality Now. Equality Now officially launched in 1992. The organization's mandate was promoting gender equality and raising awareness around issues impacting women globally. The group was ambitious, initiating large and small projects around the world. Equality Now celebrated its 30th anniversary in 2022, marking a milestone that would not have been possible without the strong foundation that Feryal helped put in place.

While Equality Now's projects were diverse and many, the one that calls for special mention was Feryal's journey to Bosnia while the Balkans were aflame with sectarian violence. Muslims in the region were under particular assault. Ever sympathetic to the underdog, Feryal visited the region with a UN Special Rapporteur to investigate reports of ethnic genocide and systemic perpetration of sexual violence on Muslim women. The findings were grim. The interviews she did left Feryal shaken and resolved to do something about the situation. In addition to raising public awareness of the atrocities committed there, Feryal would return to coordinate the reconstruction of a textile factory that would create jobs for people who were rebuilding their lives and a country after what was an intense period of destruction and near unspeakable trauma.

Feryal loved the solitary nature of an airplane and was as eager to see the world as I was. We took our share of trips, both internationally and domestically. She encouraged my weak Catholicism by taking me to the great shrines in Europe, including Lourdes in France and Fatima in Portugal. We saw Peru, hiking around Machu Picchu.

One of my favorite trips with her was a Christmastime visit to Morocco, where we laughed to see skinny Santas plying market wares in the hot sun of Marrakesh. One of our last trips was to Turkey to meet her brother and his wife in Istanbul, where we visited local markets and ate leisurely meals. This was the closest we came to going to Iran together.

• • • • • • • • • •

Feryal saw at an early age that women in many parts of the world were treated as weak and insignificant. She knew how women suffered in jails. Her independence meant exactly that to her. Her commitment to human rights was uncompromising and unrelenting. She wanted the governments of all nations to print the Universal Declaration of Human Rights (UDHR) into their passports so that everyone could see that basic rights and protection from governmental abuse have been ratified by the UN as guaranteed to all people. She visited refugee camps, death rows, homes, and soldiers at military bases with these tenets in mind.

Feryal passed away on March 1, 2017. Toward the end of her life, our relationship deepened. We spent stretches of time alternating between quiet time and intense discussions of politics and world events. I was her lifeline toward the end, and she said it outright.

She passed away at age sixty-two with Aram and me at her side. We promised her we would do our best to survive her loss and continue to create a brighter future for those in pain.

Feryal

Feryal and son Aram shared a special bond.

Feryal Gharahi with Bosnian refugees. 1993. Family Photo.

Jack, Feryal and Aram.

Feryal returned to Bosnia to coordinate the reconstruction of a textile factory that would create jobs for people who were rebuilding their lives and a country after what was an intense period of destruction and near unspeakable trauma. 1993.

Feryal was proud to be Iranian and never quit working to bring justice and human rights to her people.

Feryal In Bosnia.

Lesson Five

Get as Close to the Problem as You Can

Chapter 13

Amnesty between Tours

The late 1980s and early 1990s were like nothing I had ever experienced. Due to the popularity of the Conspiracy of Hope musicians, I was on major network news every week, sometimes more than once a week, and appeared on TV super programs such as Oprah, CNN's Primetime, 60 Minutes, and NBC's Morning Show. Scholars were calling it the "era of human rights," and Amnesty was at the center of it all.

I was never in the same city for more than two days in a row; I accepted speaking engagements at every college or high school that asked. When I landed at an airport and was picked up by the students or instructors, I was never sure of the school's prestige, but it did not matter to me. A voice is a voice is a voice. Spending a lot of time in the air traveling around, I began to get noticed there as well. Passengers and ticket agents would give up their first-class seats for me, saying things like, "Hey, you're that Amnesty guy. No, please, I will not let the plane leave with you in coach."

I never knew how to manage this brief celebrity status. I mostly just nodded and took what was offered to me. It was awkward, to say the least. Strangers would tell me about articles they read, and how they related to what they thought Amnesty should be doing.

What was far more important was the impact our popularity had on the effectiveness of Amnesty. Our name recognition was through the roof. All the airtime, coupled with the reliability of our research, gave us instant credibility.

The world was changing in our favor as well. I still remember the shocked look that our Soviet researcher had on his face when we crowded around the television to watch the Berlin Wall fall, or the tears that came to our Latin America researcher's eyes when Augusto Pinochet peacefully resigned from power in Chile. My heart still skips a beat when I think about seeing Mandela emerge from jail and thrust his fist into the air to salute the uMkhonto we Sizwe, a wing of the African National Congress.

● ● ● ● ● ● ● ● ● ●

In the spring of 1989, one of our volunteers, Jennifer Wachtell, suggested that we have a charity art show for Amnesty. At the same time, Dallas Bauman Brody Ernst asked Amnesty to start a fund for refugees in honor of her artist husband, Jimmy Ernst, a refugee from Germany and France during WW II. We had just finished the Human Rights Now tour, and we were a bit worn down from these high-profile events but Jennifer guaranteed there would be little effort required from my office. That sounded good to me.

Dallas Ernst called and said, "Let's go see Frank Stella." I told her that would be fine.

Then I had to find out who Frank Stella was. I learned he was the Bruce Springsteen of the art world. We went to his studio, which sported the décor of a mechanic's place back in Pittsburgh. Frank Stella graciously agreed to help us and donated one of his works. I got wind that Botero, a well-known artist and human rights activist, wanted to give a piece as well. I offered to pick up his work myself. I got to Botero's apartment, and he answered my knock at the door. He looked at me, closed the door without inviting me in, and went to get the piece. When he opened the door again, I got up my nerve to ask him why he painted those wonderful people in such huge proportions. He said that when he was young, he feared big people.

Leo Castelli, a firm believer in the anti-death penalty work of Amnesty, called and wanted to help. Mary Boothe and Larry Gogosian followed suit.

Alice Hunsberger and Jennifer Wachtell assembled an honorary committee headed by greats of the art world: Leo Castelli, Virginia Dwan, Ariadne Getty, Cathy Graham, Steve Martin, Jill Revson, Michael Roux, Robert and Laura Sillerman, and Justin Williams.

Robert De Niro, Sr., joined in with a gift. Blum Helman and Germans Van Eck gave us space for the show. Jay Chiat of the Chiat/Day Advertising Agency helped Jennifer organize a kick-off event attended by most of the artists. Collectively, they donated more than 150 pieces of art. We sold every piece. When the artists heard that we sold out, they donated another 120 pieces.

Art and artists are an amazing positive force for change. I got a glimpse of that power from the art show. Freedom and universality ride the artists' shoulders and they keep those feelings alive with their art.

• • • • • • • • • •

Shortly after the Amnesty concert tour and art benefit, I met Daniel Nsereko in Johannesburg to co-direct a planned mission to Swaziland (renamed Eswatini in 2018). Nsereko lived in Botswana and was a lawyer who looked the part: tall, elegant, and smart.

We were both excited to go on an official mission. We flew into Mbabane, the executive capital of Swaziland, and discovered that when the government heard we were arriving, they released the half dozen young students they had arrested for demonstrating at the University of Swaziland. We smiled and were absolutely thrilled. This was the true benefit of all the publicity. Amnesty's renown caused power to tremble.

We visited the government and thanked them for the release. Then we arranged to have supper with the freed students at our hotel. When they arrived, they were trailed by more secret police than we had at our dinner party for nine. The students told us they had received letters of support from the United States. Given the drabness of the jail, they said the colors on the stamps also encouraged them. Curious about the U.S. penny postage stamp, one of the students asked, "Who is Thomas Jefferson?"

• • • • • • • • • •

The notoriety sparked by the Conspiracy of Hope tour, which continued later with the Human Rights Now and Chilean concert tours contributed to an already strong political influence. Instead of having to send our interns down to newsrooms to cajole space for a story, print, TV, and radio reporters from all over the world were calling our office regularly, asking for quotes on Nicaragua, reports on reforms in China, and opinions about presidential candidates in the U.S.

I was called a "nemesis of third world thugs" by *U.S. News & World Report*. I am not sure I deserved the label, but I was proud to wear it.

Because of the increased income, the budget of the research department in London was large enough to hire more researchers and pay for their travel. More research helped generate more action.

The influx of money, members, and chapters necessitated a bigger staff at the New York City headquarters. We had around eighteen people on staff when I started at Amnesty in 1981. By the time the HRN tour was over, we had about one hundred people working for us. And we were still hiring. Many of our board members applied for jobs with us. We worked to hire a staff that looked like the U.S. and included Blacks, whites, gays, and people from as many different backgrounds as possible.

We tackled new issues. We had the money, the capacity, and the energy, so why not expand our goals? We grew our vision along with our organization.

The death penalty was increasingly being utilized as a form of punishment. Although reserved for the worst crimes, such as murder, it was too frequently imposed on those too poor to hire a good lawyer, guilty or not.

Later, Moira Stanley and Ian Gray from my old Walk for Development days authored a book about the death penalty. Their idea was to give the kids who joined us in big numbers after the Amnesty tours an answer as to why they should oppose the death penalty. Moira and Ian compiled a series of interviews to answer those questions. *A Punishment in Search of a Crime: Americans Speak Out Against the Death Penalty* brilliantly relays the stories told to them by lawyers, clergy, prison personnel, inmates on death row, and families of murder victims. Not only does the penalty not deter crime, it is meted out with alarming inequity.

Our efforts to eliminate the death penalty were not entirely successful, but we saw a gradual shift in public opinion and greater limits placed on its use. As I write this, in 2024, twenty-three states in the U.S. have eliminated the death penalty.

• • • • • • • • • •

The Reagan Administration cut funding for federal programs such as free school lunches, drug treatment programs, and homeless shelters. As the safety nets disintegrated, more people were jailed nationwide. Drug use and addiction prompted stealing, prostitution, and other desperate acts which put more Americans in prison.Reagan espoused the trickle-down theory of economics but money from the top was not trickling down. It was hitting a snag or stopping altogether before reaching the middle class. Public perception was that crime in America was skyrocketing. News reports of murders, kidnappings, armed robbery, and other horrible crimes gave Republicans an excuse to "get tough on crime." Even some Democrats jumped on that bandwagon.

Amnesty set a goal to stop the killing of death-row inmates. Charles Fulwood, who directed Amnesty's division fighting the death penalty, suggested that first we find out what Americans thought about the death penalty. Republicans were frequently on television touting polls saying that Americans still supported the death penalty. Did they?

Charles was good at both statistics and detecting lies. He began by breaking down the statistics. He suggested we take our own poll to acquire more nuanced information. We found that Americans supported the death penalty but with some clear caveats. The majority did not support the use of the death penalty for someone with developmental disabilities, under the age of twenty-one, or in a case where there was evidence of racial bias.

Amnesty had to jettison its former strategy of waiting to protest until after a governor had signed an execution order. Charles pointed out that we would be more likely to be successful if we talked to prosecutors and defense attorneys while a trial was ongoing. Once an order of execution had been signed, it was legally and politically almost impossible to stop the execution. We had to make people both in and out of the system were conscious of the unfair use of the death penalty. We employed the same technique that had been so successful with our concerts. We chose prisoners who were facing the death penalty and made their stories the focus of our campaign. We publicized their names and ages, their backgrounds, the circumstances of the crime for which they had been convicted, and the "fairness" of the trial. We tracked the statistics. The more we dug, the worse the situation seemed. Our researchers reported that minority defendants received the death penalty far more often than white defendants, particularly if the victim was white. Conversely, if the victim was Black and defendant was white, the death penalty was less often doled out.

Indigent defendants often received a shoddy defense. Public defenders were overworked and often were not even familiar with their clients' cases. They lacked the resources to check alibis, hire psychiatrists, and otherwise mount a decent defense.

Charles was plugged into the community of civil rights activists around the country and helped us garner support. Soon, we were meeting with the NAACP and the Southern Christian Leadership Conference (SCLC). We sponsored, with the SCLC, a "Death Penalty Awareness Day."

I met Robert Badinter, the French defense lawyer who successfully led the push to abolish the death penalty in France, at one of my first annual meetings of Amnesty International in

1983. His speech was long and thoughtful. Robert was the French Minister of Justice under Francois Mitterrand and later served as head of the French Supreme Court. I asked him for help with our anti-death penalty fight.

Mary Daly set up an interview at *The Washington Post* to start the media coverage for Robert's visit. We were ushered into a conference room.

Colman McCarthy, editorial writer for the *Post*, stomped in. He slammed his tape recorder on the table and began questioning the French Minister of Justice with: "Have you closed all the prisons in France yet?" Robert said that he had not.

Colman was not finished insulting the French Minister. Next he asked, "Have you moved back those trees on the highway because they were responsible for Camus' death?"

Again, Robert demurred. Colman stormed out in disgust. Robert Badinter turned to me and said, "Ah?" I took to translate as "What the hell?"

I had no answer. After a few minutes, Colman re-entered with his tape recorder and did a standard interview.

• • • • • • • • • •

Feryal, in her second year at Georgetown, studied case law at a university in Aix-en-Provence, France. Supreme Court Justice Harry Blackmun was one of the visiting professors for that program. In the course of his lectures, a case concerning the death penalty came up.

After class one day, she surprised me with the news that we were going to Justice Blackmun's home in Aix for dinner. The invitation came after Feryal told him in class that his position to vote for death on a 1967 death penalty case "made him just like dictators who punish misbehavior by killing."

On the way to Blackmun's house, I asked whether she really compared him to a dictator in front of the entire class. "Well, of course, Jack," she said, "and so he invited me to dinner."

As Director of Amnesty USA at the time, I had the benefit of that organization's research and findings on how the death penalty was administered in the U.S. Over dinner and wine at a table in Justice Blackmun's chateau, we talked about the use of death penalty in America and about Black men, who disproportionately ended up in the electric chair. We talked about how the American system of justice was stacked against poor people. And we talked about how Black men usually faced an all-white system of judges, juries, and lawyers. Justice Blackmun and his wife said that our findings and assertions were not surprising.

At the end of the night, after we had the cheese plate and another glass of wine and then a final, final drink, Justice Blackmun stopped me as I was leaving. "Stay strong, will you, Jack?" he asked. "With all due respect, sir, it is not me that I am worried about. Thank you for this lovely dinner, and evening."

What a couple we made and what an evening. I wished my mom were alive to hear about how we used our voice with Justice Blackmun to create a better future in a more just world.

Two years later, when the Supreme Court refused to hear a case involving the validity of the death penalty, Justice Blackmun issued a dissenting opinion stating that he would "no longer tinker in the machinery of death."

Justice Blackmun's law clerk said that Blackmun was struggling to "reflect the wisdom gained, and the frustration endured, because of 20 years of enforcing the death penalty on the court."

In 1989 when Donald Trump ran a full-page advertisement in *The New York Times* calling for the death penalty, I made sure Amnesty responded forcefully.

Speaking at a Conspiracy of Hope press conference in Washington, D.C.

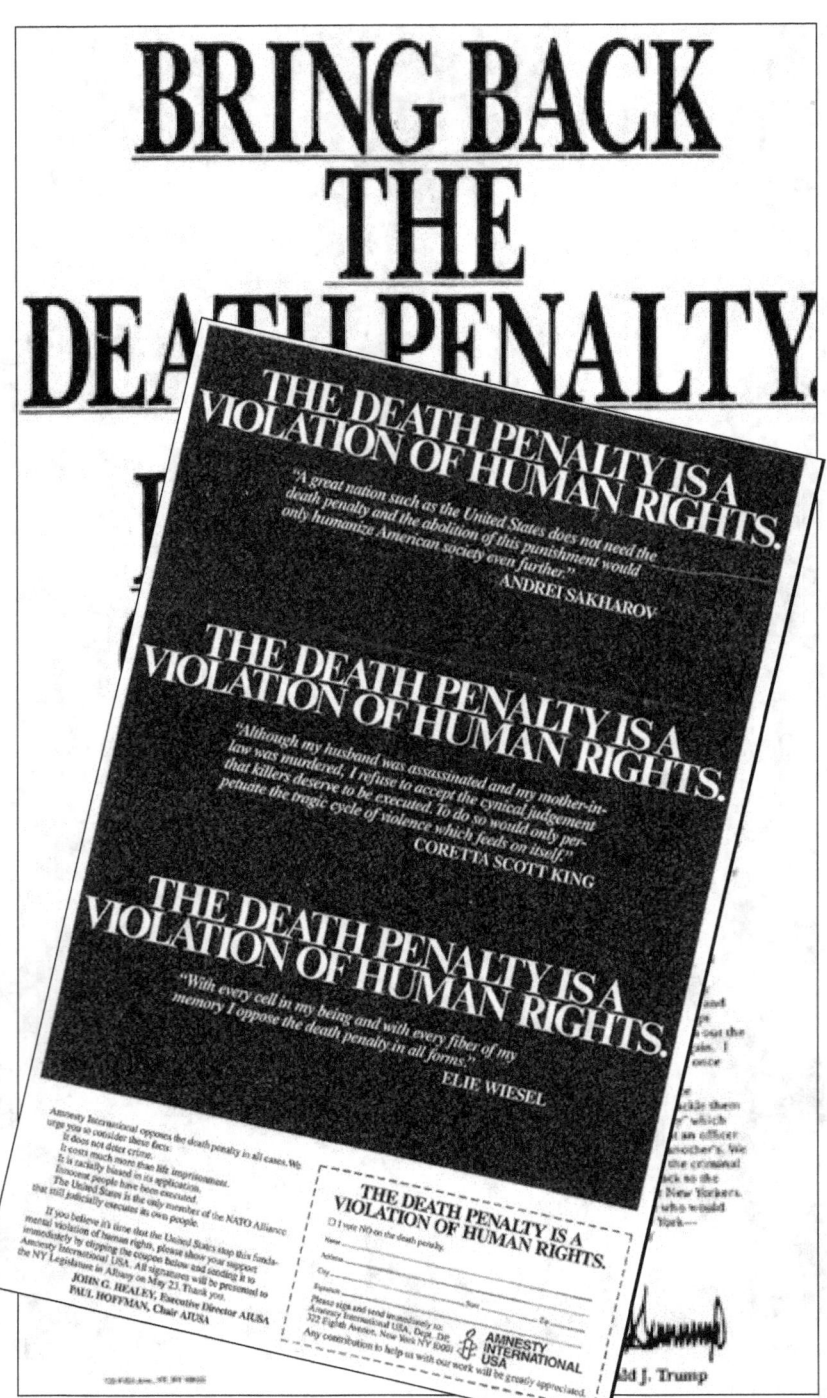

When Donald Trump suggested reviving the death penalty in a 1989 New York Times ad, Amnesty responded in force.

Chapter 14

Human Rights Now Tour

1987-1988

The call that woke me one morning to tell me about the 40th anniversary of the Universal Declaration of Human Rights (UDHR) came from one of my predecessors, David Hawk. David and Mary Daly had supper the night before and had discussed the need to do something special to acknowledge the Declaration. The Conspiracy of Hope tour had been successful, and from that experience, I knew music was a powerful tool.

Amnesty had attracted a new American generation of human rights activists and a growing, paying membership. Feryal pushed me to "Go bigger. Governments can be fooled by perceptions and presumptions. If Amnesty acts big, governments will think Amnesty is big."

The problem was how to get that concept of power, size, and influence across to governments. We thought we could use music. Instead of touring just the USA, we would tour the world.

The UDHR is universal, and the tour had to be as well. To travel the world over, we had to balance our concert locations. We had to play enough large concerts in hard-currency countries to be able to afford to play in countries with little or no hard currency. It was in the poorer countries with no hard currency that Bill Graham and I were most interested in playing. By 1987, I had watched six years of the Reagan Administration's policies on human rights issues abroad and at home. Its commitment to human rights was as ephemeral as a cloud: squeeze it and it disappears.

George H. W. Bush was better. His staff had considerable appreciation for human rights, though it was still limited. Terror is a tactic that some governments use to control people. Many people were tired of governments operating that way. I felt there was a growing river of consciousness for justice forming in the mountains that had to spill out onto the plains eventually. I could not stop torture, a policy of rape, disappearances, and the brutality of governments, but I could provide a moment of respite and solace and allow the victims to know that there were people and an organization that cared. Our artists could tell the story of the tortured and abused using music. The resulting publicity might help.

My team at Amnesty was ready and willing to go again. My nucleus of Magdeleno (Leno) Rose-Avila, Mary Daly, Charles Fulwood, Jessica Neuwirth, and James Radner were up to the task. Curt Goering would easily replace me again in the office. Communications, law, and administration were solid. The tour would take me away from the office for a year, so the strong home base was pivotal to success.

I went back to Bill Graham for help, and he agreed to produce the tour. Claude Isakov and Bill Pace, our advance team, set up the London office in Hampstead Heath. Improvisation was crucial to our operation. When we could not get a phone installed, we "rented" the phone from next door by punching a hole in the wall and using the neighbor's phone from 9 a.m. to 5 p.m.

I did not want this tour to be a repeat of the last tour that had focused on Amnesty. Instead, I wanted to celebrate the full Universal Declaration of Human Rights (UDHR) and urge that its provisions become law in as many countries as possible. It was also my small way of saying thanks to Roosevelt for saving my family. It was past time for signatory UN member countries to enforce the

UDHR. It was also past time for the non-signatory nations to sign on to UDHR. At that time, less than five percent of the world's population had ever read it or knew of it. When I was asked about the UDHR in the interview for the job at Amnesty, I responded ambiguously that the UDHR restrains the powerful and helps the poor. "That's gotta be a good thing," I said with a laugh.

Naturally, I called Peter Gabriel and Sting. Both agreed to join us. Peter said, "I want Youssou N'Dour of Senegal along." That was fine with me, and we were off to a great start. Jackson Browne called and said that I had to hear this new voice, Tracy Chapman. Bill said, "We should take her; she's got a guitar and nothing else. That works."

Graham set my next task, saying: "We need a steak, Jack. Get me a steak. We have potatoes, vegetables, salad, gravy, and dessert, but no steak. And there are not many steaks in the world. So, get me a steak." We needed a strong closing band to be the steak. I went to see U2 in Los Angeles at the A&M studios where they were recording. Bono and the boys loved the idea of joining the tour but believed they could not do it with their already overloaded recording and filming schedule. I tried to convince Bono that the film they were producing was coming too early in their career. They disagreed. Not having U2 join the tour devastated me.

Bruce Springsteen was the most popular and famous musician in the world at the time. His angst-ridden lyrics appealed to all. He wrote songs about inequality and racism, lyrics that lined up well with our message. He could sell out an entire stadium within hours of tickets going on sale.

The problem was none of us knew anybody in the Springsteen camp. After much debate and thought, Bono suggested that we call Frank Barsalona, the president of Premier Talent, promoter of the Rolling Stones and the Beatles, who had helped U2 in their rise to fame.

When we explained that the tour would be a vehicle to promote the UDHR, Frank signed up. He promised to get me an appointment with Springsteen.

With Frank in hand and right before I was to meet Bruce in the bowels of Madison Square Garden, I ran into Herb Alpert and Jerry Moss. They, along with Gil Friesen and Gary Gersh, were the anchors of the Conspiracy of Hope tour, so it was a meeting of old friends. They helped calm me down.

I found Bruce sitting alone in a darkened room on a big velvet sofa. He was tired because he had just performed an epic two-hour concert. I sat on a chair next to him and started some small talk, thinking he would want to chat for a while. Bruce interrupted me politely and asked, "Why are you doing a music tour for The Universal Declaration of Human Rights?"

I explained that "The UDHR is an essential legal document. Most people do not even know it exists, but all governments should be responsible for upholding it. The anniversary provides us with an opportunity to give the UDHR visibility. We need to take the message beyond the West and show our solidarity with people in Africa, Asia, and Latin America. We want to play the world so the millions of people under oppressive regimes are no longer suffering in silence."

He asked what I wanted him to do. I told him that I needed him for a six-week tour. I knew it was a huge request to make. Bruce said, "I'll do it."

I froze. I could not comprehend that he had just agreed to drop everything and join us. Bruce must have expected a more enthusiastic response than my silence. "Are you happy or what?" he asked. My answer, because I was still speechless, was to give him an enormous bear hug. We had our steak.

The UDHR would finally get heard around the world. My thought leaving the room was, "You got Bruce in three minutes and U2 in eight minutes. Jack, you do keep your meetings short."

● ● ● ● ● ● ● ● ● ●

Ian Martin, Amnesty's Secretary General, was awarded an honorary doctorate from the University of Essex in 2003. Among the many accolades, the presenter said:

"Speaking to people who worked in Amnesty at that time, what is striking is the way they describe Martin's management style. One said that Martin created an environment in which he could just get on with his work. If it was not broken, he did not fix it. When he did fix something, it happened so smoothly that it did not disrupt the work being done. That must be the highest tribute that can be paid to a senior administrator. Another simply said, 'He's a class act."

This was my experience with Ian throughout my time at Amnesty. When we started planning concerts, he stood behind the decision to create a legal firewall between the concert work and the rest of Amnesty's work. So, our first task was to organize a separate nonprofit called The Concerts for Human Rights Foundation. To many of Amnesty's board, it existed only for insurance purposes in case of a tragedy. But the members of the Concerts for Human Rights Foundation upheld the firewall as strictly as we could. This resulted in a few battles between the groups. Ian Martin stood up for the separation between the groups, and he helped immensely.

Along with the need for steak, we had to evaluate the cost and the potential profit or loss of the tour. Graham and I wanted to schedule concerts in countries most in need of using the power of music to advance human rights, but these were the countries that would generate a loss. The profit from wealthier nations needed to support those countries.

Our team estimated that we would need $5–$10 million even if we sold out the stadiums where audiences paid for their tickets in hard currency. Nations like Russia and Zimbabwe had soft currency. That meant Amnesty received zero return from tickets. We required a team of three hundred employees and two DC-10 jets for six weeks. Amnesty advanced $250,000 to get us started. Those funds ran out fast once we began placing holds on the jets and sixteen stadiums.

When the Amnesty funds ran out, we asked Peter Gabriel to play a televised show in Italy and give us the cash. He did. With Peter's help, we kept going. It never ceased to amaze me how quickly top artists contributed to help spread the message of human rights, and when they did, their voices thundered.

Eventually, we decided to alter our usual policy and find a corporate sponsor. This risked compromising Amnesty's credibility; we did not want it to look as if we were beholden to any corporate interests. We approached Paul Fireman, Joseph Labonte, and Angel Martinez, Reebok's top executives in Boston. They quickly agreed to underwrite any losses of the tour for up to $10 million and to advance $2 million to get the tour started. In accordance with Amnesty rules, Reebok could not use the concert to advertise its products and the Reebok logo would not appear with the Amnesty logo. As part of the agreement, Reebok could use T-shirt sales to help recoup some of its investment.

Next we had to convince the top brass at Amnesty to support this slightly unorthodox pairing of a sneaker company with the UDHR. We dragged the Reebok representatives in their tailored suits to the Amnesty boardroom in London where the board members sat together at one end of the table and bellowed questions at Reebok's representatives.

The Reebok people did well, fielding every question thrown at them: the working conditions for producers of their sneakers, shipping of their merchandise, and where and how they obtained materials. The Amnesty board members, finally, seemed to have exhausted their vast supply of questions.

Then IEC member Peter Duffy asked, "Do you use leather in your shoes?" Before anyone else could answer, I did. I simply said, "Yes, Peter, and you are eating a chicken sandwich."

We had our financial backing. We were ready to go. Reebok, after consulting with our team, decided to set up an annual event to honor young people under thirty for their human rights work.

There were three key issues to resolve before the tour. Bill Graham and I wanted to play Turkey, but the research department of Amnesty claimed that people in Turkey did not appreciate rock music. Their real concern was with religious fundamentalists. We knew that Turkey sold the second highest number of rock and roll albums in Europe. Bill and I lost that round. The tour was not to go to the Middle East or Near East. This reasoning remains a mystery to me even now. The second decision was where to finish the tour. Bill and I wanted to close the tour in Argentina, although a finale in the U.S. or Europe would have been more financially sound. But we wanted to choose a place that had seriously debated human rights, where the battle had been won, courageously and openly.

The final debate was whether to do a concert in India. Bill and I strongly argued that we should not play a concert there. The deal just did not look right to us. *The Times of India*, the largest newspaper in the country, was the sponsor. However, the chair of Amnesty mandated that we play India at any cost, so we acquiesced. She repeated, "At any cost."

The HRN tour was not an easy one. Reporters and music historians called it one of the most complicated tours produced up to that date. What the audience sees on stage is the polished product: the happy songs and the moving stories. But that vision is the result of months of planning, organizing, negotiating, publicizing, and managing staff internally and externally. The strain of flying around the world for six weeks with several groups of musicians and the huge entourage required to make the performances work meant tensions were bound to surface periodically.

Music is a hard business. It is a tough business. Other benefit concerts like Live Aid encompassed many performers, but only two shows. The Conspiracy of Hope ran for two weeks with a year of planning. The Human Rights Now tour lasted for six weeks after another year of planning. The upside was the power of the message multiple voices brought.

An unexpected outcome was the lifetime friendships created between artists during the tours. In 2014, twenty-five years after the HRN concluded, I smiled as I watched Springsteen on stage at the Kennedy Center paying tribute to his friend Sting, who was receiving the Kennedy Center Award; it was a friendship that germinated during HRN.

I always valued these great performers. Not just for their commitments to the tour, but for their kindness, passion, and steadfastness for the cause over the years.

However, before the victories came the trials. Artists and their managers are used to getting their own way. Managers customarily make hard and fast decisions. They do not enjoy collaborative decision making. Amnesty was all about meetings and moving slowly, especially given the international status of the tour. The international movement had no structure to deal with the tour, although they tried to exercise control despite the separation provided by the firewall. Each Amnesty section where the tour played thought that they oversaw the tour as well. These tensions made the tour more work than fun for me.

I had anticipated a tough go of it, but some surprises left me dumbfounded. One battle came while reaching agreement with the Springsteen camp. Bruce agreed to join us for six weeks and give up a $21 million tour. But a clash of personalities surfaced between Bill Graham and Frank Barsalona, who was arranging for Bruce to join the tour. Frank claimed that Bill was not referring talent to Frank as they had previously agreed. Frank was determined to get an apology. Bill would not apologize.

Because this conflict had nothing to do with me, I stayed quiet and looked for a chance to flee to the bathroom and escape. But Frank said, "Jack, I do not want Bruce Springsteen on a Bill Graham tour. I want him on an Amnesty tour, and you must be the producer of this show. You are the promoter. It is your tour."

I groaned, regretting I had not made a clean escape. I feared Bill thought I had helped finagle the move. Not only did I not dream it up, but I also dreaded the job. My role was human rights, promoting the message and image of human rights and doing press work. I did not want to run a tour. I was Bill's angel on the Conspiracy of Hope tour and now on the Human Rights Now tour, I would be the devil. The boss. Furthermore, Bill was my friend. He made the COH tour an enormous success. I did not want to do this one without him. The night ended in the middle of Madison Avenue with Bill screaming at me, "Where am I?"

The inability of Frank and Bill to resolve their differences had a profound impact on the tour. I was caught in the middle of two powerhouses of the music industry. It ruined the relationship between Bill and me. He died tragically in a helicopter crash on October 21, 1991, without our having reconciled. His mates at his firm told me that he was about to do so. While I was the nominal producer of the tour, George Travis, Bruce's tour manager, was the real head of the tour. He and his team worked hard and well. Bill Graham's team under Michael Ahern produced the San Francisco, Costa Rica, and India concerts. There were no mistakes anywhere.

The most dangerous struggle came about when the head of Columbia Records went to Bruce after all the arrangements had been made and told him that Amnesty was an anti-Israeli group. Bruce called me and asked me to come to New York to discuss the accusation. I grabbed Amnesty's annual report, flew up from Washington, and sat down for a lovely French meal with Bruce and Patti Scialfa, then a member of the E Street Band; this was several years before they married. While Amnesty did not bow to any government, speaking truth to all in power, we certainly did not go after any nation or people with bias. At the end of the meal, Bruce asked me about what his record company had said. I thought for a minute and said, "Well, let's go together to Israel and the Occupied Territories and examine every claim by Amnesty regarding Israel and the Israeli Defense Forces."

Bruce asked, "You would do that?" I said, "Of course."

We said goodbye, and I said, "If you want to pull out, call me. If not, let's do the tour." Bruce Springsteen did the tour. We kept our steak. The discussion on Israel was the first of many times that Bruce proved he was much more than a famous musician. He cared deeply about issues and proved it by continually requesting a thorough briefing on human rights issues. He listened carefully and used the information to speak out during concerts. He was as good with words as he was with music.

Bruce Springsteen and the E Street Band used their Stockholm concert on July 4, 1988, to announce their participation in the HRN Tour. I was on ABC's Good Morning America early the next morning. Right before my segment, there was an announcement that the U.S. Navy had blown an Iranian commercial flight out of the sky and no one survived. It took my breath away. The interviewer asked me why I was so serious. I thought it was more than obvious why. Innocents dying are the essence of human rights.

Bruce understood this essence and supported the work completely. He sent Amnesty $250,000 even before the kickoff in London's Wembley Stadium. He brought Jessica Neuwirth, our HRN attorney, and me to Berlin for a concert behind the Iron Curtain. Later, when the tour was closing out, he took us all to Ireland for a party, a real party. It was lots of fun for an Irish ex-priest like me. Instead of adopting former prisoners of conscience as we had during the Conspiracy of Hope tours, we included human rights activists and survivors in the tour. They joined us on the plane and served as informative resources for the musicians, the crew, and the press: Arn Chorn of Cambodia, Navanethem "Navi" Pillay of South Africa (later the UN Secretary for Human Rights), Charlotte Holdman (who did anti-death penalty work in the USA), Veronica De Negri of Chile, and Alicia Portnoy of Argentina all participated as voices for their nations.

Robert Johnson and Prudence Fenton organized what we called our sixth band. This band was the UDHR in animation. Johnson and Fenton had traveled to an animator's event in Europe to ask if any animators would do a spot of the UDHR. The result was a powerful animation of the UDHR translated into each native language spoken on the tour. Often all it takes is asking.

● ● ● ● ● ● ● ● ● ●

The Human Rights Now Tour grew from a crazy idea I hatched with my staff at Amnesty. Many of the board and our members thought we were insane. They argued that a music tour might trivialize human rights issues. Some chapters of Amnesty even refused to allow the tour to come to their countries. The editors of the *New Republic* agreed with them. They attacked me regularly for trivializing human rights, and they thought that corporate underwriting was a mistake. They wanted Amnesty to get rid of me. Obviously, I did not agree. The tour could only broaden the audience for our message. We wanted to include all, and that meant entertainers, audiences, and corporations. Both founders of Amnesty, Benenson and MacBride, gave us their blessings. We sold out every concert. A year after the tour, Amnesty tripled its worldwide membership. Each concert started with, "Get Up, Stand Up," by Bob Marley to honor Bob and set the stage as an activist movement. The crowd size and their response met the call of the song. They stood up.

London, England
Promoter: Harvey Goldsmith, Avon House
Audience: 82,000

The Human Rights Now tour opened on Sept 2, 1988, in London at Wembley Stadium. The artists entered the stage together to open the show with Bob Marley's "Get Up, Stand Up." As the rest of the artists left the stage, Senegalese pop star Youssou N'Dour brought the stadium to its feet with his pounding performance of his song "Nelson Mandela," who was still in prison at the time.

Though it was still daylight, we had Peter Gabriel play next. Later, Peter's mother gave me a word or two about putting her son on stage during the day. I was used to standing up to managers fighting for top billing for their artists, but I was no match for Peter's mother. I did not make that mistake again. After Peter Gabriel's set, Bill Graham came to me and said, "Your turn."

It was my turn to use my voice to motivate 82,000 ticket holders to the role they could play in advocating human rights. I always liked to give the crowds something concrete to do to help the movement. The response was heartwarming and gave our tour definition if anyone had doubted it would. During concerts, we distributed copies of the UDHR and had the audience sign petitions. Tracy Chapman followed next. She was a new artist and wildly popular. The crowd sang along: "While they're standing in the welfare lines/ Crying at the doorsteps of these armies of salvation/Waiting time in the unemployment lines/Finally the tables are starting to turn."

Sting dedicated his song "If You Love Someone, Let Them Go" to the children in jails in South Africa. Then Bruce Springsteen stepped out to the first few notes of "Born in the USA," and the crowd was ecstatic. Our press secretary, Mary Daly, was crucial to the success of both the Conspiracy of Hope and Human Rights Now tours. After the opening show in London, the tour was widely covered in the States and across Europe, leading the way to drawing huge crowds in every city. Just as he had done with the Conspiracy of Hope, Robert Hilburn provided excellent coverage of the concerts for the *Los Angeles Times*.

Paris, France
Promoter: Gérard Drouot Productions
Local Artist: Michel Jonasz
Audience: 17,000 (twice)

Two shows were performed in Paris at an indoor stadium. Sting and Bruce sang a duet of "The River." Tracy Chapman gave an outstanding performance. French singer Michel Jonasz was popular with the crowd. Everyone agreed the Paris show was better than London. The team was starting to gel musically. One gap of credibility came when Amnesty's chair Franca Sciuto read a letter from French Prime Minister Jacques Chirac.

The reading violated the tour's strict policy of impartiality. Providing a government with the ability to contribute to our message weakened our freedom to speak the truth about potential abuses in all countries without regard to political forces. I did not want the prime minister addressing our tour. We still had fourteen countries to go. I did not want a governmental message each night, especially one in the United States from Ronald Reagan.

Budapest, Hungary
Promoter: Laszlo Hegedus, Multimedia Organization
Local Artists: Janos Brody, Hobo Blues Band
Audience: 56,000

In Budapest, we were behind the Iron Curtain, but it did not feel like iron. The authorities said we could not distribute the Universal Declaration of Human Rights (UDHR), so we got the house lights thrown on, and we tossed thousands of copies of the UDHR into the crowd for anyone to grab. The concert opened the door to Amnesty to do more work in Hungary with local artist Földes László, lead singer of Hobo Blues Band, receiving special permission to play despite having been banned in nine out of nineteen counties. Janos Brody, another banned artist, also performed. His record dedicated to the UDHR in the late 1960s was particularly fitting.

Turin, Italy
Promoter: Fran Tomasi
Local Artist: Claudio Baglioni
Audience: 58,000

By the time the tour hit Turin, the artists and crew were ready for their first day off. This worked out well because the concert there was the last of the season, and the whole city was in party mode. While the others were off relaxing, the rest of the organizers and I were putting out fires. We were still trying to get a show in the Soviet Union; we were increasingly concerned about the demands being made in India, and one of the Japanese concerts had been canceled. There was no time to rest.

Barcelona, Spain
Promoter: Juan Arzubialde, Promotions DPM
Local Artist: El Ultimo de la Fila
Audience: 121,000

Barcelona was exceptional for the quality of the music and the size of the audience—121,000. The Spanish section of Amnesty had pleaded for a place in the tour schedule. In a nation recently released from Francisco Franco's control, the show was regarded as a celebration and "feast" for human rights. The Barcelona show lasted until 4 a.m., and our whole team felt the European leg of the tour was a rousing success.

The message was getting out; petitions were collected, and the artists were sincerely passionate about the issues. It was at this concert that I first got to know Pino Sagliocco, who in 1990 took me to the top of the National Stadium in Chile. The song "Biko" by Peter Gabriel, was sung by 121,000 people that night, and was earth-shattering.

San Jose, Costa Rica
Promoter: Barry Roberts, Bill Graham Presents
Local Artist: Guadalupe Urbina
Audience: 25,000

Bruce asked me to tell him stories about some of the people and the issues facing Latin America. With his extraordinary intelligence and deep empathy, he quickly got up to speed. He shared those stories passionately during his performances. San Jose, Costa Rica was played on the back side of a hurricane. We lost $50,000 worth of equipment, but the audience never lost focus. They traveled to the concert from all over Latin America. Central America was a small region that lost more than 300,000 people to wars and human rights abuses in the eighties.

On the flight from San Jose to Toronto, Paul Fine of 60 Minutes, came to the front of the plane and asked if he could speak to Bruce. I told him that while we are in flight it is inappropriate to disturb the artists. It was their only time to relax. He decided to go up anyway and spend time with Bruce. When he returned, he told me, "You need not worry, Jack. We had a great visit." That was the last leg for the 60 Minutes folks. They were off the plane from then on. We had a policy, and we followed our rules.

Toronto, Canada
Promoter: Arthur Fogel, CPI Concepts
Local Artist: k.d. lang
Audience: 16,000

In Toronto, I met John Humphrey. He was the United Nations employee responsible for typing up the UDHR and had worked under Eleanor Roosevelt. John was the only critic who could have hurt me if he had been unhappy with the tour. I was worried about his reaction to music, rock, big planes, Reebok, etc. I was afraid he would tell me to get back to the activism that mattered. "This tour," he said, "is the best thing that has ever happened to the UDHR." I left Toronto on a cloud.

Montreal, Canada
Promoter: Arthur Fogel, CPI Concepts
Local Artist: Michel Rivard
Audience: 78,000

A sold-out crowd of 78,000 Canadians joined the movement in Montreal. Singer-songwriter Michel Rivard joined the concert. In 1988 he won two Felix awards: for Concert of the Year and Male Singer of the Year. My staff and I visited the Indigenous tribes outside of Montreal to get their blessing and gave them a batch of tickets. Because of this concert, Amnesty chapters started in every school in Quebec.

Philadelphia, USA
Promoter: Larry Magid, Electric Factory
Local Artist: Joan Baez
Audience: 102,000

Philadelphia is one of Bruce's hometowns. All the artists, now joined by Joan Baez, played to a crowd of 102,000. The press conference was massive. Reebok asked to be at the dais, but as grateful as I was for their support, I said "No." It was in the contract that sponsors would not be up front. There was talk of withdrawing their support, but I recognized them from the podium, and they were fine. We also removed a big Reebok shoe that had been put in the stadium. Philly coverage of the tour was beyond expectation. The crowds and the media came out to support Bruce. It was a hometown party.

Los Angeles, USA
Promoter: Brian Murphy, Avalon Attractions
Local Artist: Joan Baez
Audience: 94,000

The Los Angeles concert ran into some turmoil because it was on Yom Kippur. Many months before, I had asked Harvey Goldsmith, Bill Graham, and James Radner, who were all familiar with Jewish traditions, whether playing on this date was advisable. "No problem," they had said. It turned out to be a problem, and we were criticized for holding the concert on a Jewish holy day. I called an old friend, Rabbi Freeling, for his advice. He told us to start the concert as late as possible on that day. We delayed as much as we could, but we lost some of our audience because of Yom Kippur.

Oakland/San Francisco, USA
Promoter: Bill Graham, Bill Graham Presents
Local Artist: Joan Baez
Audience: 50,000

On the flight from Los Angeles to San Francisco, I was informed of a union picket line around the hotel we had reserved. Upon arrival, I asked the musicians to wait on the curb. I met with the owner of the hotel for an hour trying to work things out. He spent the entire time accusing the union of causing trouble. The artists continued to sit on the curb while I found another hotel. Most of the people on our bus, Sting and Bono, for example, were not used to sitting around on curbs. It is an understatement to say that I felt pressure to find appropriate rooms. We remained loyal to the union, saying "no thanks" to crossing the picket line.

Healeys do not cross picket lines. We stayed elsewhere. My insistence that we support the union and not break a picket line did not resonate well with the chair of Amnesty, Franca Sciuto. She believed my action was outside of the scope of Amnesty. I told her she was right. It was in the UDHR. Furthermore, we were in the U.S., and I was the executive director.

I told the headquarters that this was my decision. In addition, this was on a UDHR tour run by Concerts for Human Rights Foundation, not an Amnesty campaign.

Next, I received a telephone call from a representative of the United Farm Workers Union. He announced the union would be picketing the concert that evening. I was happy to tell him that we had changed hotels and were not crossing picket lines. But he was not interested in hotels, he was calling about grapes. We had non-union grapes in our food arrangements, so we were breaking the Cesar Chavez grape boycott. The United Farm Workers grape boycott was a human rights issue. I promised the man that there would be no "scab grapes" at our show.

The morning of the show, I called my regional director Leno Avila. Leno had grown up as a farm worker, worked with Cesar Chavez, and eventually lived in Los Angeles.

I asked him to find a couple of local kids who could get to the food platters before they made it to the concert. I needed them to steal the grapes. All of them. At the show that night, there were large, gaping holes in the food displays between the cheese and the celery, but nobody asked any questions, and the pickets did not show up.

Mother Jones interviewed the group and provided great coverage of the HRN tour. But it was a reader's letter to the editor that touched me most:

> *"The riveting article on Jack Healey, ("Jailhouse Rock," Dec. 1988) is a testimony to a great American whose crusade against human rights abuses has echoed around the world. In this reader's opinion, the following words by Healey are the touchstone in David Beer's searing article. 'On Americans' ignorance of the carnage and repression in El Salvador, Healey laments: 'Sixty thousand people have been killed there and we're still arguing about the damn Vietnam War.'"* —B.J. Snelgrove, Barrie, Ontario

Tokyo, Japan
Promoter: Seijiro Udo, UDO Artists, Inc.
Local Artist: Ryudo Gumi
Audience: 42,000

Japan's head of state Emperor Hirohito was on his deathbed, so Tokyo's performance was almost canceled. He rallied however, and the show went on. The show was a great success. *Time* magazine put the tour on its cover.

At the end of the show, we foreigners experienced a bit of culture shock watching in awe as a revved-up rock and roll audience morphed into a calm and orderly recessional with fans filing out one by one as their rows were called.

We had a goal of performing in Moscow and to do a show that would draw crowds from all over Eastern Europe. We had faith that such a concert would prove that contact between young people in the U.S. and the USSR was possible. The more people we talked to in Moscow, the more aggressively they seemed to keep losing the application, the forms, or the permit.

On the flight from Japan to India, we got word that the Kremlin turned down our request to play in Moscow. Disappointed, Peter Gabriel suggested that we fly the plane over the USSR. The Kremlin would surely force the plane to land and when we made this unexpected landing, we could just get off the plane and start playing—no need to concern ourselves with such trivial matters as international incidents or jail. On that suggestion, the pilots froze. Then they ran back to the cockpit, not to be seen again, no doubt thinking "These people are crazy." To me, Peter had the real spirit of the tour, and I felt like he was channeling Eleanor Roosevelt.

New Delhi, India
Promoters: Bill Graham Presents, *Times of India,* Aryn Muttreja, Amit Chandra
Local Artist: Shankar & the Epidemics
Audience: 60,000

New Delhi, India, was the best and the worst stop of the tour. It is not easy to get two DC-10s to fly in and out of India in a three-day period. *The Times of India* sponsored the concert, paying all expenses and donating $50,000. In return, any money made at the event was to go to non-related political nonprofits. Bill and I had warned the leadership of Amnesty not to play India due to a conflict of interest, because the newspaper planned to use the concert as its birthday bash instead of as a human rights event.

When we arrived, *The Times of India* executives told us that Amnesty could not be at the dais that night nor could the chair of Amnesty, Franca Sciuto, speak at the press conference. Sciuto called a meeting of the artists and claimed she never gave us instructions to play in India at any cost, yet she had. Bill Graham and I were not liars.

By this point in the tour, nerves were frayed, and this confrontation was deeply wounding to Bill and me. It was especially unfair to Bill, who as a volunteer and dedicated supporter worked tirelessly day and night and became the moral leader of the tour. That bruise took a long time to heal.

The vitriolic exchange eroded our support among the artists. They were upset and asked me what they should do. "I am going to the press conference," I said. The artists, Bill, and I fulfilled our contract even though it ruffled the feathers of the Amnesty chair. We all addressed the human rights issues of Asia and India. Bruce did a great interview saying, "This is not a birthday bash."

Athens, Greece
Promoter: Nikos Sachpasidis, Half Note Productions
Artist: George Dalaras
Audience: 70,000

The Athens concert sold out in seven days thanks to its outstanding promoter, Nikos Sachpasidis. His father had his feet broken in the military takeover in Greece and later died from those injuries, so this tour was especially important to him.

It was Sting's birthday so in the Greek tradition of celebration we broke dishes all night. It was especially timely because Sting had advocated strongly to include Greece in the tour. It was a fitting time to celebrate, and we raised another $1 million in hard currency.

Harare, Zimbabwe
Promoters: Neil Dunn, Dunn Gould Associates,
Andrew Zwe, and Avon House
Artists: Ilanga and Oliver Mutukudzi
Audience: 60,000

Africa was a new experience for many of the artists and our crew. We took the time to let artists and crew see the amazing sights of the Zambezi River at Victoria Falls in the north.

Ten thousand South African apartheid-era soldiers came to the concert. Our team gave many tickets to anti-apartheid student movements. Our promoter's new father-in-law handed out those tickets as a favor to his son-in-law. His father-in-law turned out to be General Walls, the man who had led the fight to keep the apartheid system in Southern Rhodesia (now Zimbabwe). I was asked during the press conference about this ironic transfer of tickets. All I could say was that President Robert Mugabe had given amnesty to all fighters after Southern Rhodesia became Zimbabwe and ended apartheid, so the amnesty must have included Gen. Walls.

Phyllis Naidoo, the ANC representative in Zimbabwe, came to the concert and spoke to Springsteen and Sting about how important the concert was to her personally, and to the ANC.

During his performance, Bruce knew there were thousands of South African soldiers in the audience. Bruce spoke directly to these young men. "I guess there are a lot of young guys out there tonight who are of conscription age for the South African army. You are being required to support a government that is at war with its own people. I do not envy your position," he said.

"But we are here tonight to celebrate the 40th anniversary of the UDHR. My prayer for the young men is that you use your hearts and voices in the struggle for the dignity and freedom of all the African people. Whether it is systemic apartheid in South Africa or economic apartheid in my own country, where we segregate our underclass in ghettos of major cities, there can be no peace without justice. Where there is apartheid—systematic or economic—there is no justice. And where there is no justice, there is only war!"

Then he played Edwin Starr's song "War," and the stadium, which had been silent during the speech, joined in. Ted Koppel interviewed ANC's Thabo Mbeki on Nightline. He was Mandela's successor as President of South Africa. Koppel asked Mbeki if the concerts embarrassed him. He answered that they were in solidarity with the anti-apartheid movement, and he welcomed them.

Abidjan, Ivory Coast
Promoter: Jules Frutos, S.O.S.
Artists: Johnny Clegg and Savuka
Audience: 50,000

West Africa is Senegalese singer Youssou N'Dour's home, and he shined with a special glow that night. Earlier in the day, while he was out shopping with other artists, they could hardly move because of the large crowds gathering to see Youssou. We added Johnny Clegg and Savuka from South Africa to this concert. Their manager made the mistake of asking whether Clegg and Savuka could close the show that night because we were in Africa. I agreed to speak with Bruce, who had no problem with the idea. He was happy to get to bed early. The manager, however, learned a lesson about closing acts. Most people, thinking that the show was over, left the stadium when Bruce left the stage.

Sao Paulo, Brazil
Promoter: Luiz Niemeyer, Mills and Niemeyer Promotions
Artist: Milton Nascimento
Audience: 28,000

The Brazilian concert gave Sting the opportunity to highlight his deep interest in the Indigenous people of Brazil. Brazilian singer and songwriter Milton Nascimento warmed up the crowd with an intensity that was overwhelming.

Peter Gabriel's set, usually the emotional anchor of our tour, was marred when a fan tried to rush the stage during his performance of "Biko." The crowd's attention turned to the fan who had to be tackled. This disruption was a big loss for Brazil.

Mendoza, Argentina
Promoters: Carlos Gomez and Daniel Grinbank
Artists: Markama, Inti-Illimani, Los Prisioneros
Audience: 60,000

For many of us, the highlight of the Human Rights Now tour was Mendoza, Argentina. Chilean dictator Augusto Pinochet had refused permission for us to play in Santiago, so this was our answer to him.

Shortly after the Conspiracy of Hope tour, Sting asked Mary Daly and me what he could do to further help Amnesty and the human rights movement. We told him to do what he does best, to write a song. Then we handed him our research on Chile. Sting wrote "They Dance Alone," which tells the story of the Mothers of the Plaza de Mayo, who for sixteen straight years held weekly demonstrations in both Chile and Argentina to keep alive the memory of their husbands and sons who had been disappeared under Argentina's dictatorship. As of this writing, they have been marching for more than forty-five years and some of them are still marching, alongside their grandchildren. The song became an international anti-Pinochet anthem, just as "Biko" by Peter Gabriel came to be the international song against apartheid.

When we landed in Mendoza, dozens of women lined the exit from the airport. They shouted Sting's name repeatedly to thank him for the song he had written and performed. The women held signs with pictures of their loved ones who had disappeared at the hands of the regime. They wanted us to see the faces of the men they had lost, bodies never returned, causes of death unknown, crimes unclear. More than 3,000 political activists, teachers, and ordinary people.

Chileans poured across the border to see the concert, to disavow the abuses of Pinochet and to celebrate the election the previous week in which Pinochet was soundly defeated. More than 60,000 came to that concert from Chile and Argentina.

Sting invited the families of the disappeared of both Argentina and Chile to join him on stage as he sang their anthem. Many credited the song for the election victory.

The security team, crews, managers, and Amnesty staff were overcome with the beauty of the scene, grateful to witness this healing moment when music met human rights.

Buenos Aires, Argentina
Promoters: Carlos Gomez and Daniel Grinbank
Local Artists: Leon Gieco and Charly Garcia
Audience: 68,000

The next night in Buenos Aires, our performance continued to highlight the brutal excesses of the Argentine and Chilean regimes. The Mothers of the Plaza de Mayo protested in town squares every Friday from 5 to 6 p.m., carrying photos of their sons and daughters.

Slowly, the rest of the world became aware of the mothers in the town squares in Argentina.

Throughout the tour, we had been talking about torture, apartheid, starving children, unjust wars and brutality but we had been somewhat removed from the pain others suffered. In Mendoza and Buenos Aires, seeing the women with those sad pictures made the tragedy of their situation immediate. These two women's groups carried the long fight for human rights in Chile and Argentina. Sting took the time to meet with every one of the women who wanted to meet him. During the concert, he brought them all up on stage with him. They danced to the song that he had written for them, dedicated to their lost loves.

The Final Concert: Istanbul, Turkey
Promoters: Twelve young people of Turkey
Audience: Sold out

Amnesty had not allowed our human rights concerts to perform in the Middle East. There had been no explanation, but Bill Graham and I were deeply disappointed by this inner sanctum decision. For two years after the end of the human rights tour, my secretary Claude Isakov kept getting calls from Istanbul asking when I was coming there for the last concert of the HRN Tour.

Finally, I went to Turkey on vacation. I called the number that had been left with Claude and said I would be coming to Istanbul. Because I had been loudly critical of human rights abuses in Turkey, I had some worries about possible arrest, but I figured it would be worth the risk to see such a great city.

When we landed, I told my friends that if the agents grabbed me, they should go to the other side of the airport and get help. When I got to the customs agent, instead of interrogating me, she smiled and said, "Come with me." She led me into a room filled with journalists and other people. I asked, "What am I doing here?" A woman answered, "We are the last concert on your world tour."

"Where are we playing this concert?" I asked. She told me we had a venue opposite the Hilton Hotel. I asked, "Who are we?" The answer was, "Victims of torture, victims of political imprisonment. But we are all citizens of Turkey; there is no difference among us."

That was good enough for me. I went to the microphones and raged against human rights abuses during the impromptu press conference. I am not sure how many understood me, but I bluffed my way through it. Nine people, all smoking, drove us to a spot in Istanbul where a big poster of the Human Rights Now tour was splashed across a wall.

I recalled how at the very beginning Bill Graham and I wanted to have at least one concert in the Muslim world. We had suggested Istanbul and a few other places. I remembered the assertion that Turkey was too fundamentalist, despite being the second biggest consumer of rock music in Europe. This was surreal.

I went to the venue on the day of the concert around 5:00 p.m. thinking I would look around, say a prayer, and get a feel for the place. As I approached, there were many people outside. I moaned, thinking the gates should be open, letting people in early. I entered the venue to find it already packed. I could not believe it. I looked up and saw only big white sheets hanging from each corner of the venue. I had to get out of there because their hugs were too much and too strong for my little frame. The crowd was ready for rock and roll. I headed back to the hotel with glee. "We sold out again," I laughed. Of the twenty-two total concerts held for human rights, twenty-one were completely sold out.

I returned at concert time. I was told that the sheets in the corners were set up to show the videos of the Human Rights Now tour. This was the connection, the relationship, the bonding. It was an expression of the decency of the Turkey organizing crew. On their own, they somehow felt the need for our Human Rights Now tour to be more inclusive and corrected the mistake. I could not believe it.

The first band got into gear and let it go. The response was magical. People were weeping and hugging, and the people of Istanbul began a process to rotate the crowd in and out of the venue so everyone could participate. Donations were pitched into buckets all around the venue. I spoke through a translator to the crowd. My energy almost carried me through the microphone, I was so moved. After the live bands played, the Human Rights Now tour bands were played from video. I joined the enthralled Turks, watching the songs of Springsteen, Sting, Peter Gabriel, Youssou N'Dour, and Tracy Chapman, cherishing this final moment of the tour. The artists' spirits filled the venue and were cheered as if they were there. "Biko" by Peter Gabriel stole the night. We celebrated in a disco until the sun came up.

On the way to the airport, they bought me a beautiful prayer rug. They asked me, "What do we do with the money?" My answer was that they should give it to the victims of torture. "Just do it as a committee so it is always honest."

That concert is still my favorite of all time, and I had nothing to do with it. It was their dream and their reality. It was December 21, 1990. Two years had passed between the official last concert and the true final concert of the Human Rights Now tour.

Though neither the U.S. government nor the United Nations ever recognized the accomplishment of this musical tour, the concert in Istanbul spoke to the energy of a universal hope for human rights for all.

I can only hope that, as one reporter wrote, "Do not be surprised if a few years from now you find the Universal Declaration of Human Rights printed in your passport. That's Jack Healey's latest project, and what Healey wants—at least when it comes to human rights efforts—he often gets. Or, more accurately, he makes happen."

• • • • • • • • • •

Fortunately, the challenges we faced during the tour did not have a negative impact on its bottom line. The final cost of the tour was $26 million. Reebok had sponsored us for up to $10 million, but because the tour itself raised a total of $23 million, we could decline the balance of Reebok's offer. It was their seed money that gave us the financial base we needed to get started. The concerts were filmed by Larry Jordan and sold by Phil Kent through the offices of the Creative Artists Agency, netting $2.5 million for Amnesty. There were three airings on HBO, which, along with the live concerts, tripled Amnesty's membership. Amnesty was lifted to a new level as a worldwide charity.

The glory of the tour went to the artists, but also to the roadies. These unsung heroes, directed by George Travis, Michal Ahern, and the promoters in each of the venues, kept the tour on track and the musicians ready. Every artist was on time. We ran a frugal operation.

An article in the *Los Angeles Times* by John Voland (9/23/88) showed my mood at the time:

> *Though he cited the successes of the tour in promoting human rights causes, Healey was plainly concerned about the toll that the global rock tour — now at the halfway point in its six-week schedule — was taking on the staff and crew. "The guys who set up and strike the lighting and sound gear for each show have started calling me 'Mr. 24,'" Healey said with a smile, referring to Article 24 of the Universal Declaration of Human Rights, which calls for "reasonable limitations of work hours."*

Charles Fulwood, the media person who followed Mary Daly, said that after the concerts, when Amnesty's growth was exploding, "If you sat next to someone on an airplane and told him that you worked for Amnesty, he would treat you like a damn saint."

Most important to me was that the Universal Declaration of Human Rights finally got a moment in the sun. The real impact of the world tour was that it unleashed the spirit of human rights. New human rights groups sprang up all over the world.

Promo photo of Bruce Springsteen, me, and Sting for the Human Rights Now tour. Photo by © Ken Regan/Camera 5.

Human Rights Now press conferences were held in each concert city to draw attention to the Universal Declaration of Human Rights. Photo by: Ebet Roberts.

With Peter Gabriel at Human Rights Now press conference in Tokyo.

Human Rights Now musicians: (l-r) Peter Gabriel, Joan Baez, Youssou N'Dour, Tracy Chapman, Sting, and Bruce Springsteen. Photo by: Ebet Roberts.

Jon Landau, Nils Lofgren, Peter Gabriel, me, and Sting helping the Universal Declaration of Human Rights finally get a day in the sun. Photo by: © Neal Preston.

Human Rights Now tour artists Youssou N'Dour, Sting, Tracy Chapman, Bruce Springsteen, Clarence Clemons. Philadelphia, 1993. Photo by: Ebet Roberts.

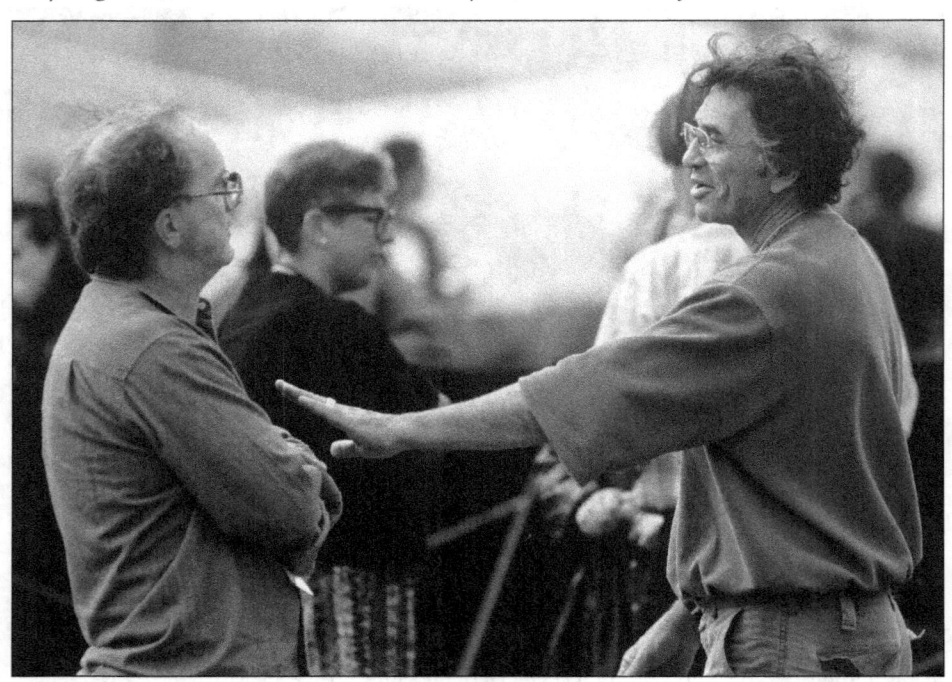

Bill Graham telling me what to do again. India, 1988. Photo by: © Neal Preston

Peter Gabriel played a concert prior to the tour to raise money to pay for the tour.
Photo by: Ebet Roberts.

Chapter 15

Amnesty after Human Rights Now

When the concerts ended, Amnesty was a different place for me. There was a renewed interest in human rights. I appeared frequently on television and radio to talk about human rights. I was asked to talk about U.S. foreign policy, Amnesty's goals for the future, and the conflicts of the day. Oprah, *60 Minutes*, and the morning shows wanted interviews. I was so busy that I was never in the same city for more than two days at a time, and one university began to run into another, as did conference rooms, and studios.

All this publicity was great for Amnesty. Its name recognition skyrocketed, along with donations and its political clout. Many of my goals had been achieved. However, I was less happy personally with the attention my role at Amnesty generated. I was not comfortable being the center of attention. I was much more comfortable organizing events and letting people such as Sting take center stage. The only part I enjoyed in all the frenzy was meeting people and motivating crowds to do more. Random people on planes and trains and in diners would tell me what Amnesty should be doing. Some of them were ill-informed, off base, or totally insane, but there were also people who genuinely cared and who shared great ideas. The first human rights tour heightened Amnesty's profile in the United States. The second tour had the same effect around the world. Human rights groups were making gains. All Latin America watched the Conspiracy of Hope live on MTV. The genie was out of the bottle, and the message of founder Peter Benenson was spreading. This would continue until 9/11.

On my way to the Vienna Human Rights Conference in June 1993, I joined a small youth group called Earth Train. Together we visited Bosnian refugee camps in Croatia. Most refugee camps move in slow motion, and these were no different. One afternoon, I was sitting next to Edin, a Bosnian refugee watching a soccer game. I nudged him to get into the game. He declined numerous times. I told him I had never played soccer. That astonished him. Finally, I asked him why he would not play, and he answered, "Because the kids and parents I played with in my village raped and murdered my family." My lame but spoken answer was, "Edin, I hope the day will come when you can run freely on that field."

The Vienna Human Rights Conference was set to redefine the role and nature of human rights work within the United Nations. The American government was present in full force, led by John Shattuck, former vice chair of Amnesty USA. John was a good man, but he did not react strongly enough or quickly enough to the atrocities taking place. President Clinton's team proved to be weak and ineffective. The massacre of 8,000 Bosnian boys and men and an estimated 40,000 rapes of Bosnian women and girls speak to that weakness. Shattuck later admitted that the international community and the U.S. s showed a "failure of imagination" regarding the war.

The first thing the Chinese government did during the conference was to bar the Dali Lama. So, Li Lu, one of the leaders in Tiananmen Square protests of 1989, and I led a march and set out to block doorways in civil disobedience. I went to the Kurds and Kashmiris requesting that they defend me if we got into trouble. They readily agreed. We caught the attention of the press and ended up on the front page of *The New York Times*.

The next day, the conference denied entry to the women of Vukovar, Croatia, whose husbands had been executed by the Serbian militia. One hundred sixty-three men and one woman, all hospital patients, were executed.

Again, we stopped traffic for as long as we could.

I was thinking what a travesty of a human rights conference it was. The restructuring of the Human Rights Commission in Geneva had the same result: not much. The United Nations Human Rights Commission was hijacked by human rights violators who said all the right things, but with no intention of standing up for the values of the true advocates who attended the conference.

"Your shame must become your glory," were my words to those who had been abused. "Let your life and the light of the world shine on the injustices of anyone who would do harm to his fellow man. Where there is truth, the people of the world will rally around that light and your shame will become your glory."

Amnesty addressed gay rights. Historically, Amnesty would "adopt" as a prisoner of conscience anyone who was arrested for advocating gay rights but not those who were actively gay. Many at Amnesty, especially in the U.S. and German sections, wanted to enlarge our tepid support for gay rights to support advocacy and activity. Other Amnesty sections viewed this effort as too Western or premature for their countries. The gay rights issue came close to getting to the floor for a vote in Brazil at the bi-annual meeting of Amnesty worldwide. However, the elites of the organization quietly tabled the measure until the next bi-annual meeting to be held in Japan. I thought it was a sly move and knew to watch carefully during the meeting in Japan.

Sure enough, in Japan, when a staffer representing the governing body asked me if we could table the measure again, I was ready.

"No, and hell no! It must go to the floor. We will not put this off for another two years. If it does not reach the floor, the U.S. section of Amnesty will resign. If it loses in a vote, so be it, but the members have the right and obligation to vote on it today."

The issue of gay rights deserved open debate. When the initiative reached the floor, it passed unanimously with a big cheer. It was 1990 and we were years ahead of many groups in advocating an important and meaningful change.

• • • • • • • • • •

George Herbert Walker Bush (Bush 41) was sworn in as president in 1989. In the first year of his presidency, he supported the military government of El Salvador against a Marxist group called the Farabundo Marti National Liberation Front (FMLN). Like a weak cover of a bad song, the Administration supported the government against the Marxist group just as the Reagan Administration had done in Nicaragua. And just as in Nicaragua, the government-allied militias attacked clinics, schools, and farms—the FMLN's base of support. The government of El Salvador targeted Catholic priests who preached liberation theology. These courageous priests publicly demanded an end to economic apartheid and supported land redistribution.

The attacks did not deter the U.S. from funding the government of El Salvador. Even the gruesome death of Archbishop Oscar Romero, shot while saying Mass on March 24, 1980, did not slow the flow of money. As the situation for ordinary citizens in El Salvador deteriorated, refugees packed up and began walking thousands of miles north to cross the U.S. border. They became undocumented workers and refugees with uncertain futures. The story had been under-reported, both because of pressure from the Administration not to look too closely, and because it was difficult to find anyone in the U.S. from El Salvador who was willing to talk to the press for fear of retribution either from U.S. Immigration and Naturalization Service or the government at home. El Salvador became another killing field.

At dawn on November 16, 1989, 50 Salvadoran soldiers surrounded the Pastoral Center at the University of Central America in San Salvador and demanded that the priests come outside and lay on their faces in the courtyard.

Fathers Ignacio Martín-Baró, Ignacio Ellacuría, Amando López, Segundo Montes, and Juan Ramón Moreno were shot dead as they prayed on the ground. Father Joaquín López, the priests' housekeeper, Elba Ramos, and her sixteen-year-old daughter, Celina, were shot and killed inside the house.

The soldiers spray-painted slogans on the walls and gate to incriminate the guerrillas. Days earlier, the FMLN had launched a major offensive against the military in San Salvador. Father Ellacuría had tried to negotiate a peace deal involving the ouster of top military officers.

Ted Koppel, of the television show Nightline, one of the most influential news outlets in America at the time, called me. He was planning to have the ambassador from El Salvador on his show, and he had some questions he hoped I could answer. I confirmed the report and told Koppel that the Amnesty research department in London had a witness who could verify the connection between the government and the killing spree.

Over the weekend, *The New York Times* broke the story. The Salvadoran government denied responsibility and blamed the rebels. Witnesses stated that the Jesuit compound had been surrounded by soldiers in the previous days.

Dick Cheney was Bush's Secretary of Defense and was instrumental in the decision to support the Salvadoran government. When the story broke, Cheney appeared on the Sunday talk shows, saying that there was no way to know who did the killings.

ABC asked that I be ready at 6 a.m. Monday to give Amnesty's side of the story. I told the producers that what Cheney said on the weekend talk shows was not true. The United States and Cheney knew exactly who was responsible for those murders. America must stop aiding this regime.

We published report after report, with irrefutable evidence that government soldiers had committed the murders.

The New York Times and *The Washington Post* stayed with the story. Slowly, the public began to question and then reject the Administration's explanation. And for once, the story and the truth survived. Finally, the horrors of Central America were becoming known. Cheney's blatant lies were exposed. During the Reagan and Bush Administrations, Central America lost 300,000 lives in conflicts supported by the U.S.

Bono continued to stay involved with Amnesty after the 1986 Conspiracy of Hope tour. He flew to El Salvador with some of our Amnesty researchers. He spoke with people who had experienced the civil war firsthand and with members of organizations helping victims. Bono came back and wrote the song "Bullet the Blue Sky" for U2's Joshua Tree album that came out in 1987.

Students on college campuses began to voice concern and to protest the U.S. involvement in El Salvador. Some young people organized "die-ins" in front of the White House where they would quite literally play dead outside 1600 Pennsylvania Avenue, demanding an end to U.S. support for the regime.

On December 2, 1980, Sister Dorothy Kazel, laywoman Jean Donovan, and two Maryknoll Sisters, Maura Clarke and Ita Ford, were abducted, raped, shot, and then buried together in a shallow grave. They had been helping the poor of El Salvador.

Five men, believed to have been ordered by military generals to kill the women, were tried, convicted, and sentenced to thirty years. Two of the five murderers were released early for good behavior. The two generals who are believed to have given the orders retired in 1989 in Florida. The Reagan Administration awarded one of these generals the U.S. Legion of Merit, a high military honor.

Human rights abuses in El Salvador were given some light by writers Larry and Paul Barber during two episodes of *21 Jump Street* in 1989 and 1990. They highlighted the issue of deportation from the U.S. and disappearances in Central America. U2 and Peter Gabriel donated their music. It was a brave and rare moment for national TV.

• • • • • • • • • •

In 1990, Saddam Hussein ordered the Iraqi military into neighboring Kuwait, supposedly in response to a dispute over oil production quotas. Amnesty published a report about the invasion of Kuwait. The document, detailing torture and killing of Kuwaiti civilians by Iraqi soldiers, was not particularly unusual. Amnesty published perhaps thirty similar reports about different countries in the same year.

President George H. W. Bush chose to use this particular Amnesty report for his own purposes. He wrote an opinion piece that was published in 450 college newspapers around the country. Following his special assistant Elliott Abrams' lead, he cherry-picked facts from the Amnesty report and used it to support the war that his Administration was planning to start against Iraq.

The incident that stood out in our report and the one that the President, the Secretary of Defense, and the pundits obsessed about was the one about the babies. Buried in the long report was a charge that during the invasion of Kuwait, Iraqi soldiers had pulled the plugs on more than three hundred incubators in the premature infant ward of a hospital, and that all the infants had died. The President described this action as "Hitlerian."

I wrote a response that was published in the same college newspapers, stating that the Administration was twisting human rights information for political purposes.

In the middle of this controversy, the Amnesty report itself came under fire. Middle East experts stated that there was no evidence to support the claim about the babies. They noted that no hospital in Kuwait had three hundred incubators.

The House of Representatives asked me to testify about the findings in the report. I called Ian Martin, Secretary General of Amnesty's International Secretariat, for advice. He spoke to the researchers who had authored the story. I asked a researcher from Human Rights Watch, who had done his own research and was among the main critics of our report, to join us on a conference call with the Amnesty researchers who authored the report.

An hour into the call, the Amnesty researchers were debating loudly, and we were getting nowhere. The call ended with Human Rights Watch unconvinced by Amnesty's research and our team defending its information. I could only assume the London research team had acted in good faith and I stood by them. The report was already in the hands of Congress and the White House.

The hearing room was larger than I had expected. All members of the Foreign Affairs Committee were present. After introducing me and the other speakers, the chairman of the committee asked me to read my statement. In front of the congressional committee and the press, I presented the Amnesty International report and said the researchers at Amnesty were particularly good at their work. I backed the report, never dreaming that they would use one report to justify an unjustifiable war.

Weeks later, I was sitting at my desk drinking coffee. I idly turned on the television and was shocked to see that the United States was in the process of declaring war on Iraq. The vote in Congress was narrow; the Senate passed the declaration 52-47 and the house 250-183. Seven senators who voted for the war cited the story about the infants and the incubators in their remarks.

Months later, after coalition forces had launched their assault to "liberate Kuwait" and drove out Iraqi forces, reinstated the Emir in Kuwait and caused the deaths of hundreds of thousands of Iraqis, we found out that in all of Kuwait there were fewer than 130 incubators.

At least 500,000 children died of hunger because of the trade embargo the UN imposed on Iraq in the aftermath of the war. Some 400,000 Palestinians were expelled from Kuwait as punishment for supporting Hussein.

Amnesty's report could not have been true. The damage had been done. Amnesty had published and then confirmed incorrect information. Amnesty let people down and damaged its credibility. Worst of all, our work had been exploited for a terrible cause. I do not know how the researchers in the International Secretariat got the story so wrong.

It took a year for Amnesty to issue a public apology, further burning those of us working for Amnesty.

Lesson Six

Music Is the Magical Newspaper

Chapter 16

National Stadium of Death

1990

T wo years after the Human Rights Now tour had been denied permission to perform in Chile, we had our chance. The director of the Chilean office of Amnesty, Ramón Farías, asked Amnesty USA and me to help Amnesty Chile stage a two-day concert in Santiago.

Chileans had endured great suffering over the 16 years of Pinochet rule, and many had worked bravely and tirelessly to win back their democracy. Pinochet's government had suppressed dissidents with violence and death. But in 1990, Pinochet was forced to step down after an electoral defeat that he could not manipulate. The Human Rights Now tour had celebrated that election in Mendoza, Argentina, two years before, and we were eager to close the circle by bringing music back to the people who had forced Pinochet and his brutal, blood-tinged regime to cede power. Chile had succeeded in doing what so many social movements and leaders claimed was impossible: take out the bad guys without bloodshed. Santiago was truly a city on a hill. It was a huge victory for Chile, Latin America, and the human rights movement around the world.

Sting was my first call. He helped with the other Amnesty tours, but his song, "They Dance Alone," was particularly meaningful to the mothers and widows of Chile. I said, "Sting, we have to go and re-baptize the National Stadium. Your song was destined to be sung in Santiago when the time was right. This is the right time and the right place."

He agreed instantly. Peter Gabriel, Jackson Browne, and Irish rock star Sinead O'Connor also said yes. Ruben Blades, a Panamanian musician, lawyer, and actor who had joined Sting on the "They Dance Alone" recording, was pleased to be invited and joined the celebration. The young American pop stars, New Kids on the Block, were extremely popular in Chile, so we invited them to play even though some people feared that they were too lightweight for this kind of show. I thought their youth was on their side and they proved themselves in the press conference by giving strong, articulate interviews.

I wanted Wynton Marsalis, the great American jazz trumpet player, to play this show. When I contacted Marsalis' manager Ed Arrendell, he asked, "Why do you want a serious jazz performer, one of the best the world, to play in the middle of a rock show?"

Good question, I thought, and I had a good reason. "Back in 1973, Secretary of State Henry Kissinger and the Nixon Administration helped Pinochet topple the Allende government, replacing an elected leader with a military man who suppressed democracy in Chile. They know the worst of what Americans can do," I explained.

"What I would like the Chileans to see at this concert is the best of what America can do for others. Jazz is a truly American genre, created by Americans, especially the Black community. Wynton is the best jazz player to represent the American people and our decency as a people. Chile saw the indecent America, now they will see the decent America."

Ed was convinced, as was Wynton, who joined the concert roster. The Chile section of Amnesty recruited Inti-Illimani; a Chilean group banned during Pinochet's rule. They were a part of the Nueva Cancion (New Song) movement celebrating Indigenous cultures in Latin America and supporting the political struggle for indigenous rights and social justice. Inti-Illimani had been on tour in Italy during the 1973 coup d'état and they were not allowed to return to Chile. They remained in Italy until 1988 and had performed in Mendoza, Argentina with the Human Rights Now tour. Luz Casal, Congreso, Los Ronaldos, and Fernando Saunders also joined the roster.

The artists were solid in their commitment to human rights. They learned how to use their celebrity to further the growth of the movement and spread the message. The day after the concerts, Jackson Browne went to a prison where two journalists were being held as political prisoners. He managed to help put enough pressure on local authorities that the journalists were released from jail while he was there, and he left with them.

Sting said in an interview:

"I think you would have to be blind, deaf and dumb not to know that this was more than just an entertainment. I am not sure what percentage of the people who came to see us will go away with a seed planted inside them. I do not know how long that seed will take. But I believe very strongly that in ten or fifteen years, when these young people who came to our concerts inherit the political and social infrastructures of their respective countries, the seed that has been planted about human rights will come to fruition."

The two-day concert was called "Desde Chile: un Abrazo a la Esperanza" (From Chile, A Hug to a Hope). The stadium was buzzing with energy, excitement, and hope. We wanted this to be one of the biggest human rights events ever held in South America. We wanted the world to celebrate Chile's bloodless human rights victory.

The venue was the National Stadium of Chile in Santiago, a site that epitomized the treacherous years of General Pinochet's military dictatorship. It was used as a massive holding pen in the weeks following the September 11, 1973, military overthrow of President Salvador Allende's government. Thousands of Chileans were imprisoned, interrogated, tortured, and killed in the stadium. Survivors reported that inmates were grouped by colored discs. Prisoners who had red discs were certainly going to be executed, while those who had either yellow or black discs stood a small chance of surviving. Prisoners were herded and penned like sheep, sleeping more than one hundred men to a cell. They were packed so tightly that the only way they could sleep was by lying in rows and alternating feet and heads.

Occasionally one of the prisoners would be taken away for interrogation. If they came back at all, they returned to the cell bloody and barely able to speak. The interrogators would beat the prisoners across their heads with wooden bats.

Bruce Springsteen's and U2's production teams added their technical power and ability to the vision and capable hands of film and music producers Allen Kelman and Bob Koch, who organized the technicians to run the two-day concert and oversaw the administration. Though none spoke Spanish, they collaborated closely with the local promoter and his team.

Pino Sagliocco, the promoter for the Barcelona concert, secured twenty hours for a live television broadcast for Spain plus all Latin America, including Mexico. Arturo Vargas of Uruguay oversaw the Latin American distribution.

● ● ● ● ● ● ● ● ● ●

I had been waiting for this moment for a long time. In 1976, Orlando Letelier, an exiled Chilean diplomat and former cabinet member in Chilean President Salvador Allende's government, was working at the Institute for Policy Studies, a liberal think tank in D.C. On September 21, 1976, he and his American secretary, Ronni Moffit, and her husband, Michael, were driving to work. As they drove past the Chilean embassy, a bomb blew up their car, killing Letelier and Ronni Moffitt. Michael Moffitt survived with injuries. An investigation implicated Pinochet's government in ordering the killings. Chile's secret police had penetrated the capital city of the U.S. to murder perceived enemies of their state.

People in Washington were outraged, and a large public procession was organized for the day of the funeral. I volunteered to help and was stationed at the site of the explosion, Sheridan Circle. As I stood there, I looked up at the Chilean embassy and realized that people in the embassy had probably watched the car explode. I became determined then to get these people back one day. No one should get away with reaching into the United States to kill like that.

I headed backstage to make sure everything was running on time. The backstage was below the bleachers and the stage and was not as secure as the concert venues Amnesty had used in the past. A steady stream of people was wandering around into the backstage area, moving from room to room as if they were lost. I could tell they were neither performers nor crew members and that worried me. I needed to find the backstage crew to find out what was going on and help me get them out.

"What are all these people doing back here?" I yelled down the hall at three members of the security crew as I made my way toward them. "Get them out of here." The last thing I wanted was crowds bothering the performers. Many of the musicians had just spent nineteen hours on a plane getting there; the least I could do was guard their privacy and make sure they were not mobbed by adoring fans.

A few minutes later our attorney, Surita Sandosham, came looking for me. She explained, "Jack, you are right, they are not backstage people. But they are not looking for the rock stars either. They are trying to find the rooms where their family members were tortured or killed. They want to see where their loved ones died."

Her words jolted me back to why we were in Chile in the first place—to give this stadium back to the people. I knew we had to open the underbelly of the stadium so people could be in the presence of their lost loved ones. They wanted to pay tribute to their loved ones with flowers and candles.

"Let in as many people as you can," I said. We could work around any problems this caused. We tightened security to protect the artists and let the people in to find their places of loss and pain. Sixteen years is a long time to wait.

The next problem arose outside the gates. Even though the military no longer ran the government, the carabineros, the national police force run by the military, still managed security at the stadium. Armed guards surrounded the fenced stadium, monitoring the gates, halls, and aisles.

"Jack, we need you over here," one of the crew shouted. I followed him to one of the gates where we saw thousands of people slamming into each other as they tried to get in. The carabineros were beating people back, and I saw young men and women injured, some bleeding, and others lying on the ground. Tear gas suddenly blasted through the gate, and I found myself gasping for air. I shielded my eyes and ran to a place where I could breathe.

"What the hell is going on here?" I yelled, though no one was listening. It was pure chaos. This was real trouble, and there would be more to come if it were not handled quickly. I ran backstage looking for someone who could help me. Ariel Dorfman, Chilean poet, playwright and human rights activist, was in the middle of a conversation when I interrupted.

"Ariel, I need you to translate for me," I yelled as I grabbed him by the arm. We rushed back to the gate where people were trying to get in so we could find out why concertgoers were being beaten. The guard told us that thousands of people were trying to get in with counterfeit tickets and they did not know which tickets were authentic. We walked over to the gate and asked a young man who was trying to get in what was happening.

"They say my ticket is no good," he explained. "We paid for our tickets, but the guards will not let us in. Isn't there something you can do? Please help us."

We discovered later that someone had sold 15,000 counterfeit tickets to each show. The concert was sold out both days so we did not have extra seats, but we also could not just turn people away. Someone in Chile made $1 million off these counterfeit tickets and gave me a terrible problem to solve. Ariel and I asked a guard to take us to their leader to deal with this problem. He said there was nothing he could do and passed us off to the sergeant. I banged on the nearest door. The officer, in his highbrow military-style police hat, opened the door and let us in.

"Tell him to stop his guards from beating the crowds and using tear gas; otherwise, I'm going to have to shut this concert down!" I said to Ariel, barely able to contain my rage. "I am not going to be pushed around by these guys."

"Jack, I can't tell him that," Ariel said to me under his breath, turning to avoid facing the officer. "These people are beasts. You know the history of our country."

"Ariel, please tell them right now, otherwise I'll find someone else to translate for me or I'll really have to shut this concert down." Ariel understood that he had to convey my message. We watched the blood slowly rise in the major general's face. It was likely that this was the first time in sixteen years he'd had to listen to a civilian—and a gringo at that. The office was stocked with military hardware: grenades, rifles, bazookas, and tear gas canisters. Confronting this guy was a risk, but if we didn't, we would have a riot on our hands.

"We have to let as many people with tickets in as possible because we don't know which ones are counterfeit," I said. He did not say anything. After several pleas, threats, and arguments, he agreed to let in as many people as he could, but about 14,000 went home without seeing the concert.

Ariel and I left the office relieved we had worked something out. Even though fifteen thousand scabbed tickets made someone in Chile a millionaire, more important, the show would go on. This concert had been a long time coming, and it was time to give the stadium back to the people of Chile—to the 35,000 victims of human rights abuse—the 28,000 tortured, the 2,279 executed, and the 1,248 disappeared. Music cleansed the stadium.

People who have never lived under state-controlled media have a tough time understanding that people living in a nation under a military dictatorship don't have the full story about their government and the extent and severity of its abuses. For example, not all Chileans knew about the Caravan of Death and The Claws of the Puma, the name of a special Army unit that traveled by Puma helicopter on missions to execute supposed opposition leaders, both military and civilian.

After sixteen years of censorship, this concert became an uncensored media event that named the human rights abuses and violence of the past. It celebrated a new vision for Chilean society described by the artists and activists who watched on television throughout Latin America and the world.

Veronica De Negri, whose son Rodrigo Rojas was set on fire and killed by the Chilean police, had traveled with us on the Human Rights Now tour, speaking about her experience as a survivor of torture. We asked her to join us in Santiago to introduce the bands as they came on stage. Veronica, along with Carmen Gloria Quintana, a friend of Rodrigo's who survived being set on fire with Rodrigo, and Peter Gabriel kicked off the live broadcast throughout Latin America.

We had wondered how Wynton Marsalis would be received by screaming crowds expecting rock and roll. Our worries were wasted. Wynton and his band took the stage in their cool suits. He started to play his trumpet, and after the first few notes the whole stadium began chanting with the music.

I asked people around me for an explanation, but nobody knew what he was playing. It turned out Wynton was playing a song by Duke Ellington called, "Play the Blues and Go," which sounds like a song Chileans sing at soccer games.

Wynton had arrived several days prior to the concert and invited local jazz musicians to jam with him at his hotel. It was during these many jam sessions that he learned their song. The Chilean song had become especially popular when Chile hosted and placed third in the World Cup in 1962. Fans still sing the song at soccer matches.

Marsalis and his band brought the house down. The crowd went berserk, and they were all singing their victory song, filling the stadium with powerful voices: "We won!"

The concert rocked on for hours, and the crowd's youthful energy carried us into the night. The activists shared their stories with the crowd. Near the end, every artist came on stage to join in singing Bob Marley's rousing classic, "Get Up, Stand Up."

It was time for the closer. Sting took the stage, and the band began playing the first notes of "They Dance Alone," while the Mothers of the Disappeared slowly danced onto the stage with the pictures of their disappeared loved ones on their breasts. There was not a dry eye in the stadium as the thousands of young Chileans remembered and wept for the suffering that the disappeared and their loved ones endured. All the performers came on stage, dancing together to "They Dance Alone." As we danced on the stage in the stadium where so many were tortured and killed by Pinochet, I said to myself, "Take that for killing Ronni and Orlando in Sheridan Square."

I woke up early on the second day and drove to the stadium alone. I wanted to get a good look at this place that had been "re-baptized" by the people of Chile and the musicians with their horns, guitars, drums, and voices, who sang of a new era of human rights, freedom, and justice. I had once again witnessed music as a magical newspaper and a healing force for humanity. The National Stadium is one of the few in the world used after human rights abuses had been perpetrated in it. Usually, people or governments tear down these centers of death.

I pulled up just outside the stadium, and on the radio, John Lennon's song "Imagine" came on. I listened to the song and began to weep.

Imagine all the people

Livin' life in peace

You may say I'm a dreamer

But I'm not the only one

I hope someday you'll join us

And the world will be as one

Those lyrics echoed through the stadium that day, just as they will echo through generations. I was overcome by the reality that I, a scrappy, half-blind, dyslexic kid from Pittsburgh had been given the chance to work for human rights with people from all over the world. In the stadium that morning, I felt the significance of the place and the enormity of what had happened. I said a prayer of thanks, grateful that I had been able to play a part. My mother and Feryal had urged me to think of the victims first. This time I got it right, because I had listened to their voices and made them thunder.

· · · · · · · · · ·

James Mason Cohen, a writer who had once been my intern, put my reactions into perfect words for me as follows:

OCTOBER 1990, SANTIAGO, CHILE

There wasn't a dry eye in the Estadio Nacional, Chile's national stadium as the first notes of Sting's "They Dance Alone" faded into the night. With handkerchief-covered heads and photos around their necks, the Mothers of the Disappeared danced onto the stage in memory of the men they lost—the fathers, husbands, and sons who were disappeared by the Chilean government.

My breath was taken away by the pain and suffering that filled those words and that stadium. I think even the mountains cried that day for the atrocities that had happened there. But the concert, A Hug to a Hope, was about renewal. Held two years after the last show of Amnesty's Human Rights Now tour, it was a time to heal from the violence of the Pinochet dictatorship.

My good friend Pino Sagliocco took me to the top of the stadium where the majestic Andes Mountains swathed the 68,000 young people who were grasping for the first time the suffering their parents and grandparents had endured. We stood together, taking in the cleansing that was taking place. "This is what you've done," he said.

I knew that together we had done what we could to avenge the pain, suffering, and death that took place in that stadium. I said a silent thank you to my own widowed mother, remembering her words from long ago, telling me how I would know when I had become a man:

"When you learn to walk the highways and byways of life," she said, "and learn to listen to the weeping and the wailing of the poor, then and only then will you be a man."

The National Stadium was packed. It was a day of cleansing. © Neal Preston.

Sting played "They Danced Alone" as the wives and mothers of the disappeared took the stage. Photo by: © Neal Preston

Wynton Marsalis. ©Neal Preston 16.01 Wynton Marsalis and his band brought down the house. Photo by: © Neal Preston.

Wynton Marsalis. ©Neal Preston

Chapter 17

The Work Continues at Amnesty

J essica Neuwirth and I noticed that a vast majority of prisoners of conscience were men. These were the men adopted by Amnesty members, who wrote letters on their behalf. This effort by the grassroots supporters worked over a thousand times a year. As we looked at the data, we suspected that there was some bias toward reporting about male prisoners over women, but the research department in London told us that any such bias was unintentional.

To help address the gap in reporting on women, I decided to produce a concert to highlight women in human rights. We chose Women's Day, March 8, 1992, to stage a show in Los Angeles. Bob Meyerowitz, who had worked on the Human Rights Now tour, agreed to help me make it happen.

We created a three-hour show for the Lifetime network called "Free to Laugh" that was performed live at the Wiltern Theater in Los Angeles. The show was a mix of music and humor, hosted by Tom Arnold and Roseanne Barr. Halfway through the show, it became clear over an open mic that the couple wanted to do their whole shtick without interruption and then leave. I went on stage to correct this misjudgment on their part. I told the audience, "We're sorry, Tom and Roseanne have to leave now." They left, and other acts were finally able to get on stage. I received some nasty notes about this later, but it was well worth it. Tom called me a "sick liberal." The comic talent included Richard Lewis, Howie Mandel, and Nora Dunn. The performers were Vanessa Williams, Woody Harrelson, Jackson Browne, David Crosby, Kathy Sagal, Lily Tomlin, Robin Williams, and Sinbad. Maxine and Sally Lapiduss and Don Foster led the extensive list of contributing writers. The presenters were Anjelica Huston, Marlee Matlin, Daryl Hannah, Susan Sarandon, Andrea Martin, Richard Gere, and Marlo Thomas.

The human rights part of the show featured stories of women survivors. These survivors and activists working to free others included: Nomgcobo Beatrice Sangweni, South Africa; Ninotchka Rosca, Philippines; Veronica De Negri, Chile; and Susanne Riveles, USA. The show was a powerful mix of human rights, music, and humor and was nominated a month later for an ACE award.

• • • • • • • • • •

When William Jefferson Clinton was chosen as the presidential nominee of the Democratic Party, CNN asked me to make some comments. I walked into the room, the producer strapped a microphone to my shirt, and the commentator asked me one simple question. "What would you like to see Bill Clinton do for human rights?" I answered that I wanted President Clinton to listen.

I wanted him to listen to the voices of the losers. I wanted him to hear the stories of those who had been silenced by the international discussions—the American Indians, the Kashmiris, the East Timorese, the Palestinians, and the N'dabelli in Zimbabwe. I said he should bring them together in a big forum and ask them what they wanted their futures to look like, and how the United States could collaborate with them to achieve that future.

My frankness shocked the folks lingering around the television studio, the producers, the cameraman, sound engineers, and the like. When I walked out of the room they gave me a standing ovation. However, that speech was to earn me condemnation within the organization. Some believed I had moved too far from Amnesty's mission. I believe I was speaking for people suffering from an enormous number of human rights abuses. A new era in politics might signal new interest. It was not the first or last time I spoke truth to power and encouraged others to do the same. I have been relentlessly bipartisan in my criticism of U.S. policies on human rights from Nixon on through to President Joe Biden.

• • • • • • • • • •

Hans Wahl, a senior staff member at Amnesty, had delivered a paper in 1992 about the future of Amnesty and human rights work in general. The paper was in response to a request from my friend Ian Martin when he completed his excellent term as Secretary General of Amnesty. The presentation was to the governing body of Amnesty (the International Executive Committee). The assembly was held in London and was also a way to introduce the new Secretary General, Pierre Sane, a friend to be. By then the Berlin Wall had fallen, and the Soviet Union had collapsed.

My assessment of the most effective future for Amnesty included a change in the role of Amnesty in the human rights movement. Cameras had become a swifter messenger than pen and paper. We had to move from Gutenberg to computers. CNN footage exposed areas of abuse before Amnesty could. In the past, Amnesty reports had provided the story to the media. The paradigm had changed, and now the 24-hour news networks told the story first, which allowed for a change in Amnesty's role.

In the way that the concert tours, and music, had enlivened our mission, I saw the potential for the changing media and worldwide communication.

Amnesty could focus on in-depth research to expand the narrative. I recommended more regional offices closer to the actual work. Amnesty founder Benenson had always wanted Amnesty to move to a place such as India. Young people in small non-governmental entities can get closer to the issues of the poor and abused and respond more quickly.

Computers allowed far more expansive communication between the field and the home office. Amnesty workers in regional offices could get a better perspective on issues and were more likely to be trusted by the victims. We could make the human rights movement more accessible and more useful to people. Hans Wahl helped me with that paper, and it went over well, but my ideas were not implemented for quite a while.

We recommended:

- New human rights issues should be pursued: ethnic strife, homophobia, racism, killing, and torture necessitate expansion from the sole focus on prisoners of conscience.
- The dragon slayer has become the dragon—we need to get our fighting posture back.
- Amnesty International needs to be on the ground doing human rights work, not behind a desk filing it.
- We need to shift the focus from the sad victim image to one of strength, leadership, and inspiration.
- Amnesty International's watchful eye must strive to cover the entire globe, even if it cannot get 100%. The fact that we can be nearly everywhere multiplies our power.
- Amnesty International should be known as the hard-hitting voice of human rights.
- We must always remember how our work helps prisoners and/or victims of human rights violations, give them credit for surviving their oppression, and advocate for them through the skills and information Amnesty can provide (training, internationalizing the issue).
- Integrate development of local human rights groups into our strategy. Adopt local human rights organizations as a campaign strategy. See to it that our campaigns have a lasting impact on the ground.
- Do not be afraid to build on the successes of other human rights organizations that come up with good, innovative ideas (e.g., Peter Gabriel's Video project).
- The experience and influence of Amnesty's membership should be empowered and unleashed.

- Amnesty needs to enhance the image that it is a tough fighter for human rights on the ground. Our membership wants to act. One of the unique things about Amnesty is that we have work for members to do. If we give them real human rights work to do, we will bring activists into the movement who know how to make a difference. If we give them marginal work to do, we will get people who are only marginally active and influential.

- Co-groups (experts), who are our most astute and sophisticated resource, say they are used as automatons to move papers rather than as participants in an interactive process that uses their expertise and contacts to the limit. This must change so that Amnesty can develop the best human rights strategies possible.

- Computer communications/interactive capacity: there have to be more effective methods to involve more people in consultation and decision-making.

- Decentralize the responsibility for actions or new initiatives. Make the most of section and regional opportunities to break with policies and practices of the rich over the poor—our traditional human rights work. Give sections responsibility to plan and organize.

Amnesty had historically focused on the violation of rights specific to the Soviet Union, countries led by dictators, the Soviet gulags and torture in Africa. We no longer operated in a bipolar world, ruled by an ideological conflict between two superpowers. Amnesty needed to change by advocating for extensive human rights—not just freedom of speech and the freedom to vote. Economic rights belonged in the forefront. People desperately needed food, medicine, and housing. Our narrow focus was turning Amnesty into an instrument of Western hegemony rather than a neutral human rights organization.

I believed that in addition to economic rights, we should focus on criminal justice, the fight against the death penalty, and the necessity for fair trials. These were issues in almost every country. We also had to fight against the use of torture, but I thought we should try to do so in a more even handed manner, acknowledging police brutality in the U.S. as well as in jails in Sudan. Amnesty and its human rights effort needed to improve its emergency responsiveness: when a political prisoner was arrested, an Amnesty team had to be ready to provide support, send a lawyer, or find a local one. If a report of a death penalty case in Texas came up, we wanted to have local contacts ready to provide legal aid as well as to protest the sentence. Amnesty needed to continue to engage young people through art, music, and television. I told the crowd that I would not be at the helm of the U.S. section of Amnesty much longer, but this was the future. This prediction was my public recognition that both Amnesty and I were ready for new directions. Amnesty Secretary General Ian Martin had retired. I knew I was not far behind him.

In truth, I had been a part of Amnesty's growth from a small organization that moved quickly to a slow-moving ship I couldn't turn fast enough. We had been successful to the point of exceeding the size with which I was comfortable. I like to grab an idea, jump on a plane, head into a backstage dressing room, and get the job done. I was the eight-minute Bono meeting, not the year-long board meeting type leader. Neither way is necessarily better. Both speed and caution have value. The *Los Angeles Times* called me "irascible." I cannot argue with that. I knew my time was almost up. My style no longer suited the organization I helped to build.

The irascible label given by the *Los Angeles Times* was apt, despite a dozen years in seminary and my mother's finest attempts to make me as gentle as she. Or perhaps my wise mother groomed me to be this way, knowing I would need the tough with the gentle. Why else would she send me to handle a legal issue at the age of fourteen to get help for my brother? Why else would she tell me I would be a man only when I could stand up for those who could not stand up for themselves? With this personality and a drive to make a substantial difference quickly, it is not surprising that I offended my share of folks along the way.

By the end of the concert tours, Amnesty USA's annual contributions were $21 million, and membership and staff had tripled. I was not done with human rights work, but I was about done with coping with a massive board. For me, dealing with a board is the most challenging part of working for a nonprofit. During my twelve years, 140 board members passed through our offices, and eleven different people had been chairs of the board. Most board members and chairs were supportive, open-minded, and eager to applaud innovative ideas. However, I was stepping on the leadership's toes with mosquito-like annoyance. I was losing patience with the political games, and I had been in the crosshairs of the latest board chair a few times.

The board chair and I had vastly different styles, and it was clear that we were not going to co-exist smoothly. Things had been a little rough between us because we had gone together on an outreach trip to Europe, the West Bank, and Israel. As we were leaving together after having visited the West Bank, I was stopped at the airport in Tel Aviv. Israelis looked at my passport and began questioning me. "Give us a list of who you have visited," they said. "Tell us where you have been and what you have been doing." Airport authorities typically ask questions when one visits the West Bank. I felt it completely reasonable to tell them it was none of their business. Of course, I did not make my plane. The future board chair went on without me, leaving me at the Tel Aviv airport. Perhaps he felt it completely reasonable to let me handle the result of my response myself, but it did not sit well with me to not have his support.

My level of frustration with Amnesty's size and board was not sustainable, and I was ready to move on. No doubt they were ready for a little peace and quiet as well. I suggested we agree to a two-year contract instead of the standard four-year term to provide sufficient time for a smooth transition. I was offered a one-year contract instead. I rejected their offer. I signed a six-month non-compete clause and an agreement not to speak about the exit terms for two years. This agreement was made ostensibly to avoid questions amongst the membership and media, but it had the opposite effect. Rumors of all sorts spread as people speculated about such a sudden change in leadership. Thankfully, three directors (Philippines, Australia, and Ireland) with the support of the full International Executive Committee (Amnesty's worldwide governing body) put an end to all such rumors by breaking the silence and saying some incredibly kind words to the membership about my role at Amnesty at the biannual international meeting in Boston:

...In the time since you became Executive Director, the U.S. section has grown from about 35,000 members to over 400,000, and the section's income has increased from $2 million to $21 million annually. That increased income has resulted in millions of additional pounds being available through the international assessment. It has meant our movement could undertake new areas of activity, increase the number of countries we research, and strengthen its campaigning capacity. Today the U.S. section contributes about one-third of the international budget, and the translation of that extra money into action is the realization of your dream of a more effective worldwide campaigning movement.

In his remarks at the start of this Council, Curt remarked on what it was like to be part of the U.S. Section in this international movement, describing it as being somewhat like an elephant trying to do ballet.

Yet on the HRN! stage in Buenos Aires you showed us you were prepared to do somersaults for this movement. However, too rarely have we let you know how much we have appreciated your commitment to human rights and AI work worldwide.

In your time as Executive Director, you have challenged this movement to face new developments and to widen our horizons. The rock tours were the most obvious of these to us internationally. Through them, millions of people became aware of human rights and AI's work. Recently, Pierre Sane mentioned that it was the HRN! tour which led to him joining AI. We never imagined the rock tour would recruit our next SG. Maybe the IS personnel office will have to modify its recruitment process to incorporate music. Yet there are a great many other movement initiatives with which you have been associated which may not be widely appreciated.

From your recognition that with more supporters we will be able to campaign harder and better, and an appreciation that the future of the human rights movement lies with youth, you led your section into that sector of the community. I am sure others like me have met with young people here in Boston in the last week and cannot but be inspired by their support for AI's work.

The move to more direct and more diverse actions are innovations that have inspired many of the discussions that have culminated in our consideration of SYSTEC over the past few days. On behalf of your colleagues on the movement-wide staff, I want to publicly share some things with you.

Last night someone described the developing network of senior staff throughout this movement as "a bracelet of precious stones," and we feel we have lost one of the gems.

Over the past seven years, there has been greater contact between senior staff, and you have been a driving force behind that development. Your efforts have fostered a spirit of collegiality amongst key people in this movement, particularly the Section and IS Directors; people who have often felt alone and vulnerable through their unique position in their respective parts of the movement. You pleaded for a fair deal for all AI staff.

You have tried to have this movement address the difficulties of board-staff relations. In addressing this ICM about the challenges facing this movement, Ross Daniels identified board-staff relations, and this ICM has finally acknowledged that this is an issue that must be addressed. We cannot afford to continue to lose valuable staff and board members as has happened over recent years, and finally, something will be done to stop this bleeding.

As a friend and colleague, you have shared with us your energy, creativity, and enthusiasm for new ways to make this a better world.

While many of us derived our understanding of this movement from the decisions of bodies such as the AGM and the practice current at the time, you also went back to "the source." You could convey to us the inspiration of Peter Benenson and Sean MacBride, people with whom you have spent much time, and who were instrumental in establishing our movement.

Jack, in conversations we have had, you have often remarked that whatever our position in AI we are only what our movement wants us to be. Your colleagues want you to be part of the much-needed struggle for human rights.

There are still too many injustices in the world for us to not heed your words in the final plenary in Yokohama, so let me repeat them to you, Jack: 'LET'S GO!'

—Harris van Beek, Director Australian section.

● ● ● ● ● ● ● ● ● ●

Following this and a few other tributes, the International Executive Committee gave me the privilege of addressing the meeting. Three other directors introduced me to the audience (Australia, Ireland, and the Philippines). It was quite an honor for me. I prepared for the talk by reading the speeches of Chief Joseph of the Nez Perce Indian nation in Oregon, who had fought the U.S. military on a 1,100 mile trek from Oregon to Yellowstone and up to Montana, almost reaching Canada with eight hundred men, women, and children. (Chief Joseph was trying to join Sitting Bull in Canada, who had defeated Gen. George Custer at Little Big Horn River.) I quoted Chief Joseph quite extensively to remind the audience that we were on Indian land.

Leaving Amnesty was not easy. Like an amicable divorce, there was peace and pain simultaneously. Though I was ready to head in new directions, I was going to miss these folks. Amnesty had been particularly good to me. The board had allowed me to try every crazy idea I had and supported our efforts to advance the human rights movement.

I tried to inspire the movement and emphasize the importance of its work in the future. Something good must have happened during our years because I got a standing ovation for an embarrassingly long time. I thanked the International Executive Committee for giving me such a heartwarming farewell. It was truly a healing moment.

The team of directors at Amnesty

Final farewell party at Amnesty.

Final farewell to Amnesty in response to my speech. Boston Amnesty International Conference in 1993. Photographer unknown.

Chapter 18

Human Rights Action Center

1994-Present

There is a terrible emotional cost associated with major life changes, and I was facing another one with my departure from Amnesty. At every change of my life, I had to remake myself: leaving the priesthood; working with teens to end hunger; joining the Peace Corps in apartheid South Africa. This change was the toughest. I fought anger, self-doubt, and hurt.

I was fifty-five and had almost no savings. When I started at Amnesty it was unimaginable to make big bucks at a nonprofit that speaks for the oppressed. So, while my successor started at well over $100,000, I had taken a $20,000 salary cut from my Peace Corps job to start at Amnesty at $34,000, and my salary advanced slowly over the years. Though I received a small severance, it dried up quickly. I had just stepped off a roller coaster and the room was spinning. The transition from working seventy-hour weeks to having to build my own life was disorienting, to say the least.

I started yoga and made it one of my best friends. Pulling and stretching my back muscles, I could feel my fingers reaching closer and closer. Finally, after about three weeks, I could feel the tips of my longest finger brushing up against my big toe. This gave me an odd sense of accomplishment. The next day I booked a plane ticket to California.

In San Francisco, a friend was producing a fundraising concert like none that I had ever seen before, and he asked me to join him backstage for the show. Political hip-hop duo, The Disposable Heroes of Hiphoprisy, which consisted of artists Michael Franti and Rono Tse, opened the show with ravaging beats that had the audience bopping their heads. They were followed by The Breeders, which was fronted by Kim Deal, formerly of the Pixies. A quintessential nineties act, they captured the audience with their hit "Cannonball." Then the all-female grunge band, L7, followed with thrashing guitar riffs and upbeat and screaming lyrics.

Three working class white boys from Washington State had put the show together. Kurt Cobain, Krist Novoselic, and Dave Grohl produced an incredible breakthrough album "Nevermind." It knocked Michael Jackson off the top of the charts and ushered in a whole new era of rock. Overnight, Cobain went from sleeping under a bridge to becoming one of the most recognizable faces in entertainment.

His band, Nirvana, had a stage presence like no other. Instead of the neatly toned bodies that I was used to seeing in lead singers, Kurt Cobain was about 5'9" and 150 pounds. He played every note like he was barely hanging on to the rhythm; he powered through chords with heavy distortion and the reverb turned all the way up. His raspy voice made the music hard to ignore. The light show felt like the Velvet Underground gone punk. It made it impossible for me to keep my eyes on anything but the stage.

I could feel energy filling my body again. This was a great concert for a great cause. Krist Novoselic, the child of Croatian immigrants, had become concerned about the war in the former Yugoslavia and had recently returned from a trip around Bosnia-Herzegovina where he saw the impact of the war first-hand. The show raised money for the Trešnjevka Women's Group which was working with the victims of rape in Bosnia.

During that war, a policy of mass rape was orchestrated by the Serbian military in Bosnia. They were backed by the Serbian government under Slobodan Milosevic against most of the population in Bosnia, as well as against the Croats.

The conflict was one of competing ethno-religious-nationalist identities as well as attempts by anti-Muslim Serbs at ethnic cleansing. Ethnic Serbian armies expelled the mostly Muslim Bosnians and Catholic Croats from Bosnian towns that the Serbs were trying to make fully Serbian. Though living in Bosnia, these Serbs were backed by Milosevic in the neighboring country of Serbia. For Nirvana, this conflict was both personal and political.

I talked with the artists about the goals of the concert. They had a humility about them, combined with an anti-corporate politics that was new to me. They were concerned about the way their concert would portray the victims about whom they sang. Krist noted that the media made Croatia look like it was one giant starving child, and he did not want any part in that. He also understood that there were people attending the concert who would not be interested in the crisis going on in Croatia, but there would be literature in the back for those who wanted it. Kurt seconded Krist's determination that they would not pretend they were doing more than they were.

"This is not some corporate rock, we make you feel like a hero for having donated a couple bucks to a cause kind of thing," Kurt said. Though I thought they were underestimating their own power, I was extremely impressed by their sincerity. It gave me a lot of hope. It also helped me snap out of my own quiescent state. I was beginning to imagine what it would be like to build a new organization for human rights.

I have talked all my life about "What One Person Can Do." I wanted to return to that truth. I wanted to create a one-person organization that could be as effective as a medium-sized human rights group, but with a lot less money. New technology made this possible. I did not want meetings. I wanted simplicity and its power. I also wanted to take advantage of the 24-hour news cycle, the Internet, and social media, all of which were brand new. This was the birth of the idea for the Human Rights Action Center.

● ● ● ● ● ● ● ● ● ●

On that same trip, I went to visit British rock star Joe Strummer, co-founder of The Clash, a meeting I had been seeking for years.

By the time I arrived at the pool hall, working class hero Joe Strummer, lean, with his hair in an Elvis puff, had already finished one bottle of wine. In the 1980s, The Clash had been dubbed "the only band that matters" because of band members' willingness to take on tough political issues in an otherwise stagnant time. While I fumbled around, missing shots, and sinking the eight ball, Joe was in the pocket with every shot. As we played, we chatted.

"I know this place is a far cry from London," said Joe.

"It's a far cry from Pittsburgh as well," I answered.

"The world is changing. The Labor Party in England is not what it once was, and neither are the Democrats in America. Ever since Thatcher and Reagan broke the unions, both parties have increasingly had to look toward the banks for funding," said Joe. "The poor are increasingly left out of the conversation, even on the left. It is all about privatizing this, closing that public park, making way for the mall. We live in increasingly myopic times."

"Yeah, Joe. It is depressing, but there's hope, too. Mandela is out. White minority rule has ended in southern Africa."

"Sure, sure, but my concern is about the poor. In South Africa, what type of victory will it be if the white elite is just replaced with Black elite? In England, working class kids like me could never make it today the way I was able to."

"You know the Universal Declaration of Human Rights guarantees everyone the right to health care and education. It also guarantees people freedom from the want of hunger."

"Is that a fact? So, is that what you plan to be working on, promoting that document?"

"Yeah, Joe, among other things."

"Well, then let's do something that will get the word out about the Universal Declaration of Human Rights. How about a Punks for Human Rights album? I can wrestle up all the young punks who love the Clash and get them to donate songs. All the money we make from the album can be donated to your new organization."

And that was a contract. We planned to work on the album soon. My excitement was growing and growing. Jason Rothberg, a smart and dedicated producer, made it happen.

One afternoon, I was at the offices of a new law firm opening offices in Los Angeles. I was not sure why I was there, but after a few minutes a tall, smart-looking guy walked up to me.

"Are you Jack Healey?" "Yup."

"I want to be your lawyer."

"Okay," I said. He introduced himself as Matt Burrows, and he has been my attorney ever since. Matt has become one of my closest friends and a trusted advisor on strategy and legal issues for the Human Rights Action Center.

It was settled then. I had a lawyer, a financial backer, and a musician who returned phone calls. Now all I had to do was get to work. I named the new organization Human Rights Action Center (HRAC) and it has been an umbrella for my work since 1993. I was determined to keep HRAC small enough to respond quickly. I wanted to be an advocate for places I had been to and people whom I knew. I did not want to be isolated from the actual work on the ground as I had often been at Amnesty.

•••••••••

Bosnia became our first focus. In December 1994, I had a conversation with Feryal about the unfolding genocide in Bosnia, particularly the targeting of women by Bosnian Serbs. I had seen reports of rape camps operated by the Serbs and I suggested that she travel to Bosnia on a fact-finding mission. By then, as noted in Chapter 12, Feryal and Jessica Neuwirth had started Equality Now, an organization that continues to address the violation of rights of girls and women around the world.

Feryal's trip, arranged with help from the United Nations, allowed her to collect information. She spent two weeks in Croatia and Bosnia interviewing hundreds of people, mostly Bosnian refugees who had fled their homes. She returned with a harrowing account of what was happening in Bosnia: an asymmetrical war of aggression and ethnic cleansing waged by the well-armed Serbs against a Muslim civilian population that was under an arms embargo imposed on it by the West.

She was asked to testify before Congress with two Bosnian women who were rape victims. The members of Congress at the hearing were sympathetic but reluctant to intervene. I suggested that she go to the media to publicize the plight of women in Bosnia, hoping it would generate a public outcry for a policy change.

In 1994, the United Nations formed a Commission of Experts and charged it with investigating war crimes and crimes against humanity in the former Yugoslavia. The commission hired twelve international lawyers, one of whom was Feryal. The team of lawyers was dispatched to Bosnia and Croatia for a month to probe the charges. Their findings formed the basis for establishing the War Crimes Tribunal in The Hague that has successfully prosecuted Slobodan Milosevic (the former president of Serbia), Radovan Karadžić (the president of the Bosnian Serbs), and many others for crimes against humanity and war crimes.

Feryal was deeply affected by the events in Bosnia and wanted to do something tangible that would have a positive impact on the daily lives of the people there. So, she went back to see what we could do. She came across a destroyed garment factory which had been a major source of employment in the town of Fojnica outside the capital of Sarajevo. She met with the former director of the factory, who was a Bosnian Serb married to a Bosnian Muslim. They discussed what was needed to rebuild the factory and provide much-needed jobs. The major problem was financing. After months of searching, Feryal found a group of American bankers in Sarajevo who were looking at different development projects. Feryal met with the head of the banking group, David Proctor, a man blessed with unusual intelligence and kindness. He agreed to finance the rebuilding of the factory. Feryal hastily arranged a meeting between Nenad, the former director of the factory, and several of his colleagues and Proctor to discuss the details of the financing.

Agreements were reached to reconstruct the factory. Nenad agreed that the workforce would be multi-ethnic. Serbs, Croats, and Muslims would all be hired, and war widows would be given priority.

In 1997, Feryal received a call from Nenad inviting her to the formal opening of the rebuilt factory. It was fully operational and produced sports gear. Since this was an economic success for that region, Haris Silajdžić, the Prime Minister of the Republic of Bosnia-Herzegovina, attended the ceremony and cut the ribbon. Feryal was also asked to serve as an election monitor for Bosnia.

●●●●●●●●●●

We didn't stop there. Ireland has always been magical for me. Nobel Peace Prize winner Sean MacBride and U2 had remained my friends after the concert tours. I once attended a Van Morrison concert with Bono in Dublin. I was hearing Van's powerful voice in one ear while Bono's voice was in my other as he sang along—two great Irish voices at once. It was a lovely moment in my life.

I saw U2 perform in Dublin at an indoor arena. My family is originally from County Mayo in western Ireland. Whenever I could, I would go through Shannon Airport and drive around the West of Ireland for days.

Northern Ireland had been a troubled region for seven hundred years. Tensions were high between the Irish Catholics who wanted to be rid of British rule and Irish Protestants who dominated the local economy and government, oppressed the Catholics, and relied on the British for protection. Rita Mullan, a neighbor of mine in Washington, D.C., helped me understand the difficulties of working in Ireland. Her mom had been killed by British troops, but Rita had remained committed to nonviolence. She knew who the players were in the battle zone.

I was asked to observe a trial in Belfast, Northern Ireland. The case involved the execution of Fergal Caraher and the wounding of his brother, Michael Caraher, by British soldiers. I flew to Manchester, England, and then took a short flight to Belfast. The customs people in Manchester questioned me endlessly until I finally told the customs officer, "I am done now with this."

Later, on the plane, I understood their concern, because Ian Paisley, the firebrand of the Protestants, was on the flight as well. The hostesses treated him like a rock star. My taxi ride took me by the site of an IRA hit on a meat store where several people had died. I then asked the Belfast taxi driver to take me by some spots hit by the Protestants. He passed on that.

The trial was for two British soldiers from the unit 45 Commando, Richard Elkington and Andrew Callaghan, who had fired more than twenty armor-piercing shells into Fergal's car, killing him and wounding his brother. The spent shells were later collected and hidden, so there was no evidence of who did the shooting. The Caraher family believed that the soldiers had passed the boys through a checkpoint and later that night opened fire on them as they left a nearby pub. I asked their father what he thought and what I might do to help. His answer was: "We will not get justice in this court."

IRA prisoners typically were brought to court in chains and with head coverings. The British soldiers on trial came in wearing uniforms and could walk around and speak to people.

There was another American in court. I never got his name because he wanted to keep his distance and be independent. Unbeknownst to him, his "independent guide" for the next two days was close to the IRA. The British soldiers were acquitted of killing Fergal and wounding Michael.

The Carahers looked like my family—very Irish, red faced, some big and some small. The family moved me. I asked Mr. Caraher if I could visit his farm. I asked questions about their lives. One part that struck me hard was that British soldiers would descend quite often on the Caraher farm and knock on the door. If the door were not opened quickly enough, they would break into the home, harass the children, and accuse them of being IRA members.

Mr. Caraher told me this kind of harassment was constant. I suggested we try to stop the raids or at least give families a little respite from the aggravation. I wanted to figure out how to stop this invasive practice.

When I returned to the U.S., I wanted to do something for that family. I thought that we could print large signs for both the front and back doors that would say something like "if you enter this home, you will be filmed, recorded, and a fax will be sent to ten American families telling them you are in our home unlawfully."

Each of ten American families contributed $100, with which we bought a fax machine, a camera, and a small tape recorder—the equipment needed to carry out this attempt at non-violent protection. Word spread, and many families liked the idea. Before we tried to implement the "Families for Families" campaign, successful peace negotiations began. Finally, after seven hundred years, the troubles came to a rest. Although the "Families for Families" campaign was never implemented, it was worth the exercise of finding a method for outsiders to help when a society is under severe pressure.

Much later, the wounded Michael Caraher was arrested and convicted of possessing arms and belonging to the IRA. He was later released as part of the peace agreement.

• • • • • • • • • •

Years later I wrote an op-ed piece that ran in *The Washington Post* and re-ran in the *International Herald Tribune* calling on the Irish Diaspora (mainly in Irish bars) to stop funding the IRA. The peace process needed a boost. We American Irish had to stop giving them money so that the IRA would be more motivated to seek peace in Northern Ireland. Many in the Irish community did not like this call for stopping the cash flow, and they let me know how they felt. I felt grand when an invitation came to attend the White House St. Patrick's Day celebration at the urging of the British government.

Everything was going smoothly as I joined the line to meet President and Mrs. Clinton. As I went to shake the President's hand, he turned quickly and did not allow a photo to be taken. Eventually, as happens after White House events, I received a picture in the mail, but mine was with Hillary Clinton. He remembered that during his presidential campaign I told his fundraisers, Miles Rubin and Smith Bagley, that I would not reach out to Bruce Springsteen for the Clinton camp because Clinton supported the death penalty. Shortly after they had asked for my help, then-Gov. Clinton pointedly left the campaign trail to return to Arkansas to order the execution of Ricky Ray Rector, one of the four executions performed during Clinton's tenure as governor. As President, Clinton pardoned only one death row inmate.

While I strongly opposed Clinton's death penalty stance, I appreciated his work with Prime Ministers Bertie Ahern of Ireland and Tony Blair of Britain, who got the peace process to work in Northern Ireland. That ultimately became a large part of Clinton's legacy.

• • • • • • • • • •

I find it hard to write about Joe Strummer. His music was unique, challenging, and powerful. In person, he was simply a grand friend with whom one would cry from laughter. I first met Joe at Moira Sher's home, where I had stayed for more than thirty years when work took me to LA. His former father-in-law, Tom Salter, would come by and we would spend long, strange nights filled with fun and banter. Shooting pool at Tom Salter's Hollywood Athletic Club was an experience in cheating, laughing, bumping, yelling, and friendship. Joe was so decent and caring. He missed feeling important in music, but he was not driven by fame. Meals with Joe were a true experience in existential life. They were a mixture of laughter and wine and talking to everyone in the restaurant.

When Joe rehearsed, he liked to be surrounded by the flags of many nations. For me, studio work is more yawningly called "over and over." When Joe worked on the song "Generations," Jason Rothberg, a young and talented producer, and I listened for hours. At the end of the final cut in a long recording session, I heard Joe's voice singing ever so softly and ever so kindly the words "Jack Healey." Joe had ended "Generations" by adding my name. I have always treasured this moment as my Nobel.

We produced a video to go along with the song. A pregnant woman lying in the way-back seat of a station wagon shot the video while Joe and I drove an Elvis Presley-style Cadillac along Mulholland Drive in the hills above LA. I told Joe that if we included the words of the Universal Declaration of Human Rights on the video, MTV would never run it. "Okay," he said, "let's include the same words in Chinese and MTV will never know it, but one fifth of the world will understand." I loved this plan, and we did it.

Joe used the song "Generations" on the album *Generations: A Punk Look at Human Rights*, produced by Jason Rothberg and Miles Copeland, Sting's manager at the time. Green Day, Bad Brains, Pennywise, BUGS, Jellybeans, DFL, Electric Doghouse, Good Riddance, Lagwagon, Pansy Division, Swamp Dogg, Red Ants, and the Vandals all donated their music. An artist created what can only be described as a punk portrait of Eleanor Roosevelt, with lines from the UDHR printed underneath. The album came out in 1997 to great reviews. I was thrilled.

Joe was truly a friend. One day he returned to his London home from a peaceful walk, laid down, and died. After his funeral, the local firemen drove his body around London to the pubs where he had played his music. He deserved an easy passing. It was just not that easy for the rest of us. I still miss him and his raw and vital spirit and his cheating at cards and pool.

●●●●●●●●●

Two young filmmakers, Shainee Gabel and Kristin Hahn, asked if they could interview me for a documentary and book they were producing, asking if the American Dream was still alive at the end of the 20th century. Their book and film, The Anthem, included interviews with some of my old buddies, including Studs Terkel, the great American historian and theoretician, and Hunter S. Thompson, the gonzo journalist with whom I spent surreal time during visits to his Colorado ranch. The filmmakers and I walked two blocks from my house and set up my folding chair on the steps of the Supreme Court. It seemed the most appropriate backdrop to discuss the state of the American Dream. Ironically, we were chased away and had to find another spot to complete the shoot.

●●●●●●●●●

Korea is not a country that most Americans think about much, but Amnesty could not ignore the situation in South Korea in the 1980s. The country was under military rule.

Lee Shin Boom, a former prisoner of conscience, made it out of South Korea to the U.S. on April 12, 1984. Shin Boom was young, smart, and working to help South Korea reach higher ground on human rights. He had spent time in jail fighting for human rights in South Korea; he had proven his mettle. Lee gave my staff and many others in our Amnesty meetings a better understanding of South Korean human rights abuses. He was one of the prisoners of conscience we highlighted the day of the MTV show on national TV.

I guess for this reason, Kim Dae-jung and Kim Young Sam later visited us. Both of them went on to become presidents of South Korea. Dae-jung was a natural human rights leader, having been tortured, jailed and kidnapped from Japan by agents of the South Korean government (the KCIA). Kim Young Sam was more of a business kind of guy. Kim Dae-jung was nearly elected as head of the South Korean parliament in 1971. He lost because of restrictions placed on his candidacy by the ruling party. He was placed under house arrest for publishing an anti-government manifesto. Amnesty had adopted him as a prisoner of conscience in the seventies. When Kim was released in 1980, he came to New York and asked for our help in returning democracy to South Korea. Kim spoke about South Korea at Amnesty conferences and any other events he could find.

Anti-military protesters were suppressed and dispelled with tear gas and water cannons. In 1987, the South Korean government tortured a student to death, and the country revolted against the coup's leaders. Kim Dae-jung returned to Korea to help re-establish democracy. I spoke at his going away events in New York City and Los Angeles. He was elected president in 1997 and served from 1998-2003. He won the Nobel Peace Prize for his efforts to make peace with North Korea. He thanked us publicly for our help in supporting the people of South Korea.

Years later, Feryal went to South Korea representing Human Rights Action Center. She was to interview Woo Yong-gak, the longest serving prisoner of conscience in the world as he was being released. Initially they were not going to let her in because she did not have proper credentials as a journalist. Lee Shin Boom, by then a press officer for President Kim Young Sam, heard the noise and straightened it out by telling them to let Feryal in.

"Jack Healey did more for South Korea than any other American," he told them. We were both grateful for the kind remark, and she was also able to meet Woo Yong-gak, who was released after forty-one years.

Matt Burrows and Robin Hurley, architects of the album "For the Lady," at the Aung San Sui Kyi dinner. Matt Burrows offered his legal services to the work and has become one of my most trusted advisors. ©ABImages.

Feryal Gharahi with Woo Yong-Gak, a prisoner of conscience who spent 41 years in jail in S. Korea, 1994.

Joe Strummer, lead singer of The Clash. My first celebrity endorsement and supporter at Human Rights Action Center, 1994.

A visit with young Bosnian refugees during the war. 1993. Family Photo.

Feryal Gharahi with Bosnian Prime Minister Haris Silajdzic at the dedication of the factory. Family Photo.

Top. Jack, Sting, and Brad Jenkins, an Obama alumnus. Bottom. Peter Gabriel and me. Sting and Peter Gabriel have remained devoted to promoting the principles set forth in the Universal Declaration of Human Rights.

Lesson Seven

Stay after Them

Chapter 19

Groundwork

October 14-22, 2001

Bob Patterson, a local employee of the Food and Agriculture Organization (FAO), asked me if I would do some work to raise money for small agriculture project requests presented directly by farmers around the world. I told him that I had directed the Freedom from Hunger Foundation from 1968 to 1973, which was an arm of the FAO. It took me a while to be convinced, but I agreed to do a concert.

Here is what the *Los Angeles Times* had to say about the event:

SEATTLE. *He's dumped the T-shirt and put on a good sports coat for this, a tie, for God's sake, good shoes. But his gray hair is still splaying out of his ponytail. He's still urgent, still mad. It's like they say: You can take the man out of the street, but you can't take the street out of the man. Jack Healey isn't about to let the world forget its shortcomings.*

'Do we know what the hell we're doing? What we're about?' he asks, and when no one raises a hand, he goes on. 'I'd like to think that in the last century, governments didn't do very well, and we the citizens, the average, the poor, the wounded, the confused, we are going to make it work the way it never did before ... a citizen boom that would reach out to the whole world. My God! Wouldn't that be a moment? An

—289—

earthquake. An earthquake of decency, a century of such uncommon decency that we can all look each other in the eye with equality, and justice—and something to eat.'

Healey is back...the man who spearheaded the unprecedented Amnesty International pop-rock tours in the 1980s has put together a concert series again, this one on behalf of the U. N. FAO's Groundwork 2001 anti-hunger campaign. (All) for a cause (world hunger) that has absolutely nothing to do with global terrorism. Or at least, FAO liaison officer Bob Patterson says, "not until you think about it."

Usually, producing concerts entails a search for money and talent. In this case, we had money. The bubble had broken open in the tech world, and Adobe was interested in supporting the concert to fight world hunger. After a short meeting with Adobe's staff, we were guaranteed the money to do what we wanted. Adobe generously gave us offices, phones, and financial support. They were great supporters on many levels.

Our first hire was Melanie Ciccone to be our talent recruiter. She brought her sister Madonna in as the chair of the event we called Groundwork, and Madonna made a generous contribution. We chose Seattle as the concert site. I suggested a five-day music festival because I thought an idea like the "right to food as a basic human right," might take a while for the public to understand.

Seattle reminded me of Pittsburgh when it was a thriving steel town before the bust occurred and rust settled into the factories. Seattle was in the midst of a big boom, and it gave me an eerie feeling. I wondered how long the bubble would last. Seattle's lack of mixed communities reminded me of days past as well.

Three local Seattleites helped me with the daily chores. Susan Silver managed most of the talent to come out of that area. The Westside Café owner prepared meals for the long nights, and Artis the Spoonman, a popular street performer, became the face of the concerts with the help of Bob Patterson. We shot a public service announcement of him and ran it when and where we could. The Spoonman turned out to be a walking, talking guru of human rights. We gave him the stage of TV, music, and concert presentation. He did it justice. Since Melanie managed the recruiting so well, my only contribution was to get Joe Strummer to play. Joe picked up when I called. He yelled out to his wife, Lucinda, "Jack is on the phone. Come talk to him to find out where and when he needs me."

Melanie and I met with the Starbucks people to discuss producing an album also called Groundwork. Seattle-based Starbucks was excited to help in the cause of fighting world hunger. They offered two options: $500,000 for an album up front or a percentage of the sales on the back end. We took the half million dollars and Melanie produced Groundwork, which sold in their stores for several months.

Dave Matthews and Nancy and Ann Wilson of Heart came to the press kick-off for the concerts. They were solemn and serious and spoke of their children. Dave and I spoke privately about our love of southern Africa. A large class of Seattle students was at the press event and their teacher came up afterwards and asked Dave to come down and speak with the children. In a few minutes Dave came back and said, "They want to speak to the old guy." Months later, Dave called and donated to my work.

The talent list was extremely strong due to Melanie's hard work. The first night's performance was at the 3,800-seat Paramount Theater and featured Dave Matthews, the Blind Boys of Alabama, Emmylou Harris, and Daniel Lanois. The next four nights were at Microsoft co-founder Paul Allen's beautiful EMP Museum and included Chris Whitley, The Wallflowers, Joe Strummer and the Mezcaleros, DJ Cheb i Sabbah, DJ Nasir, Afro Celt Sound System, Shawn Smith, The Gents, Ann and Nancy Wilson, Heart, Chocolate Genius, Joe Henry and Michael Franti, and Spearhead. We closed at the 18,000-seat Key Arena with Femi Kuti and the Positive Force, Mana of Mexico, Alanis Morissette, Pearl Jam, and REM. The emotional highpoint was Pearl Jam playing with Rahat Fateh Ali Khan, a Pakistani vocalist.

After the dreadful terrorist attacks of September 11, 2001, Adobe left it up to us whether to continue with the project. Most events like this were canceled after 9/11, but we were already sold out, and we went on with the show. We were glad we did. Seattle's artists worked hard and would have done even better if the concerts had not followed 9/11. We were bolstered by the fact that we could send $1 million to the small projects of the farmers in developing countries.

The Secretary General of FAO, Jacques Diouf, thanked the artists and the organizers over a long supper. Large organizations have a hard time explaining where the money is spent. We Americans are blessed with a curse and a solution. We have money for this sort of thing, but we also have a cynicism that the money might be wasted. The real issue in funding a project is that there must be risks taken for it to succeed. If you admit this, few people will want to give to that project. Risk is the necessary coin for effecting change. Our effort to supply funds to small farmers bringing in their own projects seemed reasonable and sensible. We may even have been correct.

The week of music in Seattle was a rare opportunity to speak about the issue of freedom from hunger as a basic human right. This issue is rarely addressed, even among human rights organizations. To me, freedom from hunger is obviously a human right: if you are dying from hunger and thirst, what good are human rights? Money is always short for the relief of world hunger. Seattle gave me the chance to address the issue directly as a human right, as written in the Universal Declaration of Human Rights. The Seattle show also gave me another chance to allow all thirty-nine articles of the UDHR to come to life and get exposure even if for just a minute or two.

Our final effort was to produce two 90-minute videos of the shows for FAO. These productions were given freely to all the developing countries in FAO. Billions of people got to enjoy the shows through the videos that Sandra Hay produced in her garage.

Groundwork concert. Director General of FAO, Jacques Diouf, thanks me and my team for five days of music in Seattle to fight world hunger. Photo by Fred Clarke

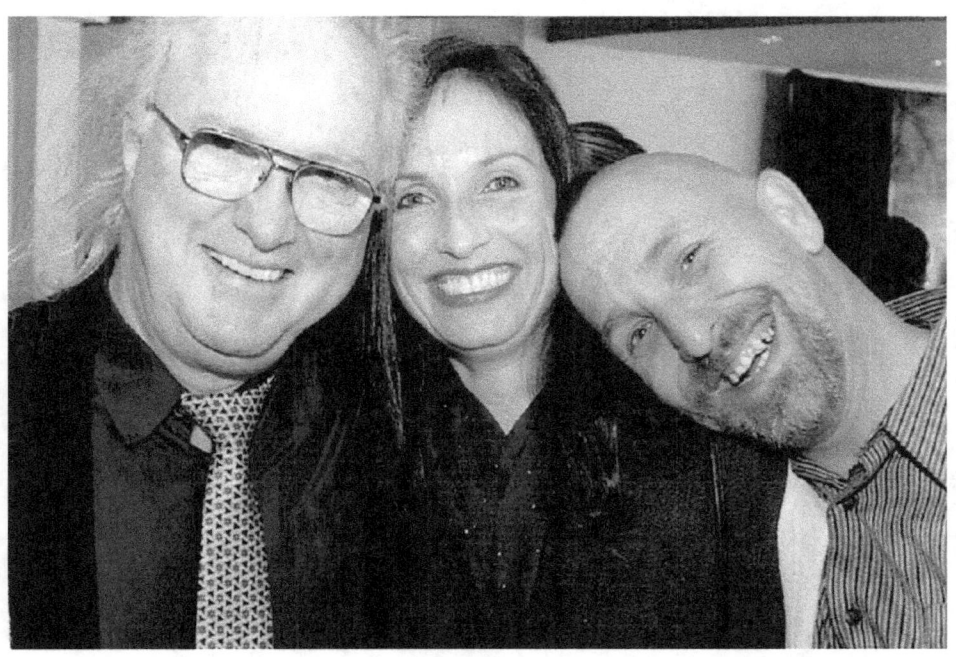

Susan Silver, manager of the Seattle talent, with Spoonman. Spoonman was famous for playing spoons every day in the Seattle market. He was the featured artist for Groundwork. My Hero.

Chapter 20

Burma

I met Michael Aris in 1990 at an Amnesty Conference in Boston. Michael was a British citizen, married to a Burmese woman, Daw Aung San Suu Kyi (ASSK). Michael had been separated from his wife since she had left Oxford for Burma in 1988 to care for her ailing mother. Once back in Burma, ASSK found herself swept up in the democratic movement there. She joined the protests and became the head of a fledgling movement advocating for democracy in Burma.

The military junta placed her under house arrest, and Michael left his post at St. John's College in Cambridge, England, and began to petition for his wife. He asked me for help, and I said "Of course." It was to become one of the longest-lasting campaigns of my time in human rights work.

All human rights campaigns must achieve goals if they are to be successful. I set these goals for our work in Burma:

- First, we needed to educate the American public on both the leader and the antagonist. This was paramount.
- Second, given the difficulty of pronouncing Suu Kyi's name, I knew we had to start there.

- Third, we had to funnel her worldwide support into one place.
- Fourth, we needed to let the world know what she looked like.

I looked to the arts and artists to help achieve these goals. Renowned artist Shepard Fairey solved the image problem through his art. Congressional staffer Jeremy Woodrum and I introduced Suu Kyi to Americans as "the Mandela of Asia." This established immediate credibility for her cause.

Amnesty had opposed the human rights abuses of the military junta in Burma. The junta was extremely repressive and imprisoned political activists; conscripted children into the military; and seized land from poor farmers. Aung San Suu Kyi was the daughter of the famed liberation hero, Aung San, so it was not surprising that she led the National League for Democracy (NLD) that pledged to unite the country's ethnic factions, restore democracy, and bring about change.

She was first placed under house arrest in 1989 and spent fifteen of the next twenty-one years under house arrest (July 1989 – November 2010). In 2015, as ASEAN put it: "In a clear showing of the people's will, Aung San Suu Kyi's party, the National League for Democracy (NLD) won 81% of the parliamentary seats and the government-backed party won only 2% of the seats." This is according to a report by the ASEAN Inter-Parliamentary Myanmar Caucus.

In 1991, ASSK received the Nobel Prize for Peace, but was prevented by the military junta from attending attend the ceremonies. Until she was released in 2010, Human Rights Action Center and its supporters devoted most of their efforts to a campaign for her release.

A few years after I met Michael Aris, a Burmese student, Zar Ni, spoke to a crowd at the University of Oklahoma. My friends Michael Johns and David Slemmons, who organized a free musical event for human rights each year at the university, were in the audience. They were moved by his speech and told Zar Ni to call me. He had started the Free Burma Campaign. We got together on August 12, 1998. Some students from American University had been arrested in Rangoon for supporting ASSK. This action gave the movement momentum. Recent college graduates Jeremy Woodrum and Dan Beeton and I joined the Free Burma Campaign and then eventually started the U.S. Campaign for Burma under the auspices of the Human Rights Action Center. We worked together for the next dozen years.

In February 1999, I visited the refugee camps and hospital of the Burmese along the Thai border. As in most refugee camps, conditions were miserable. I met some of the leaders of the 88 Generation who had helped in the victorious election of ASSK and then had to flee the country. Many of their co-leaders were in jail. In Bangkok, Feryal and I applied for visas to Burma and received them after a long interview centering on the purpose of our visit. We pretended to be tourists and antiques dealers.

At the Rangoon airport, I was lucky to meet Mr. Synge, a taxi driver who became our driver and escort. Mr. Synge spoke English and knew his way around. We ate noodles at stands along the sides of muddy roads. We toured Burma and the surrounding countryside. I saw so many pagodas I was ready to convert to Buddhism. I followed the news; ASSK had been officially "released" from house arrest but was still mostly confined to her home. I visited the U.S. Embassy in the hopes of some useful information on how to reach ASSK. "No, that will not work," they said.

I shared my problem with Mr. Synge. He said, "She gives out rice once a week to her people at the headquarters of the National League for Democracy. No one knows the schedule." I decided to watch the place and see when people showed up. I walked back and forth looking at antique stores for hours. Finally, one day there were many people going into the building and just as many soldiers across the street watching them. A white Toyota arrived and quick as a flash the lady in white jumped out and went into the building.

Feryal convinced me that she could slip inside the building unnoticed, dressed as she was in traditional Burmese garb. She seated herself on a small wooden bench and waited. Daw Suu soon appeared in front of Feryal. Feryal quietly explained who she was and asked if I could come in. Daw Suu graciously welcomed us both.

I was struck by the energy and calm Daw Suu radiated. She is a stunningly beautiful woman, tall, thin, and incredibly focused. We spoke for 20 minutes. I told her I would commit myself to her cause, and that I would not give up until democracy came to Burma. I got her autograph and a photo for a friend. ASSK asked me to take the message back to her American supporters, especially the Burmese in America: "Stay united and stay focused on the goal. We have a long way to go."

The authorities in Burma had eyes everywhere and that night I was told to leave the country. I flew out after the customs agents performed a thorough inspection of my bags, which were suspiciously short on antiques. Thankfully, we had hidden our autographed photos very well.

I went home and started the work I had promised to do. I began by learning about Burma, its colonization by England, and the long years of military rule. There was little international focus on Burma despite a long history of human rights abuses. This was a rare time when American leaders were ahead of the American people. Clinton and both Bushes supported ASSK and the Burmese people. Jeremy Woodrum, Dan Beeton, and I established the U.S. Campaign for Burma as an advocacy group dedicated to freedom for Suu Kyi.

A month later, HRAC funded a film crew to go to Burma and interview ASSK. Ebet Roberts and Nancy Anderson conducted an in-depth interview on camera with her that made the rounds for years. I wanted to give the tape to a CNN producer. He told me that CNN only covers news. I believed this was news. My response to him was that she could not call a press conference when she was under house arrest, but he stuck to his decision.

Not long after this, Zar Ni convened a quiet meeting of the exiled government and some active Burmese leaders at Harpers Ferry, West Virginia. Over the next three days, Hans Wahl, a former colleague from Amnesty, and I did our best to shape and record the meeting. It was time to nationalize the name and the face of Aung San Suu Kyi. The few Americans who had heard of her could only refer to her as "that Lady over in Asia." I thought that the least we could do was teach people her name.

With the help of Jimmy Miller and Eric Gold, who together represented him, I met with actor Jim Carrey at his home in Malibu. It was great to meet this very funny comedian, whose movies I love. I expected that elastic body of great humor to be present, but it was not. He was business-like, a warm host with a soft touch. His house was long and narrow with a great ocean view. We sat for a while on the windy deck and watched the waves. The campaign to free ASSK was in a rough spot. We were having trouble getting any attention for the cause, and we needed publicity. We wanted to make video spots featuring different celebrities describing the situation in Burma and the plight of Aung San Suu Kyi.

Within five minutes of my arrival, Jim agreed to get involved. He knew what was going on in Burma and was eager to help. He devised two plans for video spots: one was to sit in an expensive restaurant, calmly eating his meal and then stand up, look at the camera, and just scream for all he was worth. Then he would sit down and say Burma. The other one, and the one we decided to use, was designed to address the total lack of awareness about ASSK, and Burma in general, among Americans. We would do a spot of Jim Carrey teaching people to pronounce her name, thinking that the campaign would go nowhere unless people could say her name, Aung San Suu Kyi. I left feeling terrific. It was a brief meeting with a quick move to action. Just my style—human rights in action.

CNN decided that Carrey's spot was newsworthy, and its coverage helped our spot go viral. The healing power of humor delivered the traction to get our campaign going.

We followed up by planning a thirty-day campaign, *Burma: It Can't Wait*, with celebrities talking about a different aspect of Burma each day. I flew to LA three times looking for backers and was about to leave town in defeat when I stopped for a quick lunch with my good friend Dan Adler of Fanista, the first of its kind online shopping business.

Dan organized his team of Prudence Fenton and John Solomon to bring the campaign together. Prudence served as creative executive producer for the thirty-seven short videos. Kristin Hahn, Francesca Silvestri, Kevin Chinoy, Robyn Wholey, and Jorge Berlanga produced the spots. June Guterman came in for fifteen of the spots. Michael Abbott and his partner pitched in with their talent.

Joseph Fiennes, of *Shakespeare in Love*, called from London to tell me about the three-minute spot he had done. Rob Schwartz of the global advertising network TBWA in LA developed an entire campaign with our guidance. Will Ferrell and Judd Apatow kicked off our effort and from there, the project was easy.

Amy Poncher coordinated it all for the HRAC. The campaign received coverage in *The New York Times*, *Newsweek*, and the *Los Angeles Times*. We ran a new ad each day starting on May 1, 2008. The *Burma: It Can't Wait* campaign received millions of hits on YouTube. It is still frequently viewed on the HRAC site and YouTube.

●●●●●●●●●●

A terrible cyclone hit Burma on May 3, 2008. We continued with the spots and extended them to include pleas for Cyclone Nargis relief. Anjelica Huston joined Jeremy Woodrum and me at a news conference at the United Nations focusing on the devastating aftermath of the cyclone. Later that month, I found myself eating whole grain, sugar-free cookies on Jim Carrey's jet as we flew to New York so he could address the United Nations. There was no comedy when Jim said, "It's a brutal and sadistic regime that has for decades tried to quash the will of its people through mass relocation, rape, and murder." It was a brilliant talk.

Anjelica Huston, who served as chair for the campaign, helped us organize a large dinner and fundraiser at the Hyatt in Los Angeles, where we spoke to the film community about ASSK. Damien Rice sang at the dinner because he had visited the refugee camps and wanted to help. Actress and model Maggie Q did the same and brought her friends to the dinner. Sony executives Doug Belgrad and Jonathan Kadin came, as did the Mosaic staff. Mosaic covered a van with the image of Aung San Suu Kyi.

We produced an hour-long film, originally imagined by my friend Stan Salett, using the many endorsements ASSK had received and tapes showing the wide support for a free Burma. We called it *Douye*, meaning struggle, which was the word the Burmese shouted while demonstrating at the Burmese Embassy. The film included spots from President Bill Clinton, singer-songwriter Anthony Kiedis, U.S. Sen. John McCain, Anjelica Huston, REM, and Bono.

Sandy Berger of the National Security Council arranged meetings for the Burmese activists to brief the White House staff. Later George W. Bush's staff would do the same. First Lady Laura Bush was deeply interested in ASSK. Jeremy and I showed the *30 Days for Burma* videos to Laura's staff.

Matt Burrows, lawyer, arranged a meeting for me with Rhino Records founder Robin Hurley. He readily responded to our request for help, and we developed the album called *For the Lady*, a two CD set featuring the music of the best musicians in rock.

Financial advisor Lock Bingham moved from San Francisco to Memphis to help coordinate this effort for HRAC and the U.S. Campaign for Burma. Featured artists included U2, Sting, Peter Gabriel, REM, Paul McCartney, Eric Clapton, Pearl Jam, Coldplay, Ben Harper, Talib Kweli with John Legend, Bonnie Raitt, Avril Lavigne, Ani Di Franco, Damien Rice, Bright Eyes, The Nightwatchman, Lili Haydn, and the great Natalie Merchant, who was the first to sign on.

Brian Sirgutz and Levi Felix arranged for me to meet Shepard Fairey, whose poster had been instrumental to the Obama campaign. I wanted to give Shepard a gift to thank him for bringing so many young people into the last election with his art. I gave him an original art piece by Sister Corita Kent that she had given to me for my work on the Walks for Development. Shep was stunned. He had been an ardent fan of Sister Corita for years. I asked him to make a poster of Aung San Suu Kyi. Shepard kindly created the iconic artistic portrait of ASSK. His poster has become the image of her that is recognized worldwide. We printed and distributed thousands of the posters over the next few years.

My intern, Grace Powell, arranged for a Burmese child soldier now living in New Zealand to speak at a congressional hearing. Burma had tens of thousands of child soldiers. We wanted Congress to hear a direct story and see a real child soldier. Our hope was that Congress would act on this critical issue. There are over a half million child soldiers in the world.

A friend of mine, Jorge Berlanga, called me and said, "Jack, these soldiers in Burma love soccer. I will get Argentine footballer, Diego Maradona Franco, for your campaign." Diego Maradona Franco helped bring publicity to the campaign. The press copied our language, calling her the *Mandela of Asia*, which gave us a further boost.

A friend of mine in Las Vegas gave a month-long spot to our campaign on an outdoor billboard. Sylvester Stallone did a movie about oppression in Burma and kindly added Jeremy and me to the director's cut so we could discuss the non-movie version.

Friends like John Taglioli, Maria Anaya, and Steve Strauss helped me pull off a concert named *9999* on September 9, 1999, in Bangkok. Singer, songwriter, and actress Raven Symoné was the headliner. The Black Eyed Peas, while on tour in Bangkok, did a dedication to ASSK and received major headlines. 9999 is a meaningful number for many in Asia. It means bad news.

• • • • • • • • • •

Ten years after I first met her, the Lady who had inspired so many was released from house arrest. The government allowed Aung San Suu Kyi to take her seat in Parliament. The battle was not over; her party was still not in power; and the regime was still in charge, but it was a start. In 2012, when she was in the U.S. to accept in person the Congressional Gold Medal she had been awarded in 2008, ASSK's office called me. She wanted to have dinner, to meet and thank the Human Rights Action Center and others who had worked so hard on her campaign.

On a warm evening in early September, at the stately Bel Air home of my good friends Jimmy and Cheryl Miller, we hosted a dinner for 150 people. There was beautiful light from candles and paper lanterns and, most especially, from Aung San Suu Kyi herself. She sat casually among us, radiating her charm and magnetism. Lili Haydn and Tom Morello provided music. Many of the celebrities and Burmese who had been part of the Burma: It Can't Wait campaign and other activities over the years attended the dinner. Shepard Fairey spoke, and we all enjoyed precious time with the Lady.

At the end of the evening, she stood up on a small, wooden podium and spoke. "The battle," she said in her lilting quiet voice, "is not yet over. We cannot give up the fight against injustice."

Great friends: Dick Gregory, Wynton Marsalis, Jenny McCarthy, Jim Carrey, Bruno Battaglia, Jacob Donnelly, David Bruce, and Feryal and Firouzeh Gharahi joined me for my 70th birthday at Jimmy Miller's home. Photo by Daniella de Varney

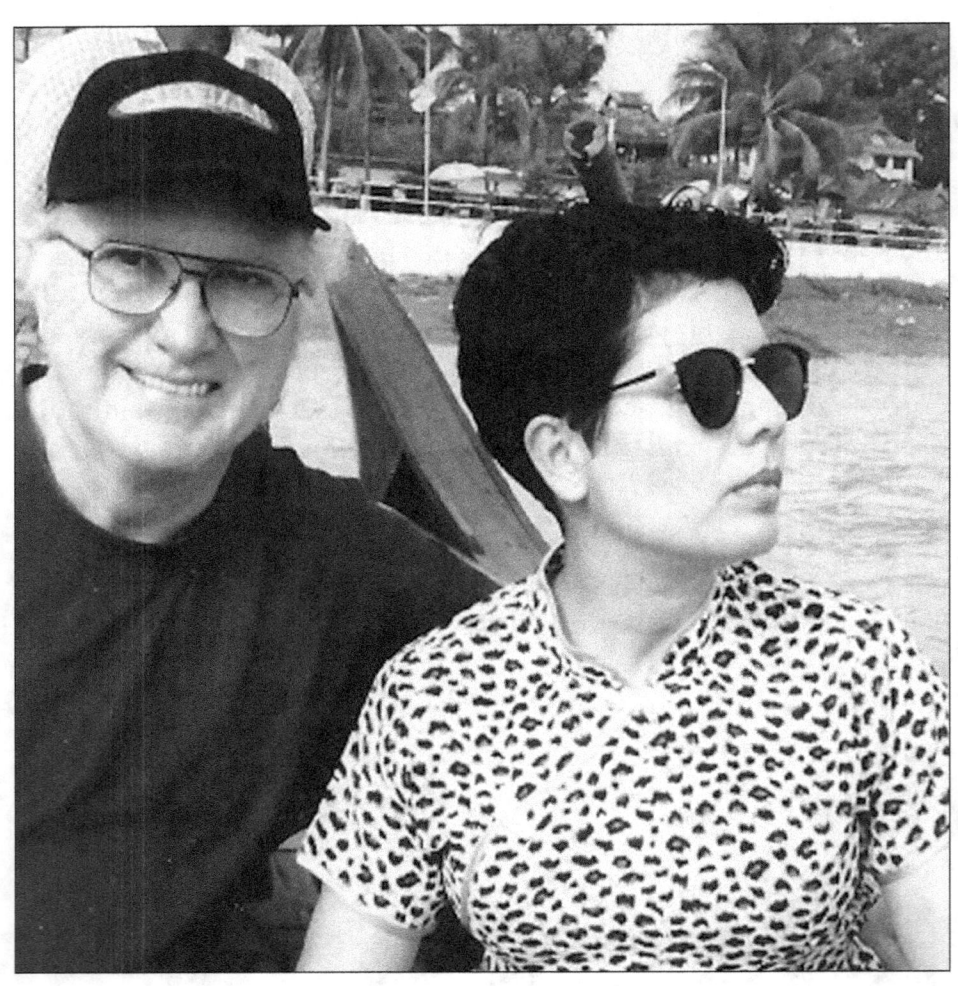

With Feryal Gharahi in Cambodia 1999. Family Photo

Shep Fairey's artistic poster of Aung San Suu Kyi made her face known to the world. © Shepard Fairey

Angelica Huston with Wendy Willis, Jacob Donnelly, Eric Torres, Tony Roman

At Harmony 1999 concert in Bangkok for Aung San Suu Kyi. Photo by Maria Anaya

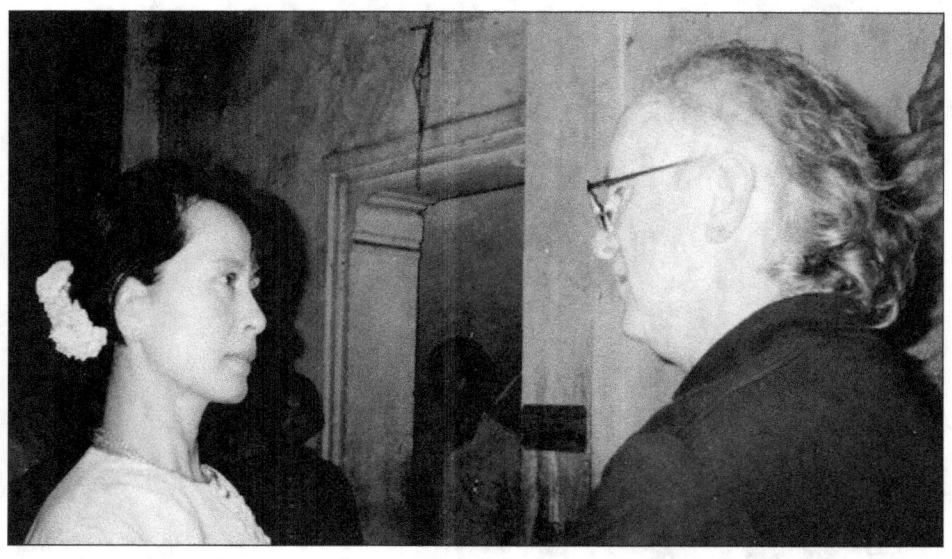

Jack with Burmese students at the screening of Douye, a documentary about the fight for democracy in Burma.

Visiting Aung San Suu Kyi in Burma at the National League for Democracy headquarters. February 1999. Photo by Feryal Gharahi

Amanda and Shep Fairey meet Aung San Suu Kyi, years after he created the iconic poster of her. ©AB Images

With Aung San Suu Kyi at dinner in her honor, 2012. © AB Images

Human Rights Begin in Small Places

Chapter 21

Heroes of Hope

I have always found comfort and power in having my own heroes of hope. Some are obvious, others are not. I heard Dr. King speak at the Lincoln Memorial, but I never met him. I did get to know Dick Gregory, Father James Groppi, Fannie Lou Hamer, and Muhammad Ali.

Internationally, I looked to Nelson Mandela, of course, but also to his lawyer Denis Kuny. A playwright, Barney Simon, inspired me, as did Chris Hani, Khalaki Sello, and Kuny during my time in southern Africa. They moved me into thought and action.

Dick Gregory won the Dawson Award in the fall of 1976 for his Run Against Hunger, and Mrs. Hamer also received an award. We were all together at a Hilton Hotel for a Black Caucus dinner when Fannie leaned over and whispered to me, "Jack, I am dying. Do not fret. I am okay. I am with Christ."

I knew she was.

• • • • • • • • •

As the head of Amnesty International's U.S. section, I was invited to give a speech at the University of Denver. Another speaker or two from a contested area of the world usually accompanied me and spoke. I was first up in a room of about three hundred people sponsored by an Amnesty chapter. Earlier in the day, I had taken the chance to pay a visit to two of my favorite Amnesty members, Marketa Freund and her mother Henrietta. These kind women lived in a tiny house in Boulder, Colorado filled with boxes and files. They were unknown to the outside world, but they were the real deal in human rights. Their arms had been tattooed by the Nazis during the Holocaust, but their hearts were marked with love for anyone under governmental oppression in Latin America.

They tirelessly made phone calls, wrote letters, sent faxes, and contributed money for the good of prisoners of conscience in Latin America. They served meals to human rights workers—luckily including me—and fussed that I was working too hard. Their purity of work always inspired me and lifted my spirits. Their humor, insight, and advice on what I should be doing next was invaluable. They never failed the movement or any of us within it. You don't have to give speeches, or even leave the living room, to be effective. That was the message I gave that evening at the University of Denver.

The second speaker was a Peruvian Indian from the Amazonian rain forest where war had been dragging on for years. He told us how he and his fellow villagers would look at the river to see how many bodies were floating by. The number of bodies floating by would be their indication of whether they should travel that day. These brave villagers continued their work for human rights deep in the jungle despite the river of death facing them daily. And then he said in his broken English, "There are two ladies who live in Boulder, Colorado, who if you can get a hold of them, can get you out of jail." He was referring, of course, to Marketa and Henrietta, who never left their home but could free prisoners in Peru. One gets a lot from people who are just the real deal. I drink from their souls.

· · · · · · · · · ·

I called on these heroes often when I faced the hardest battle of my life in 2006. I noticed a black, dome-like spot on my left shoulder and thought it was strange but chose denial and ignored it. Within a month I went to Washington Hospital Center and found out it was not only a cancer, but it was the melanoma kind, a possible killer. While the care and expertise at Washington Hospital Center was terrific and compassionate, the diagnosis rattled me and took away a lot of confidence. With my doctors, I chose surgery, which went better than we were told to expect. Fear and anger swirled in my belly as I graduated to the second floor, the land of chemotherapy and interferon. Interferon was recommended by one doctor. He said it would boost my immune system, but he terrified me by showing me the odds of cancer's return.

The treatment would require me to inject myself three times a week under the skin. Most patients drop treatment because of side effects such as depression and suicidal thoughts.

I rejected this option after a lengthy discussion with my doctor. I also checked in with Johns Hopkins Hospital, whose experts recommended that I not take the treatment.

Instead, I sprung my mind and body into fight mode. I isolated myself and pursued aggressive treatment that brought victory. I set out to get my confidence back. Fear had such a grip on me. I had even stopped flying, which I had enjoyed for so many years. During my first year of recovery, any ache, bump, or red spot scared me into becoming a terrific worrier. I had to get my spunk back. My family, friends, lawyer, and Feryal rallied me.

The Goldbergs, my friends and HRAC supporters, gave me a retreat while I recovered. I decided that I would strengthen my immune system. I got more deeply into yoga than I had been in years. I added weights and the treadmill. I added eight to ten hours of sleep. Fruit, nuts, and vegetables became an integral part of my diet, and I lost weight. It worked. I still had to get a lesser cancer off my ear and brow, but they were not melanoma. It took a year for me to regain my confidence and spirit. The cancer bullet came close, but the wind from that shell enriched my life with a new view and a new gratitude. Good friends, good doctors, good eating, and exercise are cures, too. I have been cancer-free for many years now, and I fly again.

Jimmy Miller, fellow Pittsburgh native, has been a supporter of human rights work for decades. Family Photo

With Hank and Carol Goldberg, Feryal.

Chapter 22

Haiti

February 2, 2010

On February 2nd, 2010, *Politico* ran an article by Steven Van Zandt regarding the future of Haiti. He made the important and necessary argument that Haiti must not return to a state where many of its people suffer starvation, malnutrition, the lack of clean water and electricity, and have little opportunity for decent education or health care. Steven advocated a steady hand and took steps to improve the outlook for Haiti's future.

In other words, rebuilding Haiti was a long-distance jog, not a quick fix. I could not agree more. Much of my rationale is based on my own experiences in Haiti, aiding various development projects, dating back to 1970.

I was in Haiti in 1998 to review the operations of a center that treated the victims of torture. We stayed at the Montana Hotel where many people later died in the 2010 earthquake.

To assess the general state of human rights in Haiti, I insisted we visit the prisons. Everyone wanted to know why since jails were not on the agenda. My answer was that we could learn about justice or the lack thereof more quickly in the prisons than in any other place. In the prison housing male inmates, many claimed their cases had not been reviewed by any discernible judicial process.

Many prisoners had already served their time, but they had no way to obtain release because the courts would not hear their cases. The courts often did not hear cases for weeks or months.

We visited two prisons for minors. As far as I could tell, both were unconstitutional by the standards of the Haitian Constitution. The facilities were astonishingly inadequate, lacking basic resources such as bedding and medicine. There was one bed for 162 boys. The medicine cabinet contained two aspirins. The juvenile girls had organized their prison room into areas that resembled their economic system, with the richest girls bunking at the door exiting the facility and the poorest girls bunking at the door entering the facility.

This look into the prison system said it all. I met with many Haitian lawyers who were prepared to right the system and do what was needed to fix it, but the situation was beyond their ability to repair. Haiti was a country where human life was not sufficiently valued. More than half the nation was under the age of eighteen. The government did not seem to work for anyone.

In contrast, the Center for Victims of Torture was an extremely well-run organization headed by Dr. Herve Razafimbahiny and gave much solace to those who came to it. I recommended that its funding be maintained so the Center could continue its work. Despite this recommendation, the United States government, for whom the report was written, made the decision to close the center.

Haitians saw their democratically elected leader Jean-Bertrand Aristide removed by an American secretary of state and exiled to the Central African Republic (CAR). Aristide moved from CAR to South Africa, where he lived while seeking permission to return to Haiti. Aristide was allowed home in 2011 after seven years in exile. Our government's interaction with Haiti has been a mixture of good and bad.

When I was at Amnesty, I arranged to charter a boat to go into the Windward Passage to pick up lost Haitian refugees who were out at sea and in distress. I wanted to return to the U.S. with the refugees and get arrested in solidarity with them because President Clinton was preventing them from fleeing their oppressive circumstances. Under law, the United States government has an obligation to take in refugees and hear their cases. In my view, President Clinton was wrong to turn Haitian refugees away, and I wanted to confront the Administration. The right to escape from harm is basic and guaranteed by law. Clinton violated international law by having the Navy pick up those folks and return them to Haiti. Unfortunately, during my one day at sea, I did not encounter any refugees to save even after we sent a plane up to search.

Steven Van Zandt was right: a new paradigm needed to be put into place. Haitians deserved nothing less. The devastating earthquake of 2010, killing more than 300,000, was followed in 2021 by a second earthquake killing another 2,200 people. To make things even worse, the island had been blasted by hurricanes multiple times in recent years. Infrastructure was demolished. Their government hit a standstill and in 2021 President Jovenel Moise was assassinated, causing the country to descend further into chaos. The problems in Haiti are far more complex than can be easily managed. Still, we cannot give up. Haitians deserve a better future.

Lesson Nine

Never Forget

Chapter 23

Defend Our Native People

As children, my brother Mike and I would head to an old movie theatre in Crafton, outside of Pittsburgh, to enjoy Friday night movies. The price was a dime, and it was a double feature, too. Per usual, we cheered for the soldiers chasing the Indians. On the way home, Mike would tag me to be the Indian and chase me home. I also played the game when I explored alone in the woods near our Oakwood home, imagining I was brave and strong. It was this child's game that sparked my interest in Indian history and people.

In 1972, as director of Young World Development, I joined friends Barbara Body of the Children's Foundation and Anselm Rothchild, the Buffalo leader from Freedom from Hunger, on a trip to Nebraska for a seven-day fast on an Indian reservation. Fasting was not new to me, but it was more difficult in the heat of the summer. Father James Groppi was along, and he jokingly said, "If they fast, they will think they are under Rome."

We were searching for inspiration. We wanted to clear our minds and find fresh vision for a future beyond the Walks. The walkathon concept had worked so well for YWD, organizations with a bigger footprint began to copy the idea. It was time for a new approach. The tribal leaders led us through the fasting process in a positive way. They spoke of their history, their struggles, and their hopes. That visit opened my eyes to the issues Native Americans faced. It was less than one hundred years since the 1890 Wounded Knee massacre, and the Native people were neither assimilating into American culture as the government had hoped, nor thriving on what little land the government had left to them.

The American Indian Movement (AIM) grew from the turmoil of the sixties and early seventies inspired by the Civil Rights and anti-war movements. Young soldiers from reservations were returning from Vietnam with both anger and a wish to help their own people. Several YWD chapters had funded AIM, and we had gotten to know some of their leaders, including Dennis Banks, Russell Means, and the Bellecourt brothers, Clyde and Vernon. We did not leave with a new fundraising tactic, but we found something more important on that Nebraska reservation. We left inspired and ready to put ourselves to work again for the common good.

In early 1973, my attention, like that of the rest of the nation, was riveted on the American Indian Movement after it took control of the village of Wounded Knee on the Pine Ridge reservation in South Dakota. They held it for seventy-one days to bring attention to the poverty and neglect people were experiencing on most of the nation's Indian reservations at that time. It dominated the evening news for weeks. There was an attempt in Milwaukee by Dick Gregory, Father James Groppi, and Marlon Brando to influence the occupation so there was no bloodshed. Both Groppi and Gregory, as close friends, filled me in on news of this event. Despite their efforts to keep the peace, two American Indian men were killed, and a federal marshal was badly wounded during the long siege.

Tensions remained high at Pine Ridge after the Wounded Knee occupation ended. In June 1975, another gunfight erupted at Oglala, some fifty miles from Wounded Knee. This time three people were killed: FBI agents Jack Coler and Ron Williams, and Native American Joseph Stuntz. Two Indian men, Bob Robideau and Darrell Butler, were tried in Cedar Rapids, Iowa for the deaths of the two agents, and found not guilty on the grounds of self-defense. This left only Leonard Peltier to face charges. He had fled to Canada and was facing extradition hearings. He was eventually returned to the

United States, but the circumstances of his extradition were widely questioned. A mentally disturbed young Native American woman named Myrtle Poor Bear was coerced into signing three separate and conflicting affidavits. This did not become clear until much later when it was too late to help Peltier.

He stood trial in Fargo, North Dakota, in 1977. He was convicted and sentenced to two life terms, to be served consecutively. Ironically, he would have been acquitted if he had not fled to Canada and had been tried with his friends in Iowa. The fairness of the trial was immediately questioned by Amnesty International. Amnesty sent an observer to the trial. The observer found the trial to be short of real justice for the man. A retrial was requested in 1975.

My interest in the story began when I became director of Amnesty International in 1981. In most of my talks at colleges and universities, I called for Peltier to be retried, along with Geronimo Pratt, who was convicted after another dubious trial. I raised the alarm for these two leaders, but Amnesty rules prevented further work on the cases themselves. American imprisonment cases were left to other sections and the international secretary in London.

I met a half Cree and half Ojibway Canadian Indian by the name of Larry Morrisette in late 1993. We were at a meeting in California organized by Sue Kiel, a former South African activist. I welcomed this new friendship, knowing I could learn different views from a man who was deeply immersed in the issues. I learned in quiet and easy conversations the history, traditions, and ways of life of the Plains Indians as Larry saw them. Many questions were answered. Larry's friendship enriched me deeply. In fact, when I decided to leave Amnesty, I went to the Winnipeg Council with him in the hopes of gaining some wisdom and to settle my mind on my future.

Years later, at Human Rights Action Center, when I was asked to be part of a British documentary being filmed about the life and times of Leonard Peltier, my response was "Gladly." We did the shoot, and I was saying goodbye to the camera crew when my cell phone rang. It was Leonard beseeching me to help him with a new clemency campaign. My answer was yes once again.

I started by reviewing the strategies used during the clemency campaign run during the Clinton Administration, which had almost succeeded. At the last minute, President Clinton granted clemency to Marc Rich, a major donor who had been convicted of racketeering and trading with Iran in violation of a trade embargo. Leonard was passed over. Many suspected Clinton feared political repercussions if he granted two high profile pardons. He told his supporters that he did not know how to sell the release of Leonard to the American people. The rejection was greeted by dismay in Indian country.

With that experience in mind, we determined to take a different approach during the Obama years. We would work to convince the American people to support clemency and then let them put pressure on President Obama. We ran a YouTube video every month or two. By the end of the Obama Administration, half of Hollywood and many America's best musicians were asking for clemency. It let the public see Indian life through their own eyes, their own faces, and their own history.

In the last few days of the Obama Administration, most of us in the "Free Leonard Peltier" clemency campaign were optimistic that President Obama would release him along with other deserving prisoners. Alas, that was not to be. We learned that President Obama would not grant clemency. Our campaign failed. Leonard Peltier remains in prison.

Leonard has been behind prison walls in some of America's most notorious prisons. Today he is being held at the maximum-security prison USP Coleman I in Florida. Because the prison is almost 2,000 miles from his home on Turtle Mountain in North Dakota, visits from family and friends are rare. He has held on to his sanity by teaching himself to paint and has produced some beautiful art. He has maintained a sense of humor and a deep religious faith.

We will stay with this story. This is a campaign I still hope we can win and must win in the name of justice. Readers wishing to support this ongoing effort can find more information on YouTube or at humanrightsactioncenter.com.

A Conspiracy of Compassion For Leonard Peltier
An appeal to President Biden

Jack Healey, Human Rights Action Center

During the holiday season, people of all religions come together to celebrate their faith and share their hopes for the coming year. We use the quiet moments of the season for reflection and reconciliation. One opportunity for healing and reconciliation would be for President Biden to offer compassionate release for Native American Leonard Peltier. Now 77 years of age, Peltier has been in prison for the past 45 years. He is one of the longest serving prisoners in the United States.

Peltier's supporters have included Nelson Mandela, Saint Mother Teresa, Coretta Scott King, Wilma Mankiller, the late Chief of the Great Cherokee Nation and Judge Gerald Heaney of the Eighth Circuit court of appeals. Musicians by the dozens have called for his release. Recently Senate President Pro Tempore Patrick Leahy of Vermont has joined the late Senator Daniel K. Inouye of Hawaii in calling for his release. Pope Francis has spoken twice to two Presidents about Peltier's immediate release. He once said that very long prison terms ARE the death penalty. We believe that he has asked President Biden to free Leonard and we pray that it is true.

Many great lawyers have climbed the now dusty walls of the legal case. Former U.S. Attorney James Reynolds, who originally helped to put Peltier behind bars, has courageously spoken out in a letter to President Biden seeking to end Peltier's decades long incarceration. Amnesty International and the U.N. High Commissioner for Human Rights have long called for a new trial and his release. Peltier suffers from diabetes, a heart condition that led to emergency open heart surgery three years ago. He is almost blind in one eye and has unresolved prostate issues. He has a very concerning untreated abdominal aortic aneurysm.

We can take a righteous step toward reconciliation in Indian country and allow this now elderly prisoner to go home. This holiday season would be a perfect time to re-lease Peltier. Today he is being held at the maximum-security prison USP Coleman 1 in Florida. Because this prison is almost 2000 miles from his home On Turtle Mountain in North Dakota, visits from family and friends are very few and far between.

Please President Biden give a gift of compassion to Leonard Peltier.

Leonard Peltier has been in prison since 1977. He has been eligible for parole since 1993. It is time for clemency. Photo by Dick Bancroft.

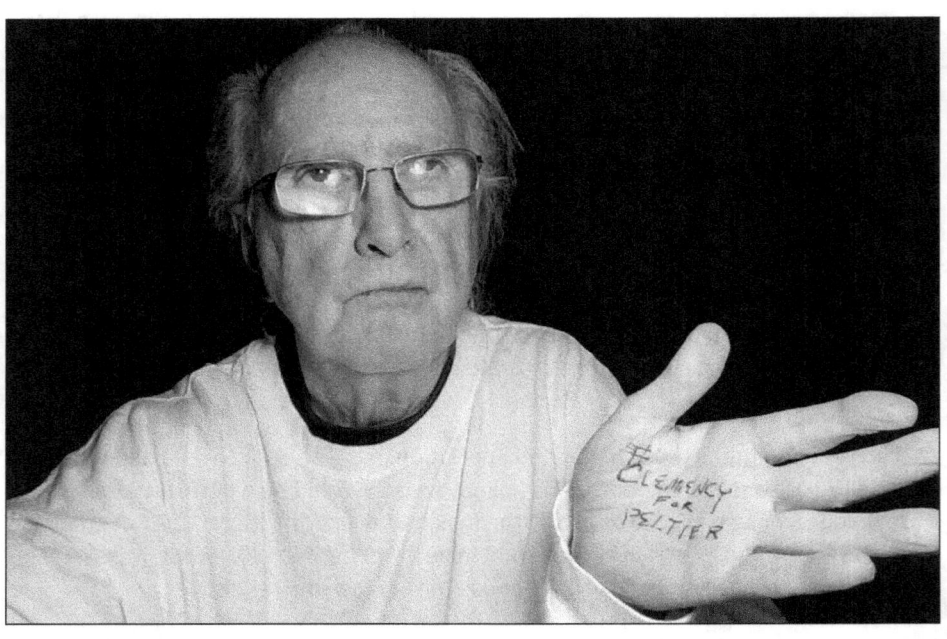

During the Conspiracy of Compassion campaign, supporters wrote the message on their hands and uploaded social media sites

Chapter 24

Vengeance in Taiwan

In 2012, Professor Jay Tu of North Carolina State University wrote me concerning the plight of the former president of Taiwan, Mr. Chen Shui-Bian. Mr. Chen was jailed for corruption—real or imagined—immediately after his two terms as president of Taiwan. Jay believed no one was paying attention to this prisoner's treatment in jail or the false charges against him. At first, I did not see much of an issue, as I got the same impression as everyone else—Chen was a corrupt politician. Jay continued to send me articles and updates. Finally, after many phone calls and email exchanges, Jay said to me, "Jack, please take this case over. It is a real human rights issue."

There had been a few writers reporting on the conditions of the prison. A U.S. congressional delegation went to Taiwan for the inauguration of the second term of President Ma Ying-jeou. While there, a congresswoman from Miami insisted that the rest of the delegation not even raise the issue. The charges against Chen were nonviolent, and he was ultimately found innocent of most of the eight charges. Yet he was sentenced to twenty-seven years for corruption. The law in Taiwan caps the maximum sentence to twenty years unless it is for life in prison. The background on Mr. Chen was important for me to understand. He came from the green side, represented by the Democratic Progressive Party (DPP), the party of those who were born and raised in Taiwan. The blue side, called Kuomintang (KMT), was controlled by those who followed Chiang Kai-shek to Taiwan from China after he lost to Mao Tse-tung in 1947-1948. The KMT ruled Taiwan under martial law from 1949 to 1987 and had only two presidents, Chiang Kai-shek and his son, who each served until dying. The KMT held every presidency from 1987-2016, except from 2000-2008 under Mr. Chen. He was a success story of the new Taiwan. In jail, for good or bad reasons, Mr. Chen remained a symbol of the Old Taiwan under military rule.

I had visited Taiwan twice, once while it was under military rule, once right after martial law was lifted. But this story was not on my radar until Jay called.

As I considered it, I wanted to make sure the Human Rights Action Center (HRAC) was doing the right thing. I sent two friends over to visit the man. Hans Wahl and Harrell Dinkies were expecting to see a healthy man who once had been a great corporate lawyer, mayor of Taipei, and President twice. Instead, they found a weakened old man with all kinds of ailments. HRAC published articles on the *Huffington Post* to call attention to the issue. I could not figure out why so few human rights groups and congressional folks were looking out for this man with the usual letters, visits, congressional mentions, etc. He was forgotten and in bad health.

Our blog posts, along with a few dedicated supporters, kept pressure on the Ma government, and eventually Mr. Chen was moved to a bed in a hospital room. The history of rushed doctor visits and drive-through hospital exams, the inhuman prison conditions—23.5 hours a day trapped in a small cell under bright lights and surveillance cameras, no bed, no table, no flush toilet, no hot water, and little time out of the cell—broke this man's health and mental powers. He was declining quickly.

Some solid voices started to come into the picture, Republicans and Democrats, including Senators Sherrod Brown of Ohio and Dick Durban of Illinois. HRAC's articles appeared regularly. The secretary general of Amnesty International visited and added his voice. Professor Jerome Cohen of New York University School of

Law, whom President Ma brought to Taiwan as his mentor, even spoke up and called for medical relief. More people in Taiwan started to join the loyal few supporters of Mr. Chen. The HRAC blogs were reaching a larger audience and gaining traction. The election of the new mayor of Taipei, Ko Wen-je, in November 2014, put pressure on the Ma government to release Mr. Chen. This new Mayor was the chair of an unofficial, voluntary medical team advocating medical rights for Mr. Chen.

Mr. Chen gained medical release in January 2015. The people of Taiwan celebrated, and I was surprised to learn that my face and writings were all over Taiwanese television as having played a significant role in getting him home.

Without money. Without fame. Just action. Impact is all that matters.

Former President of Taiwan, Mr. Chen Shui-bian, served a number of years in jail, but with the help of his friends and HRAC, we were able to send him home. Photo by Bryan Chen.

Lesson Ten

One Person Can Lift the Whole Damn Thing

Chapter 25

Words Have Power

Sometimes I think that the garbage dumps of the world, where hungry children gather their daily sustenance, might be the best place to drop as many copies of the Universal Declaration of Human Rights as I can. This neglected document, written by a committee chaired by Eleanor Roosevelt in 1948, remains one of the best-kept secrets in the world. Western and Eastern powers have neglected it. Who will wake up these governments to the UDHR and its power, its vision, and its promise?

It just might be one of those children hunting for a bite to eat in a garbage dump. There is a great river of consciousness in the world that wants governments to behave and leave people alone in their lives and beliefs. Rather than throwing people into jail to torture or kill them, we need to turn the power of government into a force for unity, sustenance, and strength of character.

Power, real power, comes from agreements—written, signed, and kept. The Constitution and the Bill of Rights are examples. Now is the time for the Universal Declaration of Human Rights. It is time to let it become the "common standard of achievements for all peoples and all nations," as proposed in its preamble. Progress in interpretation and implementation will fluctuate just as it has with the Constitution, the Bill of Rights, and the Civil Rights Act of 1964, but it should become our shared aspiration.

By the 100th anniversary of the UDHR, we pray that the wealthier countries will be flying drones over the poorer countries to help feed the hungry, clothe the needy, and protect refugees rather than to kill. The mighty are mighty only if they do not dance on the heads of the poor.

The Human Rights Now tour of 1988 was not merely a symbol of hope. It was a clarion call to have the UDHR printed in the passports of every nation. It is the best idea I believe I ever had.

Hank and Carol Goldberg, generous supporters of Human Rights Action Center, once asked me why I continue in my human rights work. I reminded them of the song "Little Victories" by Bob Seger. It is about the power of little victories in many walks of life. It tells the story with energy and force. I feel that same energy and force when I think of the victories we have had in the human rights movement. Little victories bring big victories.

Some human rights leaders become so famous their names alone invoke their causes: Dr. King, Nelson Mandela, Aung San Suu Kyi, Gandhi, and Steve Biko. Lesser known but just as important were the unseen activists who achieved victories such as ousting the military dictators in Latin America; gaining majority rule in South Africa, Rhodesia/Zimbabwe, Southwest Africa/Namibia, and Mozambique; the Soviet Union dissolving without a violent revolution; Cambodia, El Salvador, Chile, Argentina, and Bosnia settling scores with people like Pol Pot and Pinochet; establishment of an Assistant Secretary for Human Rights at the United Nations; and the creation of the International Criminal Court (ICC).

I had the privilege of being a part of some of these achievements although the extent of the role I played varied. The true credit goes to the parade of human rights survivors and advocates who few notice. I notice them. I have met and continue to meet people from these places and times. Those who survive human rights abuses are witnesses to life and its power to survive and live and to just be. Survivors energize, inspire, and mobilize the human rights movement. Their blood and their sweat, their torture and their disappearances move us all. Nobel Prize-winning author Albert Camus spoke of those who suffer the lash and those who expose the lashing. Like Camus, I count myself as one of the latter; both those who receive the lash and those who expose it share the victory.

We the people of the earth are winning, even though it doesn't always look that way.

The battle is not left versus right, Democrat versus Republican. It is the battle between good and evil; decent and indecent; and between the power of hate versus the power of love. Torturers need to be pushed into the sun and taken to court to face trial—our own leaders, as well as those abroad.

A free people must work for an unfree people.

For several years I gave a human rights workshop at Esalen Institute. These weekend retreats were a chance to spread word of the importance of people finding their voice. Brazilian TV personality Maria Paula attended and immediately went to work for the Brazilian Indians who were being driven from their homes because of the oil and other natural resources found there.

Jack on his porch in Washington, D.C. holding a Human Rights Now publicity photo of Bruce Springsteen, himself and Sting. HRN photo by © Ken Regan/Camera 5. Porch Photo by Jane Feldman.

Chapter 26

One Person Can Lift the Whole Thing

C reating your future is not just a possibility; it is a responsibility that we owe ourselves, our families, our community, and our world. It is about shedding our limitations, accessing our strength, embracing our fears, and owning our courage. German philosopher Friedrich Nietzsche said we should dare to dream big and the whole universe will conspire to bring it to reality.

Progress in human rights is won through the unwavering dedication of many thousands of people. It requires tenacity and determination and sacrifice. We do not quit. We get knocked over and come back. We get back up on the balls of our feet and fight again. So, if you get discouraged, just come back up. Get over your own problems. Think about something bigger—go back to it.

You do not need money, status, or an Ivy League education, but you do need a vision, boldness, and willingness to access one truth—one standard—that is immutable and unchangeable. That standard/truth is the inherent dignity and equality of every human being. This is where I started, and it is what I used as the foundation of my work throughout my life. A single standard was my metric by which all governments would be judged in their display of respect for the rights of their citizens.

These days, when I give a speech, I address the most confused kids in the room. I talk to the smallest, the least educated, the least powerful. I tell them they can make a difference, because I did. I am that confused, lost, under-educated kid, too. I've got all those lesser things in my life. If they understand that some little jerk has gone before them and done it, maybe it will give them the courage to do something great.

I want students to know the world needs them. I want them to know they can make a difference. We need one champion somewhere, and each one of us can become that champion. I saw it with Dr. King. I saw it with Fannie Lou Hamer. I saw it with Mandela. I have seen it everywhere in the world. One person can lift the whole damn thing. So, become that one person and lift the whole damn thing.

When Fannie Lou Hamer told me she was dying, she asked me not to fret over her. She knew she had done her part and was ready. But she did want to give me her final challenge.

"And you...," Fannie Lou said, "keep on keeping on. Do not stop until you join me."

Yes, ma'am.

—End—

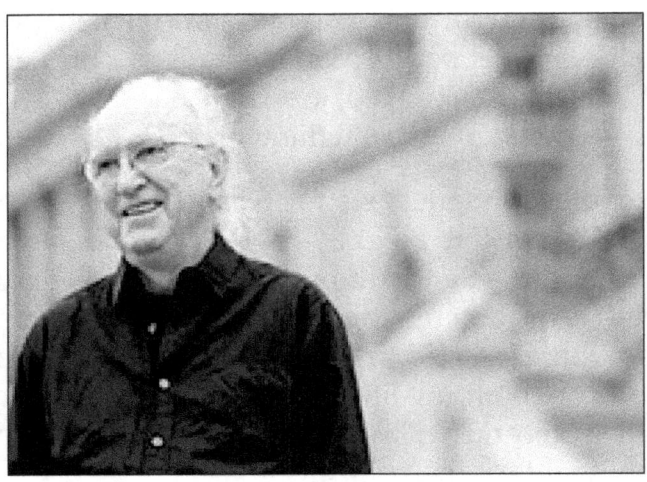

Appendices

- Acknowledgments
- Universal Declaration of Human Rights
- Honors
- Bibliography

1. Steve Starr
2. Derek Hughes, Peltier campaign
3. Charles Fulwood
4. Carolyn Todd-Larson, Bill Brieger
5. Michelle Foster
6. Barry Dane
7. Moira Sher
8. Michelle Foster, Dr. Deborah Blacker, Dr. David Brown, Matt Burrows, Jeremy Woodrum, Cynthia Okayama

Getting some love from good friend Steve Starr, 2015

Acknowledgments

The stories I share in this book are meant to inspire readers to act and to raise their voices and make them thunder. My life is proof that you do not need money, fame, or a prestigious background to make a difference in this world. You need passion. And, I have learned, you need friends and allies. Friends and supporters share equal credit for the work we have accomplished.

Feryal Gharahi always challenged me to go further and push harder. She told it like it was with irony and humor. I could not have accomplished the work of the past 40 years without her voice in my head and her brain and her heart. Aram Jafarey has taught me logic mixed with warmth.

Dick Gregory kept me laughing and focused on the goal from 1971 until his passing in 2017. No matter his fame or position, his friendship was always firm. Jimmy Miller, a fellow Pittsburgh native, has been a loyal friend and ardent supporter of the work alongside his wife Cheryl. Their dedication to freeing Aung San Suu Kyi culminated in a dinner they hosted for Aung San Suu Kyi in 2012 after she was freed. Matt Burrows has been my faithful pro bono counsel since 1992, ensuring I can focus on the work. Henry and Carol Goldberg make sure I continue in my human rights work and maintain balance. Beckie Healey deserves special thanks for her vital support of AFFHF and the Peace Corps. She was a big sister to many of the young volunteers and a steady and kind partner to me.

Heartfelt thanks go to the following people for their support and passion: Will Ferrell and Viveca Paulin, Judd Apatow and Leslie Mann, Lyle and Lisi Poncher, Phil Kent, Dan Adler and family, Fannie Lou Hamer, James Groppi, Rep. John Lewis, Reg Petty, Elsa and Norm Rush, the Freston brothers, Barry Dane, Shepard and Amanda Fairey, Simon Cole, Dr. David Brown, Don Foster, John and Maria Taglioli, David Milch, Muhammed Ali, Jason Rothberg, Amy Poncher, Jonathan Kadin, Father James Hannon, the Capuchin Order, Bob Pittman, John Sykes, Cardinal Sean O'Malley, Bishop John Corriveau, Peter Benenson, Sean MacBride, Mike Johns, Noam Chomsky, Anjelica Huston, Anca Albu, Tony Mac, Lili Hayden, Tom Morello, Maggie Q, Jae Choi, Jay Tu, Douglas Busby, David Kornhauser, Sydney Scribner, Cassa Van Kundra, Stan and Liz Salett, June Guterman, Joanne Barker, Kris Hahn, Rick Garson, Jack Magee, Michael Johns, David Slemmons, Emily Trautman, Stanley Friedman, Sheron Leonard, Charlie Hernandez, all the roadies of the four musical tours, and my seminary classmates.

Big projects build close friendships. Many of the teenagers who organized Walks for Development (Hunger Hikes) in the seventies continued into lifelong activism and remain dear friends. Their continued dedication to making the world a better place is a daily inspiration to me. To the hundreds of thousands who trekked many miles each year to end hunger, thank you. May your effort continue to your children and grandchildren. The first regional coordinator I hired at Young World Development in Los Angeles was Moira Sher. That began a friendship that has endured to this day. Moira introduced me to a variety of people in the entertainment industry. When I met her, she was married to filmmaker Jack Sher, and both became good friends. She introduced me to Joe Strummer, former lead singer of The Clash, who collaborated with me on a punk rock album for human rights.

Staff at the Freedom from Hunger Foundation, Peace Corps, and Amnesty International did the work from top to bottom, and I am profoundly grateful for all their hard work and for the many friendships formed over the years. Jeremy Woodrum, Dan Beeton, and hundreds of resolute Burmese contributed tirelessly to the work of bringing democracy to the Republic of the Union of Myanmar; I am confident they will do so again.

Once known to me only through their music, the following artists became lifelong allies in the fight for human rights and the type of friends who show up when asked. I respect each one and cherish my friendship with them: Sting, The Police, Peter Gabriel,

U2, Wynton Marsalis, Tracy Chapman, Jackson Browne, Bruce Springsteen, Youssou N'Dour, Bryan Adams, Joan Baez, Neville Brothers, Lou Reed, Paul Simon, Joe Strummer, Pearl Jam, Susan Silver, REM, and the 130 other artists who played for human rights.

My late friend Bill Graham guided this absolute neophyte through the intricacies of producing two national and international tours. The planning and demanding work for the Conspiracy of Hope and Human Rights Now tours were nothing compared to the challenge of dealing with multiple personalities, handlers, logistics, the Amnesty board, and especially me. I loved Bill and miss him. I thank the Board of Directors of Amnesty USA and the International Secretariat in London.

Finally, telling my stories was important to me because I am in awe that I was allowed to participate in these events. Putting them on paper was mind boggling. This publication was made possible only with the help of several skilled writers and editors over the past ten years.

Cynthia Okayama Dopke interviewed and recorded me for hours, meticulously transcribing stories. She captured my voice and the details that were so important to me. Mike Haack captured the historical significance of the times to put context to my story. Under his careful guidance the Maguires are remembered, and dictatorships and corrupt governments (sometimes our own) are exposed. Grace Powell edited the early versions of this work, correcting grammar and adding salient details to reveal the heart of the message. Eve Mykytyn used both chisel and scalpel to combine the two previous versions into one cohesive, readable work. Where the story bogs down for the reader, it is because I am not easy to silence and wanted every story included. Michelle (Burke) Foster took on project management and editing. She kept us all on track while ensuring my voice remained and excess chatter was silenced. Chris Reynolds, who was one of the Chicago leaders of the Walks and YWD, meticulously edited the second edition with Michelle Foster. Chris' attention to detail and expert knowledge of geography and history made the second edition much stronger. I also want to thank my intern James Mason Cohen, who wrote a piece with me about the Chile concert for his blog, which appears in this book.

Finally, I send loving thanks and gratitude to my family. I thank my father and mother as well as my brothers and sisters: Martin, Mary Olivia, Virginia, Elaine, Evelyn (Naomi), Eugene, Joseph, Agnes, Carole, and Mike for their love. My mother was well cared for by my sisters and for that I say special thanks. My brother Mike watched out for me as a young boy in our cold attic and has continued the task all through my life. Naomi was not only a faithful sister but was a second mother to me. She protected me as fiercely as I tried to protect my mother. We are an Irish clan with fire, love, and passion. I hope our collective offspring can share a bit of our family history through the stories told here.

To those with nowhere to turn, I say, "Rise." Believe in your own talent when you feel weak. Believe in your dreams and make them a reality. I know you will produce plays and poems and art and music and step into the breach when needed. Take your place. Demand your rights and protect others who need help.

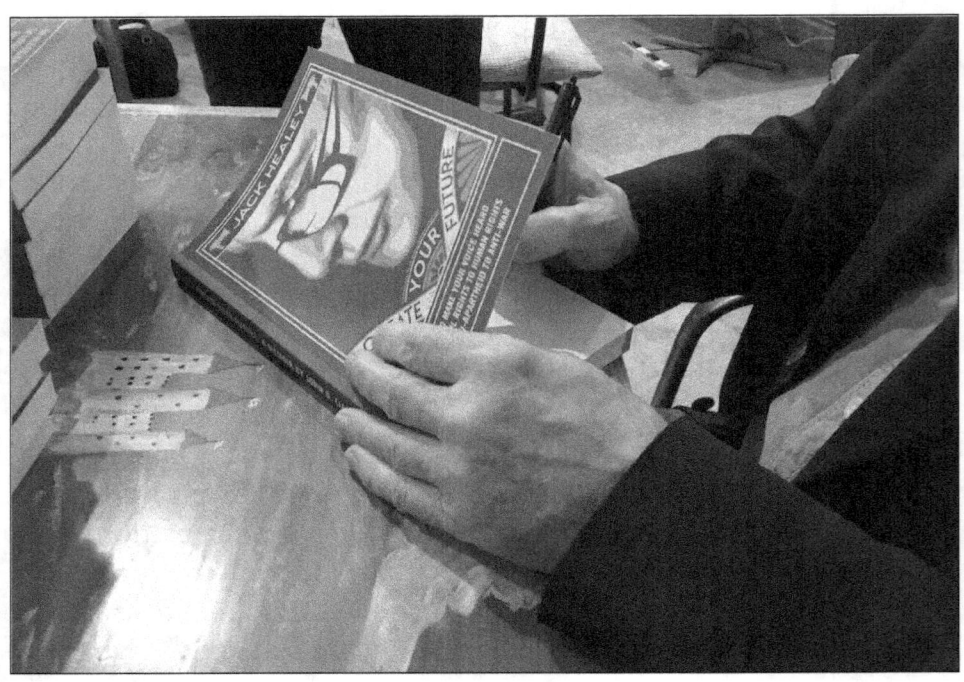

Universal Declaration of Human Rights

The General Assembly Proclaims this Universal Declaration of Human Rights as a common standard of achievement for all peoples and all nations, to the end that every individual and every organ of society, keeping this Declaration constantly in mind, shall strive by teaching and education to promote respect for these rights and freedoms and by progressive measures, national and international, to secure their universal and effective recognition and observance, both among the peoples of Member States themselves and among the peoples of territories under their jurisdiction.

Article 1. All human beings are born free and equal in dignity and rights. They are endowed with reason and conscience and should act towards one another in a spirit of brotherhood.

Article 2. Everyone is entitled to all the rights and freedoms set forth in this Declaration, without distinction of any kind, such as race, color, sex, language, religion, political or other opinion, national or social origin, property, birth, or other status. Furthermore, no distinction shall be made on the basis of the political, jurisdictional, or international status of the country or territory to which a person belongs, whether it be independent, trust, non-self-governing or under any other limitation of sovereignty.

Article 3. Everyone has the right to life, liberty and security of person.

Article 4. No one shall be held in slavery or servitude; slavery and the slave trade shall be prohibited in all their forms.

Article 5. No one shall be subjected to torture or to cruel, inhuman or degrading treatment or punishment.

Article 6. Everyone has the right to recognition everywhere as a person before the law.

Article 7. All are equal before the law and are entitled without any discrimination to equal protection of the law. All are entitled to equal protection against any discrimination in violation of this Declaration and against any incitement to such discrimination.

Article 8. Everyone has the right to an effective remedy by the competent national tribunals for acts violating the fundamental rights granted him by the constitution or by law.

Article 9. No one shall be subjected to arbitrary arrest, detention, or exile.

Article 10. Everyone is entitled in full equality to a fair and public hearing by an independent and impartial tribunal, in the determination of his rights and obligations and of any criminal charge against him.

Article 11. 1. Everyone charged with a penal offence has the right to be presumed innocent until proved guilty according to law in a public trial at which he has had all the guarantees necessary for his defense .2. No one shall be held guilty of any penal offence on account of any act or omission which did not constitute a penal offence, under national or international law, at the time when it was committed. Nor shall a heavier penalty be imposed than the one that was applicable at the time the penal offence was committed.

Article 12. No one shall be subjected to arbitrary interference with his privacy, family, home or correspondence, nor to attacks upon his honor and reputation. Everyone has the right to the protection of the law against such interference or attacks.

Article 13. Everyone has the right to freedom of movement and residence within the borders of each state. Everyone has the right to leave any country, including his own, and to return to his country.

Article 14. Everyone has the right to seek and to enjoy in other countries asylum from persecution. This right may not be invoked in the case of prosecutions genuinely arising from non-political crimes or from acts contrary to the purposes and principles of the United Nations.

Article 15. Everyone has the right to a nationality. No one shall be arbitrarily deprived of his nationality nor denied the right to change his nationality.

Article 16. Men and women of full age, without any limitation due to race, nationality or religion, have the right to marry and to found a family. They are entitled to equal rights as to marriage, during marriage and at its dissolution. Marriage shall be entered into only with the free and full consent of the intending spouses. The family is the natural and fundamental group unit of society and is entitled to protection by society and the State.

Article 17. Everyone has the right to own property alone as well as in association with others. No one shall be arbitrarily deprived of his property.

Article 18. Everyone has the right to freedom of thought, conscience and religion; this right includes freedom to change his religion or belief, and freedom, either alone or in community with others and in public or private, to manifest his religion or belief in teaching, practice, worship and observance.

Article 19. Everyone has the right to freedom of opinion and expression; this right includes freedom to hold opinions without interference and to seek, receive and impart information and ideas through any media and regardless of frontiers.

Article 20. Everyone has the right to freedom of peaceful assembly and association. No one may be compelled to belong to an association.

Article 21. Everyone has the right to take part in the government of his country, directly or through freely chosen representatives. Everyone has the right of equal access to public service in his country. The will of the people shall be the basis of the authority of government; this will shall be expressed in periodic and genuine elections which shall be by universal and equal suffrage and shall be held by secret vote or by equivalent free voting procedures.

Article 22. Everyone, as a member of society, has the right to social security and is entitled to realization, through national effort and international cooperation and in accordance with the organization and resources of each State, of the economic, social and cultural rights indispensable for his dignity and the free development of his personality.

Article 23. Everyone has the right to work, to free choice of employment, to just and favorable conditions of work and to protection against unemployment. Everyone, without any discrimination, has the right to equal pay for equal work. Everyone who works has the right to just and favorable remuneration ensuring for himself and his family an existence worthy of human dignity, and supplemented, if necessary, by other means of social protection. Everyone has the right to form and to join trade unions for the protection of his interests.

Article 24. Everyone has the right to rest and leisure, including reasonable limitation of working hours and periodic holidays with pay.

Article 25. Everyone has the right to a standard of living adequate for the health and well-being of himself and of his family, including food, clothing, housing and medical care and necessary social services, and the right to security in the event of unemployment, sickness, disability, widowhood, old age or other lack of livelihood in circumstances beyond his control. Motherhood and child-hood are entitled to special care and assistance. All children, whether born in or out of wedlock, shall enjoy the same social protection.

Article 26. Everyone has the right to education. Education shall be free, at least in the elementary and fundamental stages. Elementary education shall be compulsory. Technical and professional education shall be made generally available and higher education shall be equally accessible to all on the basis of merit. Education shall be directed to the full development of the human personality and to the strengthening of respect for human rights and fundamental freedoms. It shall promote understanding, tolerance and friendship among all nations, racial or religious groups, and shall further the activities of the United Nations for the maintenance of peace. Parents have a prior right to choose the kind of education that shall be given to their children.

Article 27. Everyone has the right freely to participate in the cultural life of the community, to enjoy the arts and to share in scientific advancement and its benefits. Everyone has the right to the protection of the moral and material interests resulting from any scientific, literary or artistic production of which he is the author.

Article 28. Everyone is entitled to a social and international order in which the rights and freedoms set forth in this Declaration can be fully realized.

Article 29. Everyone has duties to the community in which alone the free and full development of his personality is possible. In the exercise of his rights and freedoms, everyone shall be subject only to such limitations as are determined by law solely for the purpose of securing due recognition and respect for the rights and freedoms of others and of meeting the just requirements of morality, public order and the general welfare in a democratic society. These rights and freedoms may in no case be exercised contrary to the purposes and principles of the United Nations.

Article 30. Nothing in this Declaration may be interpreted as implying for any State, group or person any right to engage in any activity or to perform any act aimed at the destruction of any of the rights and freedoms set forth herein.

SOURCE: *Universal Declaration of Human Rights*

Honors

Honorary Degrees

- Doctor of Philosophy, Doctor of Humane Letters, May 31, 1987. Southeastern Massachusetts University
- Doctor of Philosophy, Doctor of Humanities, May 22, 1988. Providence College
- Juris Doctor, Doctor of Laws, May 29, 1988. Northeastern University.
- Doctor of Philosophy, Doctor of Public Service, May 27, 1989. Bridgewater State University
- Juris Doctor, Doctor of Law, May 9, 1992. Notre Dame College
- Doctor of Public Service, Bridgewater University
- Doctor of Human Letters, Old Dominion University

Honors and Awards

- Special Recognition Award, Humanitarian of the Year. MTV Video Music Awards, 1986
- Pollstar 1988 Readers Poll Award for the Amnesty International Human Rights Now tour, named the Concert Industry Event of the Year. Pollstar, 1988
- International Rock Award Tour of the Year Elvis Presley Award. The International Rock Awards, 1989
- Bill Graham Award. <u>Fox News</u>. 1991, *Billboard* magazine
- Martin Luther King Jr. Spirit of the Dream Award. House of Blues Foundation, 1996
- Person of the Week, ABC World News with Peter Jennings
- Guest editor, *SPIN* magazine
- Thomas Merton Award, 1976, for World Hunger

Bibliography

1. Biko, Steve. *I Write What I Like: Selected Writings*. Edited by Aelred Stubbs. Chicago: The University of Chicago Press, 1978.

2. Black Backlash Programs Set at Frostburg State College. *The Cumberland News*. May 16, 1968.

3. Burns, Kathleen. *The Chicago Tribune*. Hikers Cheerful Despite Rain. May 8, 1972.

4. Headlam, Bruce. For Him, the Political Has Always Been Comical. *The New York Times*. March 13, 2009.

5. Henke, James. *Human Rights Now.* Edited by Kim Ronis. Topsfield, MA: Salem House Publishers, 1988.

6. Hilburn, Robert. *Los Angeles Times*. Pop Review: Amnesty's State-of-the-Art Benefit. June 9, 1886.

7. Hilston, James. Regional Jobless Rates in the Early 1980s. *Pittsburgh Post-Gazette*. April 1983.

8. Honorary Graduates. University of Essex. April 3, 2003.

9. Houck, Davis W. *Speeches of Fannie Lou Hamer, To Tell It Like It Is*. University Press of Mississippi, 2011.

10. Kaplan, Eben. Child Soldiers Around the World. Council on Foreign Relations. December 2, 2005. https://www.cfr.org/backgrounder/child-soldiers-around-world

11. King, Jr., Dr. Martin Luther. The King Center Archive. The King Center. April 4, 1967. https://thekingcenter.org

12. Lardner, George. Abrams Pleads Guilty in Iran-Contra Affair. October 8, 1991.

13. Groovefest Raises Awareness for Human Rights. *The Oklahoman*, April 15, 1999.

14. *Report of the Chilean National Commission on Truth and Reconciliation.* United States Institute on Peace, 1993.

15. Schultz, Terri. *The Chicago Tribune.* Tireless Young Walkers Rack Up Blisters, Cash. May 9, 1971.

16. Steve Biko, Black Consciousness Movement Leader Is Buried South African History Online. September 25, 1977.

17. *The Death of Stephen Biko.* South Africa: Overcoming Apartheid.

18. Van Zandt, Steven. Don't Rebuild Haiti: Re-imagine It. *Politico.* February 2, 2010.

19. Young, Gary. The Man Who Raised the Black Power Salute. *The Guardian.* March 30, 2012

20. Ziemba, Stanley. Thousands Plan Hike on Hunger. *The Chicago Tribune.* May 8, 1971.

21. Leffler, Warren K, photographer. *Fannie Lou Hamer, Mississippi Freedom Democratic Party delegate, at the Democratic National Convention, Atlantic City, New Jersey, August/ WKL.* New Jersey Atlantic City, 1964. Photograph. https://www.loc.gov/item/2003688126

ISBN (pbk)   979-8-9901290-0-9
ISBN (ebk)   979-8-9901290-1-6

www.ingramcontent.com/pod-product-compliance
Lightning Source LLC
Chambersburg PA
CBHW071136130626
46553CB00004B/1392